AF323431

# ENVIRONMENT AND CRIME AMONG RESIDENTS IN URBAN AREAS

# Environment and Crime among Residents in Urban Areas

## A Study of Districts in Stockholm

OLOF DAHLBÄCK
*Stockholm University, Sweden*

ASHGATE

Published by
Ashgate Publishing Limited
Wey Court East
Union Road
Farnham
Surrey, GU9 7PT
England

Ashgate Publishing Company
110 Cherry Street
Suite 3-1
Burlington, VT 05401-3818
USA

www.ashgate.com

**British Library Cataloguing in Publication Data**
Dahlbäck, Olof.
    Environment and Crime Among Residents in Urban Areas: A Study of Districts
    in Stockholm.
    1. Crime – Sweden – Stockholm. 2. Criminal behavior – Sweden – Stockholm.
    3. City dwellers – Crimes against – Sweden – Stockholm. 4. Victims of crimes
    surveys – Sweden – Stockholm. 5. Geographical offender profiling – Sweden –
    Stockholm. I. Title
    364'.042'094873–dc23

**Library of Congress Cataloging-in-Publication Data**
Dahlbäck, Olof.
    Environment and Crime Among Residents in Urban Areas: A Study of Districts
    in Stockholm / by Olof Dahlbäck.
        p.    cm.
    Includes bibliographical references and index.
    1. Crime – Sweden – Stockholm. 2. Crime analysis – Sweden – Stockholm.
    3. Urban ecology (Sociology) – Sweden – Stockholm.  I. Title.
    HV7038.5.D34 2012
    364.109487'3–dc23                                                     2012004521

ISBN    9781409447054 (hbk)
ISBN    9781409447061 (ebk-PDF)
ISBN    9781409484059 (ebk-e-PUB)



Printed and bound in Great Britain by the
MPG Books Group, UK

# Contents

# List of Figures

# List of Tables

# Acknowledgment

The research reported in this book was financed by the Swedish Research Council for Environment, Agricultural Sciences and Spatial Planning. I thank Marcus Carson for valuable comments.

OLOF DAHLBÄCK
*Stockholm, June 2012*

# Introduction

How various factors affect the rate of crime committed by residents in districts of large cities is a central issue in criminology. Concern with identifying these factors and understanding their effects has generated a great deal of research. Studies have demonstrated that areas with high rates of such crime have certain characteristics. For example, areas with high rates of crime tend to have a deteriorated physical environment, many residents who lack economic resources, high rates of divorces, and great ethnic heterogeneity. Many of the relationships found are quite strong, giving rise to a series of questions about the causes of crime. How should the criminality of the residents of these different areas be explained? How does the physical and social environment in an area influence crime among those who live there? And what roles are played by selection processes that imply that different types of individuals are attracted to or locked into particular areas? These and related questions are important from a theoretical point of view and they are also of significant socio-political interest, for example in contemporary Swedish society, in which there is great deal of concern about social developments in certain metropolitan areas. Exactly how these questions should be answered has been unclear, however. It seems that there are no empirical studies in which a satisfying causal analysis of the relationships has been carried out. The purpose of the study reported in this book has been to fill this critical gap by analyzing register data of districts in the City of Stockholm.

Thus, the purpose of the study is to determine how the local physical and social environment has affected the rate of crimes committed by residents in different districts in the city. In order to accomplish this, comprehensive area data of register type are analyzed cross-sectionally and longitudinally, with care taken to separate environment's direct effects on crime from its indirect effects via the geographical selection of individuals. The analysis is based on assumptions about the significance of social control and social resources for individuals' criminality as well as assumptions about the significance of dwellings and social resources for their geographical location. Police records of residents suspected of crime are used for measuring the rates of fifteen separate types of crime, with the measurements referring to the years 1980, 1985 and 1990. The data cover most crimes registered. For many independent properties, the project has had access to individual-level data for all residents in Stockholm City. Basic independent variables describe residents' ages, sex, citizenship, families/households, socioeconomic conditions, dwellings, and moves, and most of these refer to the years 1970, 1975, 1980, 1985 and 1990.

In order to make it possible to carry out the analyses intended, it is important that there is an adequate measure of area crime. This seems to be no great problem. For the years studied, it turns out that one single factor explains an overwhelming part of the total variance of all crime rates. Furthermore, it is found that the correlations between this factor and many independent properties are about the same for the different years and that several of these correlations are very strong.

On the other hand, modeling crime as a function of independent factors is no easy matter. An important task in this connection is to find the right form of model. It may be questioned whether a simple linear form is adequate. Assumably, interaction between factors on the micro level may affect area crime. Therefore models of crime are used in this study in which crime is seen as a function that is characterized by aggregated micro-level interaction. On the micro level, the effect on crime of interaction is modeled as weighted products of independent factors within and between individuals, respectively, assuming that the weight for such a product is the same for different individuals or for different pairs of individuals. The weighted products are aggregated up to the area level. For bivariate analysis, it can be shown algebraically that the aggregate of within-individual products of correlated factors cannot be formulated on the area level in terms of means of the analyzed individual-level factors. This implies that if there is within-individual interaction between correlated factors, crime cannot be perfectly modeled on the area level using factors of ordinary types. However, the aggregate of within-individual products of uncorrelated factors can be formulated on the area level in terms of means of the factors. It can also be shown that if interaction between two different factors for different individuals affects crime in the same way for all pairs of individuals in the area, there will be area-level interaction of corresponding type. Thus, area-level interaction of bivariate type may be due both to interaction within and between individuals. These conditions have multivariate counterparts.

Naturally, knowing the effects on crime of interaction within and between individuals is of great theoretical interest. It is also of great interest to know whether crime is affected by such interaction between individuals that cannot be expressed in area-level terms ordinarily used in criminological research, but must be expressed as means of individual-level products. Should this be the case, research in area-level crime as ordinarily carried on must be modified.

Reasons for assuming that interaction exists within and between individuals are discussed in this book. Much focus is placed on interaction between social control and social resources properties. Thus, I try to find out if the two theoretical perspectives in criminological research that regard these properties as main causes of crime can be joined in the same model in this manner. I investigate empirically whether such interaction exists. However, it turns out that it is difficult to analyze the relationships between these and other independent factors and crime using cross-sectional data. The reason for this is that several independent factors are very strongly correlated with each other, which makes it hard to identify models of crime. The strategy I use to handle this problem is to analyze change data. Changes in the independent properties are as a rule much more weakly correlated with each other than are the cross-sectional values.

Another kind of strategy used in the study is to analyze the influences on crime exerted by long-term residents and by newcomers in the areas. Several local social processes can be assumed to involve the long-term residents much more than the newcomers, and this fact can be used in the analysis of the influence on crime of independent properties, including the two types of aggregated micro-level interaction.

The distinction between long-term residents and newcomers is important to consider in distinguishing the direct influences on crime of the environment in an area from the indirect influences that go via the geographical selection of individuals. The direct influences on crime of the environment can be assumed to be particularly strong for the long-terms residents, and analyzing relationships between independent properties and crime for these residents may therefore discover these influences. Indirect influences via geographical selection are easier to discover by analyzing the relationships for the newcomers.

Another way of analyzing the significance of geographical selection is to decompose the cross-sectional relationship between crime and the independent factors that govern the selection – above all the economic resources and the occurrence of dwellings of particular types. The selection entails that individuals are differentiated geographically, and factors directing the selection may be strongly related to crime cross-sectionally on the area level. However, the influence of these factors, as far as the selective power is concerned, manifests itself as only one part of the factors' cross-sectional relationship with crime. This cross-sectional relationship can be assumed to be made up of four components: the relationships caused by 1) the factors' selective influence, 2) their direct influence, and 3) their indirect, non-selective influence, and 4) the spurious relationship between the factors and crime that is due to the fact that the factors are affected by causes of crime. These components can be described in regression coefficient terms, and the significance of the factors' selective relationship can therefore be estimated as the difference between the coefficient of the cross-sectional relationship that they have with crime and the total of the coefficients of the components 2) – 4). An analysis of this type is performed in the study reported in this book.

However, what above all characterizes the research presented in this book, as distinguished from much other research on the subject, is its profoundly realized micro-macro perspective. The micro-macro link between individual-level independent properties and area crime is modeled and empirically analyzed. The last aspect is worth stressing. The study has an extraordinarily rich database. There is access to data for some years on practically all residents' values on independent properties in all urban areas. The study is probably unique in this respect.

The book is organized as follows. In the first chapter, which deals with previous research on crime among residents in urban areas, I discuss certain relationships commonly found between environment and crime and some theoretical perspectives often used to explain these findings – the social disorganization, social control, social resources, and sub-cultural perspectives. I am skeptical of much in this research, both with respect to its theoretical and methodological content, and in the chapter I present my critical views.

In Chapter 2, I discuss how offender crime rates may be affected by geographical selection of individuals and by local environment. I consider micro- and macro-level aspects of the influences in areas, and I focus on social control and social resources as causes of crime. A basic assumption made is that these two types of factors interact on the individual level in their influences on the generation of crime. I show algebraically how aggregated micro-level interaction within and between individuals may affect area crime.

The method I use to manage the problems that have hampered much previous research is described in Chapter 3. Here, various aspects of the design of my empirical study are detailed – for example, the construction of measures of individual-level and area-level independent factors and of the measure of crime. Moreover, I discuss the relevance of the data used, ways of analyzing causal influences, and the usage of models of different forms.

Chapter 4 describes the cross-sectional analyses made and their results and Chapter 5 the longitudinal analyses and their results. Both chapters include analyses using linear and nonlinear models and analyses of the significance of moves and of aggregated micro-level interaction. Chapter 4 includes an analysis of the influences from adjacent areas, and Chapter 5 includes linear analyses using both point and change data. In Chapter 6, finally, the results, which turn out to differ in several important respects from what has been found in previous research, are summarized and conclusions are drawn.

# Chapter 1
# Previous Research

## Urban Areas and Crime

The subject of how crime emerges and develops in cities is of great criminological significance. The reasons for this are obvious: crime has shown to be strongly related to urbanization – the urban environment seems to be conducive to its inhabitants engaging in criminal activity – and a very large portion of the populations in many countries lives in cities.

The existence of strong relationships between crime rates of the inhabitants of areas in large cities and other social properties of these areas seems to be a highly general phenomenon. For traditional types of crimes, similar relationships have been found in many Western countries (Wikström, 1998). In the cities studied, there seems as a rule to have been a regional differentiation as to various social factors, and several of these factors have been shown to be related to crime. In particular, it has been found that areas with disadvantageous social conditions have high rates of crime. This finding has been obtained for a variety of measures of crime and for areas of different sizes.

Most of the studies dealing with the relationship between crime rates of the inhabitants of urban areas and other social properties of these areas are methodologically simple. The most common design is probably the cross-sectional type applied to register data. The independent factors studied are typically quite similar: as a rule factors describing economic resources, family/civil status, ethnic status, and mobility are included. To a great extent, this is probably due to the fact that these factors can be easily measured by register data. Another reason may be that the research that was conducted by Clifford Shaw and Henry McKay (see below) has been influential in focusing on these types of factors. Nevertheless, it seems clear, as discussed below, that several of these factors are interesting from theoretical points of view.

Relationships of the types mentioned above – between the crime rates of the inhabitants of urban areas and other social properties of these areas – can be found in the City (that is, the municipality) of Stockholm, the capital of Sweden. However, one might think that there is reason to expect that Stockholm would not exhibit these types of relationships. Its regional social differentiation is smaller than for many other cities in Western Europe and in the USA due to the public housing policy in postwar Sweden, which has aimed at counteracting residential segregation by socioeconomic characteristics. Nevertheless, as will be shown in this book, the regional differences in Stockholm have in fact been substantial and large enough to generate strong relationships between social factors and crime on the area level.

Furthermore, postwar Stockholm is interesting to study due to the emergence and development of a variety of problematic conditions. Substantial changes occurred during the 70s and 80s in the social conditions in the city. For example, the numbers of divorced individuals and of immigrants increased strongly. New housing areas were built, some of which later became the locus of serious social problems.

There is a good deal of previous research on crime in Stockholm that makes use of register data. Per-Olof Wikström is among the more prominent of those who have carried out such research. In what is probably his most important study on districts in this city, Wikström (1991) analyzes a comprehensive body of data. The results show the same type of pattern of cross-sectional relationships between crime rates and various factors as can be found in many other studies. However, due to the nature of the data, the possibilities of performing an advanced causal analysis were very limited in Wikström's study.

## Theoretical Perspectives

The theories most often discussed in the field attribute causes of crime among residents in urban areas to one or more of the following conditions: *social disorganization*, weak *social control*, lack of *social resources*, or *subcultures* in these areas. Social disorganization theory was developed specifically to explain urban crime. The social control and social resources theories have a more general sociological character, but are interesting because social-control and social-resources factors have been found to vary geographically in large cities and to be strongly related to crime among the residents in the areas. The theory of urban subcultures refers to a variety of deviant behaviors, among these crime.

*Social disorganization* theory, originally developed by Clifford Shaw and Henry McKay (Shaw and McKay, 1969 [1942]), has played a central role in the research. According to Shaw and MacKay, social disorganization in an urban area is an important cause of crime among the youth living there. By "social disorganization" it is meant that inhabitants have poor social contact with each other and an inadequate organization of activities needed to protect their interests, for example to protect against crime. According to Shaw and McKay, disorganization may be traced back to the lack of economic resources, ethnic heterogeneity, and high mobility of area residents. This theory has been the subject of several different interpretations and revisions (Wikström, 1998), and has also been the target of much criticism (as to criticism focusing on individual-level aspects, see Farrington, 1993). In its modern form, the core of the theory seems to consist of ideas about social control.

According to social disorganization theory, more disorganized urban areas generate more criminal activity. Shaw and McKay maintained that they had shown that registered crime in Chicago was distributed in such a way that the highest level of crime existed in a zone where social organization, measured with a set of indicators, tended to be worst. Moreover, they maintained that this level of crime remained about the same over time, independent of how the population in large was constituted. Some of their empirical results, for example regarding the permanent level of crime, have been questioned or refuted (see, for example, Bursik, 1988). However, their ideas about the significance of social disorganization and its underlying factors have had great impact on criminological research. They belong to the standard repertoire of theoretical ideas in social ecological contexts.

Social disorganization theory has attracted renewed interest in more recent years, largely inspired by an article by Sampson and Groves (1989). These researchers modified the theory in several ways. For example, they introduced factors that they believed describe disorganization more directly than was previously the case. They argued that the theory had never been tested in full, because disorganization had only been measured indirectly with the three factors assumed to underlie it. They conducted an empirical study that they contended showed relationships on the area level between crime and new direct indicators. Social organization was measured in terms of local friendship networks, control of street corner teenage peer groups, and prevalence of organizational participation. Sampson and Groves' ideas and their study have strongly affected subsequent research about disorganization and crime (for example, Bellair, 1997; Sampson et al., 1997), also research with a critical stance (for example, Veysey and Messner, 1999).

The idea that networks are an important aspect of social organization has played a prominent role in modern research on disorganization and urban crime. For example, Bursick and Grasmick (1993) have argued that disorganization theory should consider not only the local networks among residents, but also the networks that connect neighborhoods with the greater society in which these are imbedded. Connections with schools, churches, the police and other institutions and agencies outside the neighborhood may be important. However, seeing general networks among residents as a factor that keeps crime down has been met with skepticism. It is a fact that there are neighborhoods with relatively dense networks among residents that nevertheless exhibit fairly high crime rates, and it has been argued that while such networks may contribute to neighborhood ability to control crime, they may also provide a source of social capital for offenders (Browning et al., 2004). Furthermore, insofar as networks do affect crime their causal status has been problematized. For example, it has been argued that networks, and local organizations and voluntary associations as well, only have an indirect effect via collective efficacy, measured as residents' views of the social cohesion and social control (Morenoff et al., 2001). In these and other modern researches testing social disorganization theory, the concept of social capital is important (Portes, 1998). Salmi and Kivivuori (2006) studied how crime on the individual level is related to indicators of social capital and various other independent factors, and they found crime to be negatively related to a number of the indicators.

Social disorganization theory has been cited in many contexts. There is probably some truth in it, but it is unclear what and how much it explains and it has been heavily critized. I myself am critical of it and of much of the research that is based on it. I think that its coupling between the micro and macro levels is unclear and that it is questionable as an explanation of neighborhood crime to the extent that the social organization referred to is assumed to be collective, that is, to exist outside the family (and, in my view, if organization is assumed to refer to the family, the theory has hardly anything unique to contribute). In actuality, tests of the theory have not yielded unequivocally positive results. For example, according to the theory, mobility is expected to have a strongly positive relationship with the crime of the inhabitants on the area level. Certainly, newly arrived inhabitants in an urban area can hardly be socially well organized. The fact is, however, that it has often been difficult to find such an empirical relationship (this is for example the case in the Sampson-Groves study). There is also much to criticize in the research that has been adduced as support for the disorganization theory, particularly regarding the methods used. I therefore believe that the possibilities of drawing conclusions about the validity of the theory from this research are severely limited. Some of my methodological criticisms are presented below.

Much of the modern sociological research on crime is dominated by theories that stress the significance of *social control*. Many of these theories are revised versions of or are strongly influenced by the "social bonding theory" propounded by Travis Hirschi in his book *Causes of Delinquency* (Hirschi, 1969). A main idea in this theory is that crime arises when individuals' bonds to the conventional society are weakened or broken (for a discussion, see Akers, 2000, pp. 105–110). There are several different types of bonds, including personal bonds to individuals not engaged in criminal activities, stakes in conventional work (for example regarding education and occupation), engagement in conventional activities, and belief in conventional values and norms. The Sampson-Laub life-course theory of social control is founded on this perspective (Sampson and Laub, 1990, 1992; Laub and Sampson, 1993). This theory focuses on the influences on crime of the social bonds created by social institutions and major life events (for example, getting a steady job, getting married, becoming a parent) and it deals particularly with how such bonds facilitate desistance from crime.

Social control theories have been supported by many studies (as to the Sampson-Laub theory, see Savolainen, 2009). Family disintegration and attachment to parents are examples of aspects of social bonds that have been found to be associated with crime (Rankin and Kern, 1994; Skarðhamar, 2009).

There are different theories built on the assumption that *lack of social resources and inequality* cause crime, and they have been used as a basis for a comprehensive body of empirical research (Akers, 2000, pp. 143–162). However, the results of the many studies made on the individual level are not, it seems, as clear as are the results obtained in studies in which social control factors are used, as least not as far as the criminality of young individuals is concerned. The association between social class or socioeconomic status or income, which are properties often used to describe social resources, and the criminality of young individuals turns out to be weak or non-existent in most cases. This has made researchers question the existence of such an association of any greater importance and has led to a long debate about the matter and to attempts to show that social class and similar properties only play a modest role for crime (Tittle et al. 1978; Braithwaite, 1981; Tittle and Meier, 1990; Dunaway et al., 2000; Agnew et al., 2008; see also Becker and Mehlkop, 2006; Ring and Svensson, 2007). Furthermore, there are several questions about the theories, for example, exactly how the lack of resources and the inequality exert an influence on crime.

Thus, the results of the research seem to indicate that the individual-level association between social class or similar properties and crime is weak at most. Furthermore, the influence of social class on crime can be assumed to be indirect, and it has been shown that controlling for various factors supposed to mediate this influence strongly reduces an association found (Fergusson et al., 2004).

However, despite the failure to find a strong relationship between young individuals' criminality and their social class or similar properties, some researchers have maintained that there is such a relationship. For example, it has been suggested that the failure is due to ignorance of the fact that the tendency to become delinquent is extraordinarily strong among individuals who experience persistent childhood poverty. Jarjoura et al. (2002) have presented empirical support for the existence of such a tendency. Thus, it seems that individuals with very poor social resources should be particularly focused when analyzing the causes of criminality. The finding of a relationship on the individual level between severe poverty and criminality has a parallel on the societal level. On this level, it has been found that the crime rates of communities are better predicted by factors that describe the existence of extreme disadvantage of the neighborhood than by factors that describe a more balanced picture of such disadvantage (Krivo and Peterson, 1996).

Social resources may refer to different things – for example, money and things having economic value, knowledge, status, and social relations. As to the economic dimension, the question may be raised whether it is the absolute or the relative economic value of resources that affects crime. It might seem that there are good reasons for focusing on the relative dimension. However, while there may be a relationship on the individual level that implies that poorer individuals tend to commit more crimes, there may on the societal level be a relationship between economic resources and crime that implies that more resources lead to more crime, because greater affluence of resources results in the fact that more objects having economic value are poorly guarded and are therefore easier to steal.

In the research, the predominating idea of how lack of social resources and inequality cause crime on the individual level is the frustration hypothesis. According to this hypothesis crime may be committed by resource-poor individuals, because poor resources lead to failure to achieve positively valued goals and to a sense of being unjustly treated – consequences that lead to frustration and to a pressure for corrective action, which may be crime. This explanation was early suggested by Richard Cloward and Lloyd Ohlin and by Robert Merton (Cloward and Ohlin, 1960; Merton 1968, pp. 185–248).

Robert Agnew has taken up and revised the frustration hypothesis (Agnew, 1992, 1993, 1999), and his theory has attracted much interest in the research in later years (Froggio, 2007; Rebellon et al., 2009; Froggio et al., 2009; Botchkovar et al., 2009). According to Agnew, the negative emotions that accompany the frustration following lack of social resources and inequality often turn into desires for revenge, which energize the individual for action. These views and emotions may be a motive for committing crime. Furthermore, Agnew has suggested that the strains associated with a lack of social resources and inequality interact with other factors, for example control factors, in the influence on crime (Agnew, 1999; 2001; 2005, pp. 109–120). This interaction could be due to the fact that while lack of social resources provides a motive for committing crime, lack of social control provides a prerequisite for this motive to be realized in action (Agnew, 1993).

Evaluating the results of the tests made of Agnew's strain theory is made difficult by various methodological problems. As to the core of the theory, the results must be characterized as mixed. As to the idea that strain interacts with social control in the influence on crime, the results are still more problematic, but some findings indicate or can be interpreted to indicate that such interaction exists (Agnew and White, 1992; Mazerolle and Maahs, 2000).

Finally, a fourth type of theory seeks the explanation of crime among residents in urban areas in *subcultural conditions* (Fischer, 1995). The fundamental assumption here is that norms and values that make people prone to commit crime can be found in their culturally determined attitudes and ideas. Two types of theories dominate. They explain urban crime by a subculture of violence or by a subculture of poverty. Subculture of poverty theories have often focused on crime in ghettos in central cities, but this is a type of environment that does not exist in Stockholm.

## Geographical Selection of Individuals and the Influence from Local Environment

The theories just discussed are not total in the sense that they can on their own adequately explain crime rates of urban areas. Instead, they may offer partial or idealized explanations, focusing on particular aspects. This is not surprising, since the social mechanisms that underlie the crime rates of urban areas can be assumed to be complex and difficult to describe in full. A micro-macro view of the matter provides insights into this complexity. Crime rates and other factors of areas can be seen as aggregates of individual data of the inhabitants. The relationship between the rates and the factors may be analyzed by considering two types of mechanisms: mechanisms producing relationships on the individual level between various properties and the generation of crime (crimes committed by the individual or by others), and geographical selection processes that imply that individuals with certain properties and certain tendencies to generate crime are to be found in certain areas. The mechanisms producing the individual relationships are of two types – those that work on the local level only and those that work on the global level. Global mechanisms are those mechanisms that work in the same way everywhere irrespective of geographical location. Local mechanisms, on the other hand, are

specific for some particular area or areas. They are dependent on the conditions –
the physical conditions and the social make-up – in this area or these areas.

Thus, in order to explain a rate of crimes committed by the inhabitants in
an area at least three issues must be considered: 1) the global individual-level
relationships between the generation of crime and various properties, 2) the
geographical selection of individuals according to some factors and the resulting
distribution of properties in areas, and 3) the influences of local properties on
the generation of crime on the individual level. There can be no doubt that the
first two of these issues are important. Certainly, there are properties that are
related globally on the individual level to the generation of crime and that are
also involved in geographical selection processes, thereby creating a relationship
between the rates of properties and the rate of crime in areas. The selection is
above all determined by the economic resources of the individuals and by the
properties of the areas, including the dwellings in these. The competition among
individuals for attractive dwellings and other local advantages lies at bottom of
this process. Thus, individuals' economic resources are a very important selective
factor, and even if these resources do not cause crime directly on the individual
level, they are related to properties, for example other resources properties and
control properties, that do cause crime, and these crime-affecting properties are
therefore geographically differentiated.

Thus, an area's social make-up may have an indirect influence on its crime
because of the selection of individuals with certain tendencies to generate crime
globally. But how is it with the direct influence of the social organization of those
individuals living in the area? Social organization should then be taken in a broad
sense. It is not necessarily a question of any formal organization. Some kind of more
permanent, informal social contacts between individuals from different families is
sufficient. As we have seen, there is research on crime committed by inhabitants in
urban areas that is based on the assumption that there is a local social organization
in these areas that affects crime. Social disorganization theory is based on this
assumption, and subcultural theory can probably also be seen as being so based
to considerable extent. Ideas of this type can also be seen as being consistent with
social control theory – social control can be assumed to work better to inhibit crime
if the local society is more strongly organized according to conventional lines.
Thus, it is or can be assumed in these theories that the cross-sectional relationship
that exists on the area level between crime of the inhabitants and other factors is to
a significant extent the result of the influence of local social organization.

However, this assumption is not self-evident. It seems that cross-sectional
relationships on the area level between crime and social factors of the types in
question do not need to be the result of a direct influence of any local social
organization at all. They can have at least two other explanations: 1) As mentioned,
if the values of crime-affecting individual-level factors are geographically
differentiated, a relationship on the area level between the aggregated values
of these factors and crime arises. In this case there is no direct influence from
conditions of the area on crime, regardless of whether these conditions are

organizational or of some other type. 2) If, on the individual level, there is an influence on the inhabitants of an area and their crime from nonorganizational conditions in the area – for example, the physical opportunities to commit crime – that are related to organizational social conditions, this may, after aggregation, give rise to relationships of the types in question on the area level. Thus, these two types of influences refer to conditions on the individual (or family) level that are not caused directly by social organization, but they lead to relationships on the area level between crime and this organization. It should be noted that the relationships on the individual level might be very weak but still lead to relationships of significant strength on the area level (see below).

There is another problem with the idea that influences from local organization give rise to relationships between crime rates and other factors on the area level, and that is that there is reason to question whether, as a rule, there in large cities really is much local organization of social life of the type referred to here. The high population density, the high degree of anonymity, and the good communications in these cities can be assumed to work against the development of such a state of things. Of course, there are networks of contacts between individuals, but these networks do not need to be locally limited. In fact, it has been found that urban residents have rather few close relationships with neighbors (Wellman, 1979). Thus, the idea of the locally limited social organization probably fits rather poorly as a description of the metropolitan environment. It probably fits the conditions of communities in rural areas better.

Considering the problems discussed above, a central question in the research on urban crime is whether and to what extent the cross-sectional relationships found on the area level between crime and other factors are due to the fact that the area environment exerts an influence on the criminality of the individuals living in the area. Looking at existing research, it is often difficult to decide whether such an influence really exists. The problem of separating the direct influence of the area on the crime of the individuals from the indirect influence of the area that is due to geographical selection has to a rather great extent been ignored in the research – particularly in older research. Researchers have often presupposed in a fairly simplistic manner that statistical relationships on the area level express a direct influence. In modern research, however, more sophisticated methods have been used (the study made by Sampson and Groves, 1989, is an example).

If the area where individuals live affects their criminality, a cross-sectional relationship between area and individual criminality would be expected to exist. However, this cross-sectional, individual-level relationship does not need to be strong in order for there to be strong relationships on the area level between crime and various factors. In a study I carried out examining the individual-level relationship between registered criminality and geographical location among young males who had resided for a long period of time in the same areas of Greater Stockholm, findings indicated that this relationship was very weak for all types of crime and for all points in time (Dahlbäck, 1996a). However, the area-level relationships that were calculated in the same data between crime, on the one hand, and income and occupational status, on the other, were found to be strong.

Thus, it was found that area-level relationships between crime and some factors were strong in spite of the fact that the individual-level relationship between area and crime was very weak. Of course, this does not mean that the individual-level relationship between criminality and area or the mechanisms underlying this relationship were uninteresting to consider in explaining the area-level relationships – had there been no influence of the local environment on individual criminality and no geographical selection that resulted in the fact that individuals with certain criminality values or certain characteristics that led to criminality tended to land in certain areas, there would have been no relationship on the area level between crime and area factors.

The results from my previous analysis of Stockholm data can be used to evaluate the influence of the local environment on individual crime. These data were affected by both of the two mechanisms mentioned – the influence of the local environment on individual crime and the selection processes that resulted in certain individuals' landing in certain areas (thus, in this study it was only the question of the influence of the local environment on the individual's own crime, not of the environment's influence on the individual's generation of crime among others). These two mechanisms can be assumed to have affected the relationship between individuals' crime and area of residence in the same direction – areas with a disadvantageous environment can be assumed to have been conducive to individual criminality, and the selection processes can be assumed to have resulted in the fact that individuals with social backgrounds that were conducive to crime tended to land in the same type of areas. Since the relationships found between individual criminality and area of residence were very weak, the conclusion must be drawn that both the relationship between area of residence and individual criminality that was due to the direct influence of the area and the relationship between area of residence and this criminality that was due to the indirect influence of the selection processes were very weak. Thus, the influence of the area on individual criminality was very weak in both respects.

However, this conclusion pertains to Stockholm and Swedish conditions. What about large cities in other countries? Focus is, as mentioned, on the influence of local environment, the neighborhood, on individual criminality. This is a subject that has interested researchers much (see, for example, Simcha-Fagan and Schwartz, 1986; Peeples and Loeber, 1994), and it seems that it has been found in most empirical studies that the proportion of the variance in criminality that is uniquely explained by the neighborhood is small (Simcha-Fagan and Schwartz, 1986; Gottfredson et al., 1991; Elliott et al., 1996; Schneiders et al., 2003; Oberwittler, 2004; Weijters et al., 2007) – thus the same result that I found for Stockholm.

A problem in much research of this type is the fact that data is nonexperimental, which means that environmental and selection influences are difficult to separate (see Duncan and Magnuson, 2003). Ideally, one might think, data should be experimental, that is, individuals who are randomly assigned to different areas should be compared with respect to their criminality. Then, the differences found could be assumed to be due to the influence of the local environment only. Actually, such studies have been made to describe the results of the Moving to Opportunity (MTO) program, which has been in operation since 1994 in five cities in USA – Baltimore, Boston, Chicago, Los Angeles, and New York (Feins and Shroder, 2005; Kling et al., 2005).

In the MTO program, low-income families having children and living in ordinary public housing or in Section 8 project based housing (a sort of privately operated public housing) in high-poverty census tracts could take part. Participating families were randomly assigned to one of three groups: 1) *An experimental group* – these families were offered the opportunity to relocate using a housing voucher that could be used only in low-poverty census tracts, and they were given mobility counseling. 2) *A Section 8 group* – these families received regular Section 8 vouchers that could be used anywhere, and they got no mobility counseling. 3) *A control group* – these families received no vouchers. The families have been followed from recruitment and their relocations have been recorded. As expected, the families of the experimental group often moved to areas that were better in various respects than the areas to which the members of the Section 8 group moved and much better than the areas to which the members of the control group moved (Rosenbaum and Harris, 2001).

Kling et al. (2005) have analyzed neighborhood effects on the criminality of the young individuals in the about 4,600 families that volunteered for the MTO program from 1994 to 1997 (see also Harcourt and Ludwig, 2006). Almost all of these families were African-American or Hispanic. The main analytic sample consists of youth 15–25 years of age at the end of 2001. Data on crime refer to administratively recorded arrests and self-reported arrests and other measures of delinquent behaviors. Several other types of data were also collected.

As Kling et al. mention, there are criminological theories that imply that moving to an environment that is better in economic, educational, criminal and other respects can be expected to have an advantageous effect on young individuals' criminality. However, that was not what they found in their study, at least not generally. True, they found that taking part in the experimental condition reduced arrests for both violent and property crimes among the young females in comparison with the control group. For the young males, it was also found that taking part in the experimental condition reduced arrests for violent crimes, at least in the short run. However, for these individuals the arrests for property crimes increased strongly after 3–4 years. The same pronounced change was not found for the Section 8 group members. Thus, it seems that the young males and females from disadvantaged backgrounds reacted in different ways to the new neighborhood environments. Kling et al. suggest that this difference is due to the fact that the boys were more likely than the girls to take advantage of the opportunities of property crimes in the affluent areas to which they moved. It seems probable, the authors maintain, that the boys were more likely to do so because they were less controlled or felt a stronger competition among peers.

Certainly, the study of Kling et al. has limitations when it comes to drawing conclusions about how crime on the area level is caused. The study is about individual criminality, not about area crime, and the individuals studied constitute a limited group. Moreover, it seems likely that relatively many of the moving individuals in the experimental group landed in areas that were rather disadvantageous in social properties other than the one considered and that the difference between the social changes they experienced as a result of their moves and the corresponding social changes of the individuals in the control group was not very large (Sampson, 2008). Furthermore, four years may be a period that is too short – other results may appear in the future. These concerns notwithstanding, the results are interesting and give something to think about. The picture they give of the relationship between environment and individual criminality does not simply mean that "better" environments always produce lower criminality.

**Critical Views of the Research**

The research on the causes of rates of crimes committed by residents in urban areas can be criticized for severe theoretical and methodological shortcomings. Below I discuss some of the requirements that need to be fulfilled in studies on this subject using register data in order that conclusions about causal relationships can be drawn. These include:

1. that the studies are longitudinal and built on panel data for the areas,
2. that the causal analysis is performed so that the direct influence of the environment is separated from the indirect influence that is due to geographical selection of individuals,
3. that the effects of micro-level processes of different types – both intra- and interindividual ones – are considered in the analysis,
4. that the many independent factors that may play a role are taken into account and controlled for,
5. that models that describe interaction are used,
6. that a method is used that implies that conclusions about actual criminality can be drawn from register data on residents' crimes.

*Using a longitudinal approach.* In studying the relationship for urban areas between the rate of crime of the residents and various influencing factors, nonexperimental data must be used. Of course, a longitudinal approach gives a much better basis for analyzing the causes of crime when data is of this type than does a cross-sectional approach. Using panel time-series data is particularly advantageous. Different factors may have effects that come with different speed. For example, moves have immediate effects, whereas some social processes have delayed effects. Determining such temporally differing effects may be important for understanding the causes of crime.

*Separating the influences in areas and the influences from geographical selection.* A fatal shortcoming of much previous research is, as argued above, that researchers have failed to separate two influences of the environment in a given area on crime: the direct influence on those who live in this area and the indirect influence that is due to geographical selection.

*Considering the aggregated effects of micro-level processes.* In much previous research, the influences on area crime that come from micro-level processes (within or between individuals) are not considered. I think that more can be done to deal with this problem, and making such an effort is among the goals of this study.

*Using a comprehensive set of independent factors.* Discussions above show that in analyzing the crime rates of residents of urban areas, several complex causal relations must be considered. Since data are nonexperimental, it must therefore be possible to control analyzed relationships for various factors. This means that several factors should be considered, which puts great demands on the access to data – demands that are probably difficult to fulfill for register data in many cases.

*Considering interaction.* In order to elucidate the causes of crime, an adequate model must, of course, be used in the analysis. The adequacy of the model depends among other things on its form. The demand for an adequate form is often neglected in the research. Linear models are often used without justification. However, it seems possible that models permitting interaction effects would give better explanations of crime than do linear models.

*Drawing conclusions about actual from registered crime.* There is also reason to criticize the measures of crime used in the research. In many cases, the measurement of the crimes committed by the inhabitants is based on register data, data that pertain to individuals suspected, apprehended or sentenced. But such data seldom describe actual crime accurately. To be sure, all crimes do not result in the perpetrators' being registered, and the probability of perpetrators' being detected and sentenced varies strongly between different types of crimes. These problems are seldom adequately treated in the research.

To the best of my knowledge, there is no study – either Swedish or non-Swedish – which fulfills all these requirements. For example, most studies are cross-sectional. The lack of advanced longitudinal studies is in many cases probably due to the fact that time series of adequate data have been difficult to obtain. However, such data do exist in Sweden.

Chapter 2

# Theory

## Geographical Selection of Individuals and Crime Rates

Forming an adequate causal theory of crime among residents in urban areas is difficult. One reason for this is that such a theory must simultaneously consider the three previously mentioned kinds of influences on crime – the global individual-level influence, the influence of geographical selection of individuals, and the influence of the local environment on those who live in the areas. One complication is the fact that some explanatory factors can be assumed to play a role for more than one of these influences. For example, social resources may play a role for all three influences.

However, viewed in and of itself, the process of geographical selection of individuals is rather easily understood in rough outline. This is essentially a question – at least in the short and the medium time perspective – of matching dwellings with dwellers. In this matching process, economic and household composition factors are crucial. Economic factors, of course, play a dominant role. In order for individuals to be able to live in an area, they must have money to pay the costs of living there. Household composition factors – for example, the number and ages of household members – are also important. Certain dwellings fit households composed in certain ways. Other factors may also play a role, for example the ethnic status of individuals and the housing policy of the local government, and the influence of some of these factors may not be as easily understood (as to the influence of housing policy, see Bottom and Wiles, 1986; Bottoms et al., 1992).

Nevertheless, much of the process of geographical selection of individuals is self-evident. This is perhaps one reason that in the research studying crime among residents in urban areas, interest tends to be focused on the direct influence of the physical and social environment of the area on the degree of criminal activity of those who live there. Another reason is probably that the direct influence is seen as particularly important from a developmental perspective. Much of the growth of population in Western societies in modern times has occurred in cities, and many researchers see urban environments as conducive to crime. In the light of these facts, explaining the urban environment's direct influence on the crimes of residents has probably been seen as more fruitful than explaining the influence of geographical sorting of individuals into different urban areas. Also in this study, the direct influence of the environment is seen as particularly interesting.

However, even if the direct influence of the environment is particularly interesting, the effects of the geographical selection must be considered when forming an overall theory of crime among residents in urban areas. People who have moved to or out of areas, as well as those who have been locked into areas and have not been able to move, may have had particular values on the independent factors, thus affecting the relationship between the crime rate and these factors in area populations. Thus, in order to uncover the direct influences of the environment, these effects of geographical differentiation must be considered.

## Micro- and Macro-Level Aspects of Influences in the Area

If there is an influence of the environment in an urban area on crime of those residing there, how should this influence be explained? This study uses an approach, in which both micro- and macro-level aspects are considered. Total societal crime among residents is seen as being affected by influences from the environment on the individuals, and the social environment is seen as composed of properties of the residents. Below, I discuss how influences on the individuals may be constituted and how macro-level conditions may arise.

Suppose that we describe societal crime in an area with the crime rate of the residents. How, then, should this crime rate be modeled? Could the model be constructed as the aggregate of the residents' choices to commit crimes, expressed according to a micro-level model of general form? That is, could individuals' choices between criminal and noncriminal action alternatives form the micro-level theoretical basis, and their aggregated choices, that is, their aggregated crimes, be seen as the dependent factor? Perhaps, but it is difficult to construct and use such a macro-level model based on a micro-level choice model, for example of the rational-choice type. This is among other things due to problems with the nonlinearity and the noncontinuous character of the micro-level model (Dahlbäck, 2003, pp. 107–133). Another approach would be to see the criminality of the individual, that is, the total number of crimes the individual commits over a specific period of time, as the product of factors in his environment and his proneness to commit crime. For example, we could see criminality as the product of the quantity of the encountered situations when committing crime is attractive and the probability that the individual will commit a crime at one such situation (Dahlbäck, 2003, pp. 164–173). Such a model would be easier to construct, although describing in a detailed and explicit way how the two factors are caused by various societal properties would be difficult, because the factors have complex causes and are difficult to measure with register data.

The individualistic approach used in this study does not apply in an exclusive or strict way any of these choice-based theoretical perspectives. Instead, the individuals forming the social environment in an area are seen as influencing crime in that area not only by their own choices about committing crimes, but also by affecting others' choices. The individuals are both potential perpetrators and potential instigators/stimulators of crime, and are both influenced and influencing.

What influences on residents' crimes come from the environment in urban areas but are not due to geographical selection processes? In principle, the environment may influence potential perpetrators in two ways – by influencing their attitudes or views or by influencing the occurrence of situations in which they may commit crime. These influences may exert themselves via the social relationships between residents. Several questions can be asked about such relationships: How are they constituted? What processes are involved? How important are they? How do residents become influenced? What residents are influenced?

There are many possible answers to these questions. Several individual characteristics may be influenced and affect crime. Examples that pertain to the individual's own criminal behavior include the relative valuation of criminal activity vs. noncriminal activity, conceptions of the outcomes of crime, the estimation of the probability of being detected if committing crime, and the tendency to act so as to land in situations when crime is an attractive action alternative. Influences may result from the individual's being involved in various local social relations, for example, relations in the home, in small peer groups, in groups of a more diffuse type in the neighborhood, in associations, or in institutional settings such as schools (these are at least theoretical possibilities, but I am, as previously mentioned, somewhat skeptical about the significance of influences of a local social organization beyond the family/household). Influences may work by various mechanisms or processes. For example, the individual may adopt particular views pertaining to committing crime because these are socially accepted or have high status, predominate and form natural reference points, or satisfy emotional demands. Moreover, various types of individuals may be influenced in particular ways.

Thus, the general picture of the influences on crime from the local social environment is complex. Many types of processes may be involved. In this study, such individual-level processes will be focused that imply that individuals are affected by social control or social resources. When put in a dynamic, societal context, these individual-level processes may give rise to macro-level processes and to macro-level outcomes that create input for subsequent individual-level processes.

For example, if the social bonds between the individuals in a society change, this can be assumed to result in a macro-level process of altered control. The bonds form a net between individuals and if a direct bond between two individuals is created, more individuals may be affected because they are spun into indirect bonds. Thus, total control is a complicated function of direct and indirect bonds. Secondly, the distribution of social resources in an area can perhaps create a situation that influences crime. If there are more social resources in the area, problems of various types that could lead to crime may be more easily handled. However, if the distribution is uneven, it may mean that inequality creates stress and crime. Moreover, concentration in areas of individuals with poor resources may lead to processes in which particular attitudes toward deviance and crime emerge.

## Social Control and Social Resources as Causal Factors

What independent factors should be used for analyzing the direct influence on crime from the environment in the areas? This question cuts to the very heart of sociological explanation of the matter, and researchers hold many divergent views on this point. My own answer to the question is as follows. Even if I do not think that a model of the crime rate should be constructed as an aggregation of the inhabitants' choices about committing crimes, I regard the choice situations of potential perpetrators as fundamental. These situations should be considered with respect to the action alternatives and their outcomes and the utility values and probabilities of the outcomes. Simplistically, it could be said that the choice is between committing crime and not committing it, and that the outcome of the commission of crime is either a successful crime or an unsuccessful crime (including punishment).

Considering this choice perspective on crime and considering also the relationships found in the research on the area level between crime and various factors, I have included social control and social resources factors in this study. These factors may play a role when individuals choose between committing and not committing crime, because they affect the choice elements that the individuals consider. I discuss below how these factors may play such a role on the individual level.

I adhere to the social bonds perspective of crime. Thus, I assume that people who have stronger social bonds of conventional type are more reluctant to engage in committing crime. From a choice perspective, this can be explained in two ways: 1) that individuals with such bonds have lower relative utility from committing crime because they risk losing these bonds and becoming unfavorably regarded socially if they commit a crime and are detected, and 2) that individuals with such bonds face higher probabilities of detection because they live less anonymously. Thus, stronger social bonds of conventional type mean that the punishment becomes harsher and its probability higher.

I focus on social control factors that describe foreign extraction and social contacts pertaining to the family/household. Such factors have shown to be strongly related to crime on the area level. It can be mentioned that in a longitudinal study of the changes in the theft rate in Swedish municipalities between 1980 and 1990, I found very strong longitudinal relationships between crime and the proportion of the population that consisted of inhabitants who were foreigners and divorcees, respectively (Dahlbäck, 1998a).

By social resources I mean such things that can be used in order to avoid and manage social problems and to enjoy social success. Social status, money, knowledge and useful social relations are, as previously mentioned, important examples. In much research less access to such resources is assumed to result in more crime. Agnew's idea that lack of social resources and inequality cause strain, which could be a motive for crime, is one suggestion of how such a relationship may arise. However, as mentioned above the evidence for this idea is not particularly strong. In fact, influences of social resources on the criminality of young individuals in general have been found to be weak.

Nevertheless, it is a fact that persons who habitually commit thefts or violent crimes tend to be short of social resources and to come from environments in the same predicament. The idea about strain is one way of explaining this fact, but there may also, one could think, be other ways. One explanation may be that the relationship between social resources and criminality is, to some extent at least, due to the fact that social resources can be used to offset a criminal career. That is, lack of these resources does not generate crime directly, but is involved in a process that may lead to more crime. If an individual has committed crime and has then landed in a situation that is conducive to continued criminal activity, for example because of negative social reactions that drive him away from conventional society, lack of these resources may leave him unable to avoid the situation. It seems that this explanation has attracted less interest in modern research than the strain theory.

The same type of explanation could apply to social problems that are not brought about by a started criminal career, but that still may lead to crime. Assumably, individuals with small social resources have a relatively small potential for managing a variety of social problems that are conducive to crime. These might include, for example, problems generated by poor social control, such as problems due to living in a disintegrated family and having foreign ethnic status.

I think that the ideas that lack of social resources causes strain and that social resources give the potential to manage various social problems that cause crime can both be combined with the idea about the influence on crime of social control. Thus, in order to explain the criminality of individuals and their criminal career, information about social resources should, it may be assumed, be used in combination with information about the social control, because lack of the resources has a particularly strong influence on the individuals' (further) criminality if social control is weak. As to the potential to manage social problems, it may also be that lack of resources in the environment interacts with social control (for empirical support, see Hay et al., 2006). Hence, two types of interaction – within and between individuals – could be considered.

To put it shortly, the reasons that social resources and social control may interact are the following ones. Assume first that poor resources produce strain. This strain may interact with social control, because it produces a motive for crime that can be more easily realized if control is weaker. Assume secondly that poor resources give a small potential for managing crime or social problems that are conducive to crime. This poor managing may interact with social control, because weaker control generates more crime and more social problems.

These ideas, which thus mean that social resources and possibly perceived inequality influence individual crime in interaction with social control, seem possible to reconcile with the results of research that no very strong direct influence of lack of resources on this crime has been found, and they would be interesting to apply to explain crime on the aggregate level. There is research indicating that interaction exists on this level (McNulty, 1999). In this study, both aggregated micro-level interaction and interaction between area-level factors are considered.

The two types of interaction between social resources and social control that have been hypothesized – interaction due to the fact that poor resources produce strain and interaction due to the fact that resources can be used to manage various types of problems that lead to crime – refer to a great extent to the same resources and control factors. They are therefore difficult to distinguish from each other – particularly, of course, if this must be done knowing only their aggregate effects, as in the study presented in this book.

## Micro-Level Interaction and the Form of Models

Most of the theories of crime committed by residents in urban areas that have been presented in the literature are vague as to how the relationships between independent factors and crime are constituted formally. The theories state that the rate of crime is influenced by certain factors, and they also characterize to some extent the relationships between these factors and crime. However, most theories do not detail in any advanced way how crime should be modeled formally. Finding accurate models on the basis of these theories is therefore no easy task. This is mirrored in the fact that most empirical studies based on these theories use very simple models. In many cases, models are simply linear, and linearity seems to have been chosen much in ignorance of the true form.

This may seem somewhat surprising, considering the individualistic perspective of the theories, for example as regards the social control and social resources theories. These theories are founded on ideas about individual behavior, that is, when applied to crime in urban areas they are founded on ideas about the behavior of the inhabitants of the areas, but researchers who use them seldom derive their models of area crime from a micro-level model of individual behavior. Instead, the micro-macro link is implicit and vague. Therefore, it would be interesting to derive explicitly a macro-level model from a micro-level model. However, it turns out, as shown below, that doing this involves some complications and may lead to models that are not as simple as the models mostly used.

Of course, the derivation of a model of macro-level behavior, that is, of urban area crime, from micro-level behavior is no great formal problem if two conditions hold: that the dependent factor in the micro-level model is perfectly explained using a linear model and that the derivation is accomplished by simple aggregation. Suppose that macro-level behavior is – as is often the case in the research – the number of crimes committed per inhabitant in the area, that the micro-level unit is the individual, that micro-level behavior is the individual's impact on crime in the area – an impact generated via own as well as others' criminal behavior – and that area crime is modeled as the mean of the inhabitants' impacts. If the individual's impact on area crime is perfectly explained by known independent factors in a linear function, the derivation of the model of area crime is straightforward. Area crime is then simply the same linear function of the means of the inhabitants' factor values.

However, if the micro-level model is non-linear and characterized by interaction, then the derivation is not, as I show below, that simple. And, actually, it seems that an adequate micro-level model must be characterized by interaction. Two types of mechanisms may produce interaction effects. First, interaction may occur due to the fact that various properties of each separate individual in an area interact in their influence on crime in the area. Second, interaction could be due to the fact that properties of different individuals interact in their influence on crime.

Thus, in the first case interaction is caused by the fact that different individual factors – for example, factors that imply that the individual is poorly socially controlled and factors that imply that the individual has few social resources – reinforce one another's influence on crime. As far as the individual's own criminal behavior is concerned (which is thus only one way that the individual may have an impact on area crime), the reason for this can, seeing the matter from a utility-maximization perspective, be assumed to be that the factors interact in their influence on the individual's relative utility of committing crime as compared with not committing crime and that this interaction effect is transmitted to the choice about the commission. However, it should be noticed that the non-continuous character of the choice's function of the relative utility complicates the analysis of the relationship between choice-making factors and choice (how this works when choices are rationally made, see Dahlbäck, 2003, pp. 19–33, 86–93, 155–162). The crime-inciting factors involved in interaction may be of different kinds. For example, they may be incidentally caused. Thus, it may be that the individual's propensity to commit crime, which can be assumed to be a function of the relative utility of committing crime, interact with the frequency of the individual's being in situations when crime happens to be an attractive action alternative (Dahlbäck, 2003, pp. 163–173).

In the second case, there is interaction between factors of different individuals. For example, if different inhabitants in an area who have properties conducive to crime are together, these properties may reinforce one another's influence on total area crime so that the influence is a nonadditive function of them. Such an interactive mechanism could easily be imagined in connection with different theories of crime among residents in urban areas, for example sub-cultural theory. A criminal sub-culture could be thought to develop only if there are a sufficiently large number of individuals with properties conducive to crime who have contact with each other.

I describe below how micro-level interaction may be modeled and what aggregating individuals' influences on area crime means for the construction of a model of crime on the macro or area level. I will, among other things, prove or make it probable 1) that interaction within individuals and interaction between individuals often lead to different models of area crime, 2) that interaction of homogeneous type between individuals leads approximately to interaction of ordinary type on the macro level, 3) that it is impossible to construct a perfect and practically manageable model of area crime in terms of means of simple micro-level factors of common types if there is interaction between correlated factors within individuals, 4) that aggregated within-individual interaction can be assumed often to be more important than aggregated between-individual interaction of homogenous type in explaining area crime.

Thus, I maintain that micro-level interaction of different types may give rise to different influences that must be considered when modeling crime. Consider first the case in which there is interaction between properties of each separate individual. Assume that we have data on the independent factors $x_i$ and $z_i$ and on several other independent factors $u_i$, $v_i$, $w_i$, ..., measured for individual $i$ ($i = 1, ... , n$) in an area. Assume also that the factors $x_i$ and $z_i$ interact in their influence on the individual's impact $y_i$ on crime in the area in the following way:

$$y_i = b_0 x_i z_i + b_1 u_i + b_2 v_i + b_3 w_i + ... + a + \varepsilon_i,$$ (1)

where the $b$ values and $a$ are constants and $\varepsilon_i$ is an error. Assume further that the crime rate studied, denoted $C$, is equal to the sum of the $y$ values of all the individuals in the area divided by $n$, the number of individuals. That is, $C$ is equal to the mean of the $y$ values or $M_y$. Then, $C$ is equal to the mean of the values of the right side of (1), and if it is also assumed that $\varepsilon_i = 0$, the following equality can be taken as a macro-level model:

$$C = M_y = b_0 M_{xz} + b_1 M_u + b_2 M_v + b_3 M_w + ... + a.$$ (2)

However, the assumption that there is no error is unrealistic, and when such an error exists there may be problems in forming aggregates for the right side of (1) – problems whose nature is dependent on how the error is constituted. Above all, problems will arise if the error contains a factor that governs geographical selection.

Nevertheless, even if such problems do exist, the mean value of $b_0 x_i z_i$ can be assumed to affect area crime, and it can be used in macro-level analysis, given that an appropriate set of other factors is also used. However, can this mean value be expressed in macro-level terms of $X$ and $Z$ in a way that is practically manageable? That is, is it possible to construct a practically manageable model of $C$? It holds true that

$$(\Sigma x_i z_i)/n = M_x M_z + r_{xz} s_x s_z,$$ (3)

where $r$ and $s$ denote correlation and standard deviation. By using (3), the value of $C$ can be assumed to be an expression that includes the sum of the product of the means of the individual-level factors and the product of the correlation between these factors and their standard deviations. Thus, the model of $C$ includes an expression that describes the effect of interaction between the means of the factors and an additional expression that describes the effect of interaction among the correlation and the standard deviations. The latter expression is not formulated exclusively in practically manageable terms – in most cases the value of $r_{xz}$ is unknown – and it cannot be formulated in such terms so that a perfect model appears.

Formula (3) refers to two individual-level factors. However, if there are more such factors that interact, $C$ can be derived by using an extension of (3). The model of $C$ will then include an expression that describes the product of the means of the factors and an additional expression that includes intercorrelations between factors and products of factors as well as standard deviations of these factors and factor products. Much of the discussion below concerning two factors, will, if properly adapted, apply to such multi-factor interaction.

Obviously, a model in which the right side of (3) is substituted into (2) is awkward to put to practical use in many research situations, which leads one to wonder if this part of (3) might be simplified. If $r_{xz} = 0$, the additional expression of the right side of (3) vanishes, and $M_x M_z$ remains. Moreover, if the correlation is very weak and the absolute values of the means are very high as compared to the standard deviations, $M_x M_z$ can be used as a good approximation of $(\Sigma x_i z_i)/n$.

However, in this study such an approximation cannot be used despite the fact that the correlations between factors are relatively weak in several cases. The reason is that the additional expression, that is, the product of the correlation between the factors and their standard deviations, has a high value in comparison with the product of the mean values of the factors, which is due to the fact that the factors are dichotomous (0,1) variables that have higher standard deviations than means. Another reason that the approximation cannot be used is that the influence on crime of aggregated interaction within individuals will be analyzed together with the corresponding influence of aggregated interaction between individuals (see below), and since the aggregated interaction between individuals as conceptualized here is approximately equal to $M_x M_z$, the full formula (3) for interaction within individuals must be used in the analysis.

For certain factors $x$ and $z$ the value of $b_0$ can be assumed to be relatively high, that is, the influence on crime of the interaction can be assumed to be relatively strong, for the following reason. If $x$ and $z$ are defined so that higher values of them are more conducive to crime, the expression $b_0(\Sigma x_i z_i)/n$ describes the influence of positive interaction between these factors for the residents in the area. Suppose that $x$ and $z$ are dichotomous factors, measured so that they have the value 1 for the crime-stimulating category and the value 0 for the other category (for many properties in the study presented in this book, the individual-level factors are constructed as such dichotomies, and the mean values of these factors are thus the percentages of the residents having the value 1). Then $(\Sigma x_i z_i)/n$ is the relative size of the group of individuals who have the value 1 on both factors, that is, the relative size of the group that can be assumed to contribute much to area crime. It is well known from criminological research that relatively few individuals commit most of crime in society, and the same can be assumed to be true for the influence on urban area crime. This means that a group of individuals who have the value 1 on two crime-conducive factors may be small but still contribute relatively much to area crime, which means that the value of $b_0$ will be relatively high.

The next issue that must be resolved pertains to the possibilities of deriving a model of $C$ from assumptions about interaction between individuals. Assume that crime is affected by the interaction between the factors $x$ and $z$ of different individuals combined in pairs and that the influence on crime of this interaction can be modeled in the same way for all such pairs. Assume further that the contribution to crime produced by one such pair of individuals is a function of the product of their factor values, and that the total amount of contributions to crime, that is, to $C$, produced by all possible pairs of individuals in the area can be expressed as a linear function of the sum of their products divided by the number of pairs. This latter factor can be written as

$$\frac{\sum_i \sum_j x_i z_j - \sum_i x_i z_i}{n^2 - n}, \tag{4}$$

where both $i$ and $j$ denote individuals from the population of $n$ individuals in the area. The expression of the sum of $x_i z_i$ above the fraction line in (4) denotes the just discussed aggregated products of $x$ and $z$ within individuals.

The numerator of (4) is made up of a difference between two expressions, each of which describes a particular type of aggregated products of $x$ and $z$ values. The first expression describes such products of all pairs of $x$ and $z$ values, irrespective of whether these values refer to different individuals or to the same individual, while the second expression only describes the within-individual products of $x$ and $z$ values. Clearly, the first expression describes much more product pairs than the second expression. The number of pairs is $n^2$ for the first expression and $n$ for the second expression, that is, the number of pairs of the second expression is $1/n$ times the number of pairs of the first expression. This means that if $n$ is a high number, which is the case in this study, the products of the second expression will be relatively insignificant for the value of (4) as compared with the products of the first expression, and therefore the second expression can be disregarded and the expression

$$\frac{\sum_i \sum_j x_i z_j}{n^2}, \tag{5}$$

be used as a good approximation of (4).

If statistical measures for the data set of the $n^2$ cases referred to in (5) are given the same symbols as for the data set of $n$ cases but with a bolder face, (5) can be written as

$$M_x M_z + r_{xz} s_x s_z . \tag{6}$$

However, since every value of $x$ is paired with every value of $z$, $r_{xz} = 0$. Thus, (6) can be written as $M_x M_z$. But $M_x = M_x$ and $M_z = M_z$, and therefore the influence on $C$ of interaction between individuals is approximately a linear function of $M_x M_z$. An argumentation of a similar type can be carried out for the interaction between three or more factors, leading to the conclusion that the influence on $C$ is approximately a linear function of the product of the means of these factors.

Thus, if the influence on crime of interaction between individuals can be modeled in the same way for all pairs, the macro model can be constructed so that it includes a linear function of the product of the mean values of the individual-level factors. However, the assumption about same modeling is not very realistic, and $M_x M_z$ can therefore only be used as a very approximate measure of between-individual interaction. In most cases, interaction between different factors of different individuals will probably arise only if the individuals have personal contact with each other. Such contact is particularly frequent for individuals who work in the same place, go to the same school, etc., and who are similar in various other respects, for example in age, sex, and other background factors, and therefore the influence from interaction is particularly strong for them (this can, for example, be assumed to be the case with young individuals who know each other and who commit crime together; see Piquero et al., 2005; Haynie et al., 2006; Andresen and Felson, 2010). However, this is difficult to analyze empirically, because in general there is little or no register data on these contacts.

If the independent factors selected for empirical study are of types ordinarily used in the research, the same argument about the restricted potential for interaction due to poor personal contact between residents cannot be adduced against the use of $(\Sigma x_i z_i)/n$ as a measure of aggregated interaction for individuals belonging to a particular group. The two types of interaction differ. When $x$ and $z$ in the expression $(\Sigma x_i z_i)/n$ are dichotomous factors, this expression describes as mentioned the size of the limited group of residents having the value 1 on both factors. The members of such a group may have contact with each other and even if they don't they may look upon themselves as being members of a group characterized by the factors. The expression $M_x M_z$, on the other hand, describes aggregated interaction between pairs of $x$ and $z$ values referring to the whole population of the area in question – the pairs from the group described by the expression $(\Sigma x_i z_i)/n$ but also all other pairs. Many individuals of the latter pairs have no personal contact with each other and they do not look upon themselves as being members of a group characterized by the factors. Moreover, the single individuals of these pairs do not themselves have combinations of values of $x$ and $z$ that are particularly conducive to crime. Thus, it seems that there will often be a greater potential for a strong influence on crime from $(\Sigma x_i z_i)/n$ than from $M_x M_z$.

I will now discuss more in detail how the two properties $(\Sigma x_i z_i)/n$ and $M_x M_z$ may be used in empirical analysis and what reasons there are for their influence on crime. I assume that $x$ and $z$ are dichotomous factors, measured as mentioned above.

The two properties should be used simultaneously. One reason for this is that they together describe the combinations of different values of the factors $x$ and $z$ in a natural and exhaustive way. Dividing the combinations into those that refer to the same individuals and those that refer to different individuals is natural for theoretical reasons, and considering all these combinations is natural in a holistic analysis of area crime. Another reason for using the two properties simultaneously is causal. The two properties can be assumed to be correlated with each other (if the factors $x$ and $z$ do not correlate with each other, the two properties coincide), and the influence on crime of one of them is therefore appropriately analyzed by controlling for the other.

Why may the two properties affect crime? That is, why may two individual-level factors $x$ and $z$ interact within and between individuals in their influence on crime? Let us first consider the property $(\Sigma x_i z_i)/n$. The reasons that within-individual interaction between $x$ and $z$ affects crime may be seen both from an intraindividual and an interindividual or social aspect. The algebraic form of the influence on $y$ indicates of course an intraindividual aspect – it is the question of the influence of interaction between the factors for single individuals on their impact on crime. On the other hand, the reason that the factors interact could be social. For example, if the individuals with crime-conducive values on both $x$ and $z$ particularly often have contact with each other or if they look upon themselves as being members of a group and are treated as such members by others, this may be a reason that they affect crime particularly strongly. Thus, the influence on crime of aggregated interaction within individuals may be the result of social processes.

Consider then the property $M_x M_z$. This property describes approximately aggregated interaction between individuals. However, it also appears in the formula of the property $(\Sigma x_i z_i)/n$. If $x$ and $z$ do not correlate with each other, $(\Sigma x_i z_i)/n$ is as mentioned equal to $M_x M_z$. However, in many interesting cases the two properties will not be equal. Suppose that they both are used in a regression analysis of crime. If the results obtained in this analysis indicate that $M_x M_z$ has an effect on crime, then it can probably in many cases be concluded that this effect comes from interaction between different factors of different individuals, because this is a type of social cause that is not described by $(\Sigma x_i z_i)/n$. However, if it turns out that crime is related to $(\Sigma x_i z_i)/n$, then it cannot be determined whether this relationship is due to a social process involving the individuals having the same values on the two factors. Moreover, if it turns out that crime is related to $M_x M_z$ when $(\Sigma x_i z_i)/n$ is not controlled for, then it is possible that this relationship absorbs effects of individuals having the same values on the two factors.

The fact that the two types of interaction differ as to intra- and interindividual causes is of interest when analyzing their effects on crime for residents who have had different possibilities of contacting each other. This is done in this study by analyzing these effects for the residents who have lived and for the residents who have not lived in their area for a long time.

I have now discussed the influence on crime of interaction between different factors, but what about the influence on crime of the same factor for different individuals? Does this influence per individual become stronger as the number of individuals having values on the factor indicating strong influences increases? This is an interesting question from a sociopolitical perspective, since it deals with the issue of whether total crime becomes greater if problem individuals – who can be assumed to influence others to commit crime – are concentrated in few areas rather than being spread among several areas. The question may be analyzed using dichotomous individual factors. Suppose again that such a factor is constructed so that the value 1 is given to individuals who can be assumed to exert influence conducive to crime, and that the value 0 is given to individuals who can be assumed not to exert such influence. The form of the relationship between the mean factor value and the mean crime rate in the area then tells us, if causally interpreted, how the influence per individual is constituted. If the relationship (which is assumed to be positive) is linear, the influence per individual does not become stronger the greater the proportion of individuals having the value 1. This in turn means that this influence can be assumed not to be affected by interaction between individuals. However, if the rate of crime grows at an increasing rate as the proportion increases (the first and second derivatives are then positive), the influence can be assumed to be affected by such interaction.

Chapter 3

# Method

## General Design

The study presented in this book is designed to fulfill the requirements discussed above concerning analytical model, method and data. It is longitudinal and built on panel register data, considers individuals' relocations in order to separate the environment's direct influence on crime from the indirect influence via geographical selection, provides possibilities of analyzing the effects of micro-level interaction, uses many independent properties, applies nonlinear models to describe the relationships between crime and independent properties, and is constructed to permit conclusions to be drawn about actual crime from registered crime. Thus, the design is advantageous for analyzing causal mechanisms.

The areas studied cover the entire City of Stockholm. For most years considered there are 83 separate areas. However, for some early years – 1970 and 1975 and surrounding years – a few of these areas were not yet built-up. Thus, there were 80 areas in 1970 and 82 in 1975. Of the areas that were not built-up in 1970, two were later to become populated largely by foreign citizens, and they have developed reputations for having serious social problems. As to the definition of the areas, see Appendices I and III.

Most of the areas had more than 4,000 but fewer than 15,000 inhabitants during the period of time studied. In 1970, about 83 per cent of the areas had so many inhabitants; in 1980 and 1990, the corresponding percentages were 89 and 87 (the numbers of inhabitants of the areas in these three years are shown in Appendix II). Many of the areas are identical to districts used in official statistics from the city government, and most people probably see them as naturally limited areas. The government uses about 130 districts, but some adjacent districts have, due to small populations, been combined in this study. There was, as expected and as described below, strong social differentiation between the areas of the study during the investigated period of time.

Values on properties for the areas were produced as follows. Information about where individuals were registered as residents was obtained by running the code of the real estate where they were registered as living against a register on base geographical areas in the City. These base areas are smaller than the areas finally used. The data obtained for individuals living in these base areas was therefore aggregated up to the larger areas. Property values intended for analysis were then constructed. For this construction, there was in most cases information about all individuals in the areas.

Data, which is only of register type, was collected mainly for the period 1970–1990. Crime data was drawn from police registers and concerned crimes that identified persons were suspected of having committed. Only types of crimes that cover the same kinds of events across the different years were used. Information about suspects registered as living in the areas was obtained as follows. The personal code numbers of virtually all suspects are registered by the police. These numbers for all suspects in all crime investigations carried out during certain years in Sweden were run against the register of the total population of the country (the "RTB register" in Swedish), and the suspects living in the areas were selected. The crime data were collected for separate years (see below) and they refer to all suspects registered as living in the areas at the 31st of December of the year in question. Thus, area and crime are connected by means of the registered addresses of the suspects.

By using official statistics, it is possible to give a very good description of many independent properties assumed to have influenced residents' crimes. The conditions are particularly favorable for the time period 1970–1990 because of the statistics that come from the censuses of population and housing ("FOB" in Swedish) for the years 1970, 1975, 1980, 1985 and 1990 (no census has been conducted since 1990).

The independent properties measured refer to several things, including the residents' sex, age, citizenship, family/household status, dwellings, economic conditions, occupational status, unemployment and moves. For these properties, data were drawn from registers at Statistics Sweden (SCB in Swedish), above all registers of RTB, relocations, FOB, taxations, and social aid recipients.

Properties refer to approximately equally spaced points in time. Reference points are the 31st of December 1970, 1975, 1980, 1985 and 1990. Crime is finally measured so that it refers to the 31st of December 1980, 1985 and 1990. However, the FOB data for the years 1970, 1975, 1980, and 1990 refer to the 1st of November and for 1985 to the 15th of September. Thus, the FOB data do not refer exactly to the reference points, but the difference in time is small. Data for age and sex pertain exactly to the reference points. However, income and social aid pertain to the entire year preceding the reference point. In order to simplify matters, I will speak of "reference year" or only "year" instead of reference point in time when it is convenient and no misunderstanding may arise.

Longitudinal analyses have been performed with the aim of making clear how independent properties have affected the crime rate after different periods of time. In these analyses, single-equation models are constructed of the relationship between crime and values on independent properties at the same point in time as crime and at earlier points in time. For example, in some analyses crime at a reference point is seen as a function of independent properties that pertain to the same reference point and, if information is available and appropriate to use, to two previous reference points. In some analyses data are lagged and in some the change in crime rate is used as the dependent variable. Both nonlinear (product) models and linear models are tested.

As mentioned, consideration is paid to the interaction that may exist on the micro level between properties. Above all, efforts are made to make clear how social control and social resources properties interact when they affect crime. Following the formal analysis above, this is done by including measures of the two types of aggregated interaction in linear models. These measures are constructed for pairs of properties as 1) mean values of individual-level products of property values and 2) products of the mean values of the properties. Furthermore, models in which all independent properties enter in relationships with crime that are of a product, function-of-functions type described below are used.

In the study, efforts are made to separate the environment's direct influence on crime from its indirect influence via geographical selection. This separation is accomplished in two ways. First, it is accomplished by assuming that the indirect influence precedes the direct influence in time and by analyzing these influences and other influences as components of the cross-sectional relationship between selective factors and crime. Second, the separation is accomplished by considering patterns of individuals' relocations, as defined by their crossing the boundary of the area. Models are used that include values of independent properties for groups of individuals who have stayed in the area during different periods of time. In most analyses, these values are weighted by the groups' relative sizes. Suppose, for example, that there are data for the individuals who lived in the area during the whole of a certain period of time as well as for the individuals who did not live in the area during the whole of this period but who had moved to the area at the end of the period. It is assumed that by using these data an analysis can be performed in which the influences of the two types are separated.

The reasoning behind such an analysis is as follows. Crime at the end of the period is seen as originating in influences from the two groups of inhabitants. For both of these groups, crime is of course influenced by processes that exert their effects irrespective of geographical location (for example, crime is influenced by inhabitants' ages and sex). Reasonably, however, crime is more strongly influenced in a direct way by the inhabitants who lived in the area during the whole period than by the inhabitants who did not live there the whole period but who had moved to the area at the end of the period. Selection processes have obviously affected the presence of the latter inhabitants in the area, and these individuals' influence on crime may be affected by the fact that they relocated. Admittedly, those who lived in the area during the whole period were also affected by geographical selection, since they may have been locked into the area. Nevertheless, the geographical selection can be assumed to have played no very significant role for the *difference in crime* caused by these individuals, as compared to the difference caused by the relocating individuals. Thus, by comparing the influence on the difference in crime originating in those who lived in the area during the whole period with the corresponding influence originating in those who did not live there the whole period but had moved to the area at the end of the period, we can distinguish the direct effect of the environment, that is, the effect on crime of local processes affecting people living in the area.

## Crime Rates

The crime data refers to the crimes that persons are supposed to have committed alone or with others. The police register suspects who are fifteen years of age or older in connection with investigations of crimes and enter information about them in the register on reported crimes. Information was taken from this register about the suspects and their participation in crime in the entire country. The most important data taken from each report in the register concern civic registration number/s/ for the suspect/s/, codes for crimes that fall within certain categories, number of crimes for each code, and year when each crime was registered. Some other data was also taken from the registrations in order to describe the crimes of the suspects and to exclude irrelevant information (cases in which events registered as crimes have proved not to be crimes or suspects have proved to be innocent have been deleted). Since persons may have been suspected of crimes after these were registered, data was collected for the three years that follow the years when the crimes were registered. Very few suspects were registered later.

The counting of crimes by the police sometimes leads to high figures, even though the criminality underlying these figures cannot be considered especially serious (for example, breaking and entering a series of storage spaces in the same basement results in one registered crime for each storage space entered). In order to offset this problem, the number of crimes for each given crime code in a report was changed so that higher numbers were given lower values. This recoding implies that no crime is assigned the value 0, one crime the value 1, two or three crimes the value 2, and more than three crimes the value 3.

The purpose of this study is to analyze the tendency of an area to generate different types of criminality among its residents. Of course, the criminality of the reasonably suspected individuals in an area is seldom a perfectly valid measure of the actual criminality among the total population in the area. A fundamental problem is that all criminals do not become suspected, and that the probability of being suspected/ detected may vary systematically in various ways – for example between different types of crime, between different years or between different types of perpetrators. Another problem is that all suspects are not guilty. However, if register data is to be used, measuring actual criminality with data on suspected participation in crime is the best method. Using register data on sentenced persons is a weaker alternative. An important reason for this is that only a very small portion of all crimes leads to prosecution. The criminality of suspects comes closer to actual criminality.

Obviously, the probability of a perpetrator's being suspected varies between different types of crime. For example, for violent crimes this probability is high as a rule and for many thefts low. Therefore, official statistics were analyzed and fifteen different categories of crime with specific mean detection probabilities were distinguished and separately measured. As indicated above, only categories that are comparable between years have been used. Some types of crime, such as fraud and embezzlement and other breaches of trust, therefore fall outside. The fifteen categories selected cover most of the crimes registered by the police, particularly traditional thefts and violent crimes. The types of crime in the categories are shown in Table 3.1.

The tendency of an area to generate criminal behavior among its residents for a reference point in time was measured according to a seven-step procedure.

**Table 3.1    Crime rates and clearance rates for the whole of Stockholm City. Uncorrected rates of crime in 1985 for 83 areas. Means and reliabilities of corrected crime rate measures for 83 areas and three reference points**

| Category of crime | Whole of Sthlm City cr. rate | clear. rate | | | Uncorr. cr. rate | Corrected crime rate measures 1980 | | 1985 | | 1990 | |
| --- | --- | --- | --- | --- | --- | --- | --- | --- | --- | --- | --- |
| | 1985 | 1980 | 1985 | 1990 | 1985 | M | Rel. | M | Rel. | M | Rel. |
| 1. Serious violent crimes | .05 | .71 | .74 | .65 | .03 | 1.74 | .69 | 1.72 | .82 | 1.91 | .82 |
| 2. Assault, not serious | .78 | .63 | .62 | .55 | .19 | 2.13 | .86 | 2.17 | .91 | 2.56 | .92 |
| 3. Unlawful threat, intrusion and similar crimes | .66 | .69 | .67 | .64 | .20 | 2.25 | .86 | 2.69 | .87 | 3.26 | .92 |
| 4. Sexual offenses | .09 | .41 | .40 | .33 | .03 | 1.18 | .54 | 1.30 | .74 | 1.01 | .60 |
| 5. Robbery | .17 | .19 | .18 | .11 | .03 | 1.29 | .76 | 1.46 | .85 | 2.74 | .86 |
| 6. Violence, threat or infringement to public official | .31 | .93 | .94 | .87 | .20 | 1.72 | .90 | 1.71 | .90 | 1.84 | .89 |
| 7. Unlawful taking of vehicle, not bicycle | 1.56 | .07 | .05 | .03 | .19 | 1.50 | .90 | 2.53 | .89 | 2.75 | .93 |
| 8. Unlawful taking of bicycle, taking of thing from motor vehicle, bicycle | 5.33 | .02 | .02 | .01 | .16 | 1.53 | .88 | 2.21 | .89 | 1.68 | .90 |
| 9. Burglary | 3.86 | .05 | .04 | .03 | .30 | 1.78 | .87 | 2.17 | .91 | 1.73 | .96 |
| 10. Other theft without burglary, petty theft, not in shop, store, etc. | 2.91 | .10 | .07 | .04 | .14 | 2.02 | .85 | 2.50 | .86 | 3.40 | .89 |
| 11. Theft and petty theft in shop, store, etc. | 1.98 | .75 | .83 | .78 | .80 | 1.92 | .93 | 2.68 | .97 | 2.29 | .97 |
| 12. Crimes inflicting damage | 1.14 | .33 | .25 | .18 | .19 | 2.03 | .91 | 2.53 | .90 | 3.12 | .92 |
| 13. Traffic violations | 1.20 | .98 | .98 | .98 | 1.36 | 1.42 | .95 | 1.24 | .96 | 1.26 | .97 |
| 14. Drug violations | .37 | .96 | .94 | .92 | .37 | 1.74 | .90 | 1.53 | .93 | 1.74 | .96 |
| 15. Tax crimes | .06 | .99 | .98 | 1.00 | .05 | 1.66 | .53 | 1.34 | .62 | 0.66 | .59 |

1) The relative number of crimes that the residents in the area were suspected of was calculated for each of the fifteen types and for each of the four years surrounding the reference point. Thus, the measure of a year's criminality of suspects was constructed as the number of crimes of the type in question that the police registered for that year per resident, with the size of the population used being the one registered at the end of the year. Although crime is only registered for persons who are fifteen years of age or older, the crime rates used for the construction of the measure of the general criminality of residents are calculated by dividing the number of crimes by the total number of inhabitants of all ages. It is appropriate to do so, because a procedure of weighting up criminality of suspects to actual total criminality is applied that makes use of figures of the total population (see below).

It may perhaps be thought that using the average population during a year would be better than using the population at the end of the year in constructing crime measures. However, it seems that these two methods produce measures of crime and of differences in crime that are equivalent in means, standard deviations and reliabilities for the 83 areas. For example, this is indicated by the fact that if the final measures reported below of crime in 1980, 1985 and 1990 are reweighted by being multiplied by the quotient of the population at the end of the year divided by the average population, the new measures correlate (with two decimal places) 1.00 with the measures used.

2) For each year and each type of crime, the obtained rates of the areas were controlled for extreme values and outliers were substituted by a value assumed to be more reasonable. Rates greater than three standard deviations from the mean were substituted by this value. Reasons for outliers may be that a small population makes crime rate measures unreliable, that extreme values occur if many suspects are involved in the same crime, that the police have temporarily directed its resources at some particular type of crime or that mistakes have been made in the handling of data.

3) For each year and each type of crime, the measure obtained was weighted up by being multiplied by a factor. This factor was the quotient of the total registered relative criminality in the City of Stockholm (the total number of crimes registered in the city divided by its population) divided by the corresponding registered relative criminality committed by the suspects living in the City. In other words, the measure was corrected for the inverted value of what could be called the clearance rate for this type of crime for the whole city.

4) In order that the final measures of criminality of the fifteen types for a reference point would have high reliability, they were constructed as the means of such weighted crime rates for the four adjacent years. For example, the measures for the 31st of December 1980 were constructed as the means of the crime rates for 1979, 1980, 1981 and 1982. For the measures, reliabilities of the split-half type were estimated (all reliabilities mentioned below are of this type, unless something else is explicitly stated).

5) The crime rate variables of each type obtained for the three reference points of the 31st of December 1980, 1985 and 1990 were divided by the standard

deviation of this variable for 1980 in order to give the variables more convenient metric properties (it may be noted that the variables still assume only positive values).

6) The fifteen crime rate measures for each reference point in time were factor analyzed (see below). It turned out that the first factor obtained in each case predominated very strongly and that the first factors for the three reference points were very similar. Thus, most of the variation in the criminality in the areas could be explained by using one single factor.

7) In order to obtain a final, general measure, comparable between reference points in time, of the tendency of the areas to generate criminality among their inhabitants, results of the factor analyses were used according to a procedure accounted for below.

This final measure refers to participation in criminal incidents registered for the total population in an area. However, one might question whether other measures referring to such participation registered only for particularly interesting subgroups of this total population can be constructed and used. Analyses were carried out to make clear whether comprehensive criminality measures for the men, the young men 15–24 years of age, and the immigrants could be formed. The above-mentioned procedure cannot be fully used in these cases, since crime rate measures for the subgroups cannot be weighted up by being multiplied by the quotient of the total registered relative criminality divided by the relative criminality of the suspects in the subgroups. This is because no measures of the total registered criminality in the city can be constructed for the subgroups. Nevertheless, there could perhaps be other ways of constructing comprehensive measures, for example, by weighting the specific crime-rate measures for suspects in some other way.

However, the reliabilities of many of the specific crime rate measures turn out to be too low for this to be reasonable to do for the young men and for the immigrants. The reliabilities of the fifteen crime measures for the three subgroups mentioned above were estimated. These reliabilities are high for most of the measures for the males, but low for the young males and the immigrants. If we count reliabilities of 0.80 or higher as acceptably high and look at the figures of the reference year 1985, we find that fourteen measures for the males, but only three measures for the young males and four measures for the immigrants, reach this limit. For the young males six and for the immigrants ten measures have reliabilities equal to or lower than 0.70, whereas there is no such measure for the males. This difference is due, no doubt, to the fact that the young males and the immigrants were relatively few.

The reliabilities of the measures for the males are very similar to the reliabilities of the corresponding measures for the total population. This is certainly due to the fact that most crimes were committed by males – the mean values of most of the crime rates for the males are about double the corresponding rates for the total population (the only exception being category no. 11, "Theft and petty theft in shops, stores, etc."). Therefore, much of the crime of males can be elucidated by simply analyzing the crime rates for the total population. Only these latter rates will be analyzed. It may be noted that there is empirical research showing that the structural sources of female and of male urban crime resemble each other rather much, at least on a high aggregate level (Steffensmeier and Haynie, 2000).

Table 3.1 presents information about the number of crimes of each type per 100 inhabitants registered in 1985 in Stockholm and clearance rates (as defined above) for the crimes committed in this city in 1980, 1985 and 1990. These crimes were committed by residents in the city as well as by other individuals, but the number was divided by the mean number of inhabitants as of the 1st of January and the 31st of December. It is clear from the table that the incidence of various types of theft is high with low clearance rates, whereas violent crimes are relatively fewer and have high clearance rates. Tax crimes, traffic violations and drug violations also have high clearance rates. For many of the types of crime, the clearance rates changed rather substantially between years. For most crimes they diminished from 1980 to 1990.

Table 3.1 also presents information about the mean values of the fifteen crime rate measures, uncorrected for clearance rates and undivided by the standard deviation of the measure of 1980, for the total populations in the areas for the year 1985 and per 100 inhabitants. The table furthermore presents information about the mean values and the reliabilities for the final crime rate measures for the reference points of 1980, 1985 and 1990.

It can be seen from the table that the reliabilities are high for most of the fifteen corrected crime rate measures, and that the reliabilities tend to increase for later years. There is a clear tendency of the reliabilities to increase when the relative number of crimes increases. However, there is a tendency for the reliabilities to increase for later years also when this number decreases. It is not quite clear how the increases for later years should be explained. It should be noted that the number of crimes for suspects has not generally increased during the period of time in question (the number of reported crimes has increased, but this is outbalanced by the fact that the clearance rate has diminished). One reason for the increases in reliabilities could simply be that the police recorded suspects more carefully in later years.


**Crime Factors**

What dimensions can be found in the fifteen variables describing crime rates for the total area population? As mentioned, the variables for each of the reference years 1980, 1985, and 1990 were factor analyzed. This was done using the principal component method. Each of these analyses gave two unrotatad (and thus uncorrelated) factors having an eigenvalue greater than or equal to 1. In each case, the first factor is very strong and much stronger than the second factor. The eigenvalues of the first factors are 8.94, 9.59 and 9.97, and the eigenvalues of the second factors are 1.23, 1.04 and 1.04. The first factors explain 60, 64 and 67 per cent, whereas the second factors only explain 8, 7 and 7 per cent, of the total variance of all variables. The correlations between the first factors and the analyzed variables are shown in Table 3.2.

**Table 3.2**  **Correlations between first factors and analyzed crime rates in 83 areas. For the reference points of 1980, 1985 and 1990. Coefficients used in constructing the general crime factor**

| Category of crime | 1980 | 1985 | 1990 | Coeff. |
|---|---|---|---|---|
| 1. Serious violent crimes | .74 | .72 | .82 | .08 |
| 2. Assault, not serious | .90 | .89 | .94 | .10 |
| 3. Unlawful threat, intrusion and similar crimes | .88 | .93 | .92 | .09 |
| 4. Sexual offenses | .47 | .49 | .57 | .06 |
| 5. Robbery | .71 | .64 | .75 | .06 |
| 6. Violence, threat or infringement to public official | .85 | .88 | .88 | .11 |
| 7. Unlawful taking of vehicle, not bicycle | .75 | .84 | .88 | .07 |
| 8. Unlawful taking of bicycle, taking of thing from motor vehicle, bicycle | .74 | .86 | .80 | .08 |
| 9. Burglary | .86 | .88 | .86 | .09 |
| 10. Other theft without burglary, petty theft, not in shop, store, etc. | .78 | .85 | .79 | .08 |
| 11. Theft and petty theft in shop, store, etc. | .90 | .90 | .92 | .10 |
| 12. Crimes inflicting damage | .89 | .90 | .87 | .09 |
| 13. Traffic violations | .84 | .88 | .86 | .12 |
| 14. Drug violations | .75 | .81 | .89 | .10 |
| 15. Tax crimes | −.07 | −.12 | −.08 | −.01 |
| Explained proportion of total variance | .60 | .64 | .67 | - |

It can be seen from the table that the first factors correlate positively and very strongly with most of the variables, and that they are very similar to each other with regard to these correlations. High correlations are found for both violent crimes and property crimes – for example, for unlawful threat, intrusion and similar crimes (correlations 0.88, 0.93, 0.92), non-serious assault (0.90, 0.89, 0.94), theft and petty theft in shop, store, etc. (0.90, 0.90, 0.92) and crimes inflicting damage (0.89, 0.90, 0.87). Four types of crime correlate weakly or relatively weakly with the first factors: tax crimes, sexual offenses, robbery, and serious violent crimes. Of these, the two types of crime with the lowest correlations – tax crimes and sexual offenses – are the ones having the lowest reliabilities. Tax crime, a type of white-collar crime, has practically no correlation at all with the factors. Considering all these facts, it seems natural to interpret the first factors as traditional crime of both violent and property types.

It may be noted that the first factors correlate more strongly with non-serious assault than with serious violent crimes, and, further, that the correlations for robbery are relatively low. Does this indicate that the factors describe non-serious crime to a much higher degree than serious crime? The answer is no. While there may be a tendency that the factors describe non-serious more than serious crime, this tendency cannot be strong. This is evident when considering the reliabilities of the crime rates. Correcting for attenuation, we find that the factors still correlate more strongly with non-serious assault than with serious violent crimes, but that the latter correlations are strong (two of them are 0.90 or higher). While it is still true that the correlations with robbery are relatively weak (however, two of them are 0.80 or higher), we also find that the correlations with burglary, which is certainly a serious type of crime, are strong (two of the corrected correlations are 0.94 or higher). In fact, for two years the correlations with burglary are stronger than the correlations with "other theft without burglary, petty theft, not in shop, store, etc." – a type of crime that must be considered less serious than burglary in most cases.

For each year, the second factor correlates most strongly with tax crimes (the correlations are 0.47, 0.96 and 0.98). For the later two years, this factor has no correlation of notable strength with any other variable. Thus, it seems that interest should be focused on the first factor for all three years. This factor explains the overwhelming part of the total variance, and if consideration is paid to the reliabilities of the variables its predominating status of course becomes even more pronounced (for example, for the reference year 1985 the first factor explains 84 per cent of the total reliable variance in the analyzed variables).

Factor analyses of the crime rates for the men in the areas give results that are very similar to the results just presented for the total populations. The first factors explain the overwhelming part of the total variance of the rates, whereas the other factors only explain minor parts. The patterns of the correlations between factors and variables are very similar to the patterns for the total populations.

The predominating strengths of the first factors obtained in the three analyses of crime rates for the total populations and the similarity between them are interesting to consider when evaluating the potential for analyzing crime longitudinally.

These facts show that it is possible to weigh the crime rates of the different years in the same way, thereby forming one single construct or factor that describes a very large portion of the rates of each year. Since the fifteen rates used describe a major portion of all crimes committed, most of the total criminality in the areas, measured as rates of registered crimes, can be described by using the single factor.

This general factor was constructed by utilizing the sets of first factor scoring coefficients obtained from the three mentioned factor analyses. These coefficients yielded factors with the mean of 0 and the standard deviation of 1. Since the rates only assumed positive values, the constant terms in the sets were negative. What was sought was a set of coefficients or weights that yield factors for the three years that are as similar as possible as the previously obtained factors. Furthermore, this set should not contain any constant term, because the factor values should be 0 when all crime rates are 0. Such sets of coefficients were constructed for the three years by using the obtained scoring coefficients, excluding the constant terms. However, the coefficients obtained were not used directly, because they yielded factors that were not equivalent in absolute metrical properties. In order to obtain coefficients that yield such properties, the original coefficients were multiplicatively transformed (all coefficients for a given year were multiplied by the same constant). The coefficients for 1985 and 1990 were transformed so that the sum of their absolute values was equal to the sum of the absolute values of the coefficients for 1980. The coefficients for 1980 were kept intact. The mean of the coefficient for 1980 and the transformed coefficients for 1985 and 1990 was then computed for each type of crime, and this mean is the new, final coefficient or weight that is used. The new weights are shown in Table 3.2. They range from 0.06 to 0.12 for all types of crime except tax crimes, for which the weight is −0.01.

Using the new coefficients, new crime factors denoted C80, C85 and C90 were constructed for the three reference years. Their reliabilities are 0.97, 0.97 and 0.99, and their correlations, rounded off to two decimal places, with the previous corresponding factors are all 1.00. They were all divided by the standard deviation of C80. Their means in final, standardized versions are 2.16, 2.51 and 2.74 – that is, on average crime has increased in the areas – and their standard deviations are 1.00, 1.28 and 1.41. C80 correlates 0.91 with C85 and 0.85 with C90. C85 and C90 correlate 0.86 with each other.

The reliabilities of the final factors for the three reference points are very high, but how high is their validity? Do these factors describe the true crime rates? This depends on how well the register data used describe actual crimes and offenders. One kind of objection that has been raised against using police register data on crime is that these data tend to be biased, because certain types of offenders are discriminated against or have a great deal of attention paid to them with the result that they get much higher records of crime than other types of offenders. Two types of such offenders are mentioned particularly often in Swedish contexts: people from low social classes and people of color or of foreign extraction, and it has been argued that many of the relationships found in police data between crime on the one hand and social class, skin color and foreign extraction on the other can be explained in this way (Diesen, 2005; SOU 2006:30). Does such bias exist for the crime factors constructed in this study?

There are no data in the study that can be used for an advanced analysis of this matter. However, there are data on relationships found between the crime measure and measures of social class and foreign extraction, and such relationships that are difficult to reconcile with the bias explanation are described below.

Variables that describe the difference in crime have been formed by taking $C90-C85$, $C85-C80$ and $C90-C80$. The reliabilities of these variables, estimated according to a formula of Mosier (1943), are 0.87, 0.74 and 0.92. In some analyses, $C90-C85$ and $C85-C80$ are simultaneously used as one dependent variable. These two differences correlate $-0.29$ with each other. The strength of this negative correlation is surely to some degree due to measurement errors in C85, since C85 enters in both differences but with different signs. However, measures of the corresponding differences between split-half versions of crime, formed so that they have no measure of C85 in common, have also been constructed. The average correlation between them is only $-0.11$.

The difference measures are based on the assumption that the crime measures for the different reference points are comparable. However, objections may be raised over whether this assumption is correct. The probability that actual crimes have been reported to and registered by the police may have varied between years due to changes in the general public's interest in reporting crime, in the ability of the police to detect crime, or in the accuracy with which the police have registered reported/detected crimes, that is, changes in conditions that are not measured in this study. It could perhaps also be that the correction for the clearance rate in the whole city does not work in the same way for different years, because the portion of the total number of crimes in the city that was committed by residents has varied. It cannot be precluded that substantial changes of these types have occurred and if they have, it would mean that it is difficult to compare crime between years. However, some models of crime that will be used are constructed to handle this problem. They include parameters that are unique for each specific year and that are used to correct for differences due to such changes.

**Independent Properties**

The independent properties describe the residents' age and sex, the degree to which they are subject to social control, their social resources, their dwelling environment, and their moves to or out of the area in question between the reference points in time (these moves can be assumed to affect social control, but are also, as previously mentioned, of interest for other reasons). Social control is described with aspects of the social contacts of the residents. It is assumed that the more superficial, short-lived and exchangeable these contacts, the poorer the control and the more prone to commit crimes the residents. Two particularly important measures of the contacts describe whether the residents are divorced and whether they are foreign citizens. Social resources are described with the occupational status of the residents, their income, their unemployment and the social aid received by their household, that is, with properties that in Anglo-Saxon research often go under the heading of "socioeconomic status" or "social class".

All measures of independent properties are constructed on the basis of data on individuals who are, have been, or will be residents in the area in question. All measures are based on information from aggregated individual data, and all measures, with one exception, are based on the mean values (that is, proportions for dichotomous data and averages for multi-valued data) for the population to which they pertain. The population used in the construction of an area measure may be the total population of the area or some part of this total population (for example, a part formed on the basis of individuals' moves to or out of the area). All measures are constructed as properties that can be used, at least approximately, in comparisons between years and between areas with different population sizes.

Most properties, for example the age and sex properties and the percentages of foreigners and divorced individuals, are perfectly comparable between years. However, some properties are not. This is the case with the income property (see below) and with the properties for which data come from the housing parts of the censuses of population and housing, that is, the three properties described below under the heading "dwelling environment". Data for these latter properties were originally collected by using questionnaires, and there were different rates of non-response for the different years. Nonresponse was rather small. For most years it cannot have been larger than two-three per cent. However, for 1990 it was probably about three per cent larger than for previous years.

The individual-level properties and the corresponding area properties have the same names, but the individual-level properties are denoted with small letters and the area properties with capital letters.

Individual-level data are of two types – basic or derived. Most basic data are of dichotomous type, meaning that a resident takes on one of two possible values, coded 0 or 1, of a property, for example the resident is either a foreign citizen or not a foreign citizen, is either 15–24 years old or not of that age, etc. In that case, the area property is simply the proportion of the residents who have the value 1 of the property. Derived individual-level data are constructed by multiplying basic properties with each other. High values of basic properties used in such constructions are assumed to be conducive to crime.

Below, I describe the basic individual-level properties. If nothing else is mentioned, measures are constructed for each of the reference years.

*Age and sex.* Six properties describe the resident's age and sex. For each sex, ages are categorized as follows: 15–24, 25–50, and more than 50 years of age. Thus, all ages of criminal responsibility are covered. The category 15–24 years is chosen because young men in these ages have shown to be particularly prone to commit crime (Yearbook of Judicial Statistics 1990, p. 60, Table 3.2.10). The age/sex categories are denoted by combining labels for age (15–24 years are labeled "yng", 25–50 years "mdl", and more than 50 years "old") and sex (males are labeled "male", females "feml").

*Social control.* Four basic social control properties are used. They describe whether the individual was a foreign citizen (Forgn), whether the individual lived in a household having a single parent (Single), whether the individual was divorced (Divor), and whether the individual had moved to the area during the last five years (Moves). In the last case, there are no data for the reference year 1970.

These properties have already been given a theoretical underpinning, and their relevance is largely supported by empirical research. In Sweden, significant relationships have been found between registered crime and foreign citizenship (and immigrant status) on the individual and aggregate levels, and this has raised the question of whether immigration is conducive to crime (Ahlberg, 1996; Martens and Holmberg, 2005; Dahlbäck, 1998a). However, the outlook of the corresponding research in the U.S. seems to be quite different – immigration is mostly not seen as harmful in the same way (Reid at al., 2005; Stowell et al., 2009; but see Hipp et al., 2009a). Living with a single parent, which as a rule means living with a single mother, should, one might think, result in less control for young individuals, and family disintegration in the form of divorce should have much the same effect. For the influence of divorces there is support in the research, but for living with a single mother the results of research are more mixed. For example, Harper and McLanahan (2004) found a positive relationship between father absence and individual criminality, but Juby and Farrington (2001) found that boys from disrupted families who lived with their mothers had delinquency rates that were similar to the rates of boys from intact harmonious families (see also Farrington, 2005). Individuals' mobility is a property that does not seem to have very strong support in empirical research as an influencing factor, as least not as a directly influencing factor, but in this study it is assumed to be important in certain contexts.

*Social resources.* Measuring social resources is more complicated than measuring other types of properties. This is, among other things, due to the facts that data in some cases are missing for some years, that resources differ for men and women, that comparability between years is more difficult to obtain and that no self-evident dichotomous dimension exists in some cases. The social resources are described with seven properties. Some of these are dichotomous. One such property describes whether the individual was unemployed (Unempl). This measure is constructed for men of all ages. Another dichotomous property describes whether the individual belonged to a household that had been given social aid (Socaid). This measure is constructed for individuals who were 50 years or younger. In both of these cases there are only data for 1985 and 1990 (employment was given a new definition in official statistics from 1985, and full data on social aid do not exist for 1980 and earlier).

The other measures of social resources are all based on two primary types of data: the individual's income as assessed by the revenue authority and the individual's occupational status as assessed by Statistics Sweden. These measures describe the conditions for men, because both income and occupational status tend to differ between the sexes and are more difficult to measure for women (many of these being housewives). Two measures have been constructed for both income and occupational status: one multi-valued measure describing the individual's value on the dimension in question and a dichotomous measure describing whether the individual had a particularly low income and a low occupational status, respectively.

Income data exist for all reference years. In raw form they cannot be compared directly between years in an absolute sense, and it is difficult to adjust them in this form so that comparability is guaranteed. In order to make them more comparable they could be adjusted by using a consumer price index, but even if this is done doubts about comparability will remain because tax rules, tax evasion and other conditions may have changed during the period studied. However, much of income's influence on crime can be assumed to be due to its relative value. Therefore, the income values of all men in the study who had an assessed income were standardized for each year, and the standardized values are used as the final, multi-valued measure on the individual's income (Incmult). No adjustment was made for the age distribution. Furthermore, each year's area-level measure of average income was standardized for all areas. The dichotomous individual-level measure (Incdich) was only constructed for men between 25–55 years of age, since many men in other ages for natural reasons had no or practically no income, which would be particularly disadvantageous if these data were used for the construction of derived properties. The measure describes whether the individual had an income that was less than the fifth percentile of all male incomes.

The standard deviation of the incomes for all men was used as a measure of inequality in the area (denoted INCSTD).

Data on occupational status exist only for 1985 and 1990. The multi-valued measure (Occmult) was constructed by assigning points to occupations as follows: unskilled workers 1, skilled workers 2, low-rank white-collar employees 3, middle-rank white-collar employees 4, officials and professionals 5. Entrepreneurs were not included. The dichotomous measure (Occdich) describes whether the individual was an unskilled worker.

*Dwelling environment.* Three properties are used. They describe whether the individual lived in a multifamily house (Mulths), in a dwelling with a public landlord (Public), and in an overcrowded dwelling (Overcr). Data come from the censuses of population and housing.

The denotations of all basic area properties and their meaning are described in Table 3.3.

Several products of individual properties are used, which, for reasons discussed below, are assumed to be appropriate for analyzing the significance of bivariate interaction within individuals. As mentioned, they are constructed by multiplying basic dichotomous factors with one another, and they are denoted with the factor names combined with the sign *. I have selected three social control and three social

**Table 3.3     Basic independent area properties**

---

*Age and sex*

YNGMALE      percentage of males 15–24 years of age
YNGFEML      percentage of females 15–24 years of age
MDLMALE      percentage of males 25–50 years of age
MDLFEML      percentage of females 25–50 years of age
OLDMALE      percentage of males more than 50 years of age
OLDFEML      percentage of females more than 50 years of age

*Social control*

FORGN        percentage of foreign citizens
SINGLE       percentage of individuals living in a houshold having a
             single parent
DIVOR        percentage of divorcees
MOVES        percentage of individuals who have moved to the area
             during the last five years

*Social resources*

INCMULT      mean income of all men having an assessed income
             (standardized value)
INCDICH      percentage of men having an income less than the fifth
             percentile of all incomes, for men 25–55 years of age
INCSTD       standard deviation of the incomes for all men having an
             assessed income
UNEMPL       percentage of unemployed individuals among men
SOCAID       percentage of individuals belonging to households given
             social aid among all residents 50 years or younger
OCCMULT      mean occupational status for men
OCCDICH      percentage of unskilled workers among the men

*Dwelling envir.*

MULTHS       percentage of individuals living in a multifamily house
PUBLIC       percentage of individuals living in a dwelling with a public
             landlord
OVERCR       percentage of individuals living in an overcrowded dwell-
             ing

---

resources dichotomous properties and combined them in all possible ways, that is, I have considered all nine control-resources pairs. The control properties are Forgn, Single and Divor, and the resources properties are Incdich, Socaid and Occdich. I have also in some contexts considered the products of the different pairs of the three control properties and the products of the different pairs of the three resources properties. Moreover, I have in some contexts considered the product Yngmale*Forgn, because being a young male and being a foreigner can be looked upon as properties that are particularly conducive to crime, and it would therefore be interesting to combine them.

In order to describe the aggregated within-individual interaction between two properties on the area level, I have taken the mean of all individual-level products of the properties, and in order to describe the aggregated interaction between different individuals for the properties, I have taken the product of the means. I have constructed all the mean-of-products variables and all the product-of-means variables for the mentioned three control properties and the mentioned three resources properties in 1985 and 1990.

For the construction of interaction properties, I have not put together basic measures of social control and of social resources into total measures of the control and resources dimensions, because the basic measures refer to different aspects of these dimensions (this is particularly evident for the control properties) and give rise to different relationships in longitudinal analysis. I use all nine combinations of control and resources properties in the analyses, because I have no distinct idea about which of them are most interesting.

The independent variables are used in three forms: in original form, in standardized form and in what could be called a "normalized" form. Standardizing variables is of course a way to achieve comparability between them. However, there is also in some contexts in this study another reason for standardization: standardized variables are particularly appropriate for product models used in this study, as discussed below.

For each property, the values at different points in time are as mentioned comparable, at least approximately. However, different properties differ in their means and variations. In order to give them a form that is appropriate for the product models while still retaining the intertemporal comparability, they have with some exceptions been normalized, and these normalized values are used in several longitudinal analyses. The variables describing each independent property, except the age/sex properties, INCMULT, UNEMPL, SOCAID, OCCMULT and OCCDICH, have been normalized by subtracting from them the mean of the 1980 version and dividing the result by the standard deviation of the same year. The UNEMPL, SOCAID, OCCMULT and OCCDICH variables have been normalized in the same way by using figures from 1985 as base values (there are no 1980 figures for these variables). The age/sex variables are in most cases only used for the same year as crime and they are then standardized. The INCMULT variables are standardized unless something else is mentioned.

## Using Data on Stockholm Urban Areas

In order for the Stockholm urban areas to be appropriate to be used in analyses of the influence of environmental properties on crime, there must have been a physical and social differentiation between these areas in the period of time studied. It is quite clear that this was the case and that such differentiation was strong for many properties. For the year 1990, this can be seen from the means and standard deviations of the independent properties in original versions, which are reported in Table 3.4. A strong differentiation is found, for example for the proportions of foreign citizens (M = 0.09, s = 0.07), of residents living in dwellings with public landlords (M = 0.33; s = 0.26), of male unskilled workers

**Table 3.4     Independent properties in original versions. Simple statistics, correlations between years and results from a factor analysis**

| Independent property | Statistics, 1990 | | Correlation betw. years | | Factor analysis for 1990 Factor | | | | Comm. |
|---|---|---|---|---|---|---|---|---|---|
| | M | s | Adj. years | 1970/ 1990 | I | II | III | IV | |
| *Age and sex* | | | | | | | | | |
| YNGMALE | .052 | .011 | .74 | .24 | .00 | −.02 | −.91 | .19 | .86 |
| YNGFEML | .057 | .008 | .63 | .33 | .25 | .31 | −.68 | .28 | .70 |
| MDLMALE | .196 | .030 | .86 | −.19 | .38 | .83 | .22 | −.12 | .89 |
| MDLFEML | .192 | .025 | .81 | −.57 | .21 | .91 | −.01 | −.21 | .92 |
| OLDMALE | .147 | .029 | .89 | −.05 | −.39 | −.73 | .47 | .09 | .91 |
| OLDFEML | .211 | .056 | .95 | .35 | −.19 | −.44 | .82 | .15 | .92 |
| *Social control* | | | | | | | | | |
| FORGN | .088 | .074 | .95 | .65 | .82 | .03 | −.39 | .30 | .91 |
| SINGLE | .101 | .035 | .93 | .65 | .64 | −.20 | −.36 | −.33 | .69 |
| DIVOR | .104 | .029 | .97 | .74 | .55 | −.08 | .75 | −.08 | .88 |
| MOVES | .373 | .074 | .69 | - | .40 | .73 | .26 | −.16 | .78 |
| *Social resources* | | | | | | | | | |
| INCMULT | 635 | 119 | .98 | .92 | −.81 | .22 | .25 | .39 | .91 |
| INCDICH | .093 | .035 | .90 | .55 | .62 | .31 | .21 | .60 | .89 |
| INCSTD | 734 | 608 | .84 | .69 | −.45 | .18 | .08 | .64 | .65 |
| UNEMPL | .444 | .041 | .83 | - | .31 | −.74 | −.29 | .32 | .82 |
| SOCAID | .180 | .062 | .94 | - | .88 | .03 | .05 | .37 | .92 |
| OCCMULT | 3.13 | .458 | .98 | - | −.77 | .52 | −.01 | .23 | .92 |
| OCCDICH | .197 | .076 | .96 | - | .86 | −.43 | −.05 | −.04 | .94 |
| *Dwelling envir.* | | | | | | | | | |
| MULTHS | .782 | .296 | .99 | .96 | .60 | .13 | .71 | .11 | .89 |
| PUBLIC | .332 | .259 | .98 | .95 | .74 | −.49 | .02 | −.03 | .79 |
| OVERCR | .067 | .032 | .93 | .58 | .75 | .31 | .27 | .15 | .75 |
| Expl. proportion of variance | - | - | - | - | .35 | .22 | .20 | .08 | .85 |

(M = 0.20, s = 0.08), of the residents living in multi-family houses (M = 0.78, s = 0.30), and of individuals receiving social aid (M = 0.18, s = 0.06). There is also substantial differentiation for the important properties of mean income (M = 635 and s = 119) and mean occupational status (M = 3.13; s = 0.46).

Maps showing area values of some of these properties and of the crime factor for the year of 1990 are shown in Appendix III. It can be seen from these maps that the independent factors and crime varied strongly geographically and that areas with disadvantageous social conditions tended to have high rates of crime. I give some brief comments on the maps. As shown in Figure III.ii, there was a strong tendency that high crime was located in areas in the outer parts of the city (areas with No. 38, 50, 51, 53, 55, 60, 76, 77, and 82; for the serial numbers of areas, see Figure III.i). These areas had relatively newly been built up, mostly with multi-family houses, and several of them had many inhabitants who were unskilled workers and who had low income (Figures III.iii, III.vi, and III.iv). Several of them also had many inhabitants who were foreign citizens (Figure III.v). This is especially the case with the areas No. 76, 77 and 82, for which the percentages of foreign citizens were about 51, 43 and 28 and for which the percentages of unskilled workers were about 47, 42 and 35.

On the other hand, as can be seen from Figure III.ii, areas with low rates of crime are found in other parts of the city. The areas with the lowest crime rates are those with No. 69, 70, and 71. They are located in the west, just outside the inner part of the city, and they were populated with people who tended to have high incomes and not to be foreign citizens or unskilled workers. Most of the inhabitants lived in houses that were not of the multi-family type. The crime rate values of these areas were much lower that the corresponding values of the areas having the highest crime rates. Actually, the areas with the highest crime rates (No. 76, 38, 77, and 82) had values that were more than ten times as high as the values of the former areas.

In Table 3.4, the mean correlations between the independent property values of adjacent reference years, as well as the correlations between the independent property values in 1970 and 1990, are reported to describe how circumstances developed in the areas. The correlations between the 1970 and the 1990 values are particularly strong, of course, for the dwelling environmental variables of MULTHS and PUBLIC – the buildings and their public landlords did not change much over the years. A strong correlation is also found for INCMULT and a rather strong correlation for DIVOR. The correlations between values of adjacent reference years are in many cases extremely strong, as indicated by the average correlations reported in the table (for MULTHS this correlation is 0.99, for PUBLIC, INCMULT and OCCMULT 0.98, and for DIVOR 0.97). For several properties, these correlations tend to be stronger for later years – the areas seem to have become somewhat more rigidly differentiated.

The various properties developed in different ways during the period studied. Some properties did not change substantially. As suggested by the correlations just mentioned, this was the case with the proportions of persons living in multi-family houses and of persons living in dwellings with a public landlord. Larger changes occurred for the proportions of men and women who were 15–24 years of age (the mean proportions decreased by about 31 and 24 per cent between 1970 and 1990 – the average population became older). Large changes also occurred for social control properties, implying that foreign citizens, single persons and divorcees became more common in the populations and that social control thus became weaker with regard to these factors. Thus, for the FORGN, SINGLE and DIVOR properties the mean values increased by about 44, 30 and 73 per cent between 1970 and 1990. The proportions in the populations with social aid and with dwellings having public landlords also became greater. Overcrowding became much less common.

As for their dispersions among the areas, many of the properties changed rather little. One important exception is the proportion of foreign citizens. Its standard deviation increased by about 139 per cent. The standard deviation also increased for the proportion of divorcees (by about 16 per cent). Thus, geographical differentiation increased for these social control properties.

Many of the variables used are strongly related to each other, as is evident from the results of factor analyses made. For example, for the year 1990 all primary independent variables have been factor analyzed according to the principal component method, resulting in four factors with an eigenvalue of at least 1. These factors account for 85 per cent of the total variance. Their correlations with the analyzed variables and their communalities are shown in Table 3.4.

Of the four unrotated factors described in the table, the first one correlates strongly with many variables, positively with SOCAID, OCCDICH, FORGN, OVERCR and PUBLIC and negatively with INCMULT and OCCMULT. It seems to describe the degree to which the population had *low social rank*. Areas with low-rank populations tended to have high proportions of individuals with social aid, unskilled worker status, foreign citizenship, an overcrowded dwelling, a dwelling having a public landlord, low mean income, and low average occupational status, respectively.

The second factor correlates strongly positively with MDLFEML, MDLMALE and MOVES, and strongly negatively with OLDMALE and UNEMPL. It seems to describe the degree to which the population was *middle-aged, occupationally active and active when it came to changing residence*. The third factor correlates strongly positively with OLDFEML, DIVOR and MULTHS, and strongly negatively with YNGMALE and YNGFEML. The factor seems to describe the *degree to which the population was aged*. The fourth factor has its strongest correlation with INCSTD. This correlation is positive, and the factor also correlates positively with INCDICH, SOCAID and INCMULT. Thus, the factor seems to describe *income inequality*.

The social rank factor has obviously much in common with social resources variables, but, interestingly, it also correlates strongly or rather strongly with FORGN and SINGLE. It has a relatively weak relationship with DIVOR, which correlates more strongly with the third factor.

In a corresponding factor analysis of the 1985 data, the first factor obtained is very similar to the first factor obtained for 1990, while other factors do not have counterparts that are equally similar. For earlier years, the fact that the UNEMPL, SOCAID, OCCMULT and OCCDICH variables are missing of course makes a difference. However, the general picture is that a social rank factor and life-stage factors were very important over the years. It seems that social rank aspects of the structure in the areas were continuously reproduced (cf. Andersson and Bråmå, 2004).

The strong correlations between independent variables make for a problem when analyzing cross-sectional relationships between crime and these variables. One way of avoiding this problem is to analyze changes in the variables and in crime (this method is more closely discussed in subsequent sections). For most independent properties, the correlations between their changes are much weaker than their cross-sectional correlations. I give some examples of this by comparing the cross-sectional correlations for 1990 with the correlations between the changes 1985–1990 for some properties. For FORGN and SOCAID, the cross-sectional correlation is 0.79, while the correlation between the changes is 0.25. For FORGN and PUBLIC, the corresponding correlations are 0.51 and 0.13, for DIVOR and MULTHS 0.88 and 0.02, for INCMULT and OCCDICH –0.82 and –0.37, for SOCAID and OVERCR 0.67 and –0.05, for OCCDICH and PUBLIC 0.80 and 0.16, and for MULTHS and OVERCR 0.65 and 0.02. However, the same kind of relation between the two types of correlations is not found for the properties of men and women in the age categories. For these properties, the cross-sectional correlation and the correlation between changes are about equally strong.

As discussed above, the areas analyzed in this study can be characterized as natural neighborhoods – that is, it is impossible to choose some other geographical division of the city in order to obtain appropriate units for the study, at least in most cases and to a large extent. Much the same is true for the temporal aspect of the choice of the units. Censuses of population and housing must be the main sources of data, and it is therefore impossible to choose any other points of reference than the ones used. Of course, it can be argued that there is a theoretical universe of areas that also pertains to other points in time. However, it can hardly be argued that the selected set of units is a random sample from such a universe. On the contrary, the set selected is characterized by strong limitations and dependencies. Under these circumstances, it is natural to consider the data selected as not being a sample and to refrain from any attempts at making statistical inductions. This is also the position taken.

**Direction of Influences**

This book presents analyses of cross-sectional area-level relationships between crime and social factors, based on the assumption that the social factors may have influenced crime but that crime has not influenced these factors. Is this assumption about the non-reciprocity of influence true? May crime influence social factors of the types studied? This question will now be discussed.

The question has attracted a good deal of interest in the research on crime in urban areas. The assumption about non-reciprocity has often been made, but has also been challenged by several researchers, mostly with regard to measures of crime that pertain to the *offenses committed in such areas* (for a review, see Hipp, 2010). Results of this type of research may be thought to have some relevance for research on *offenses committed by residents in the areas*, and I will therefore discuss them.

Thus, some researchers have argued that there are reciprocal influences between crime and social structure in urban areas. Several of them have argued in about the following way. People prefer living in areas with low rates of crime. Thus, crime affects the attractiveness of areas. The attractiveness affects the costs of housing. Individuals who can afford it move to or remain in low-crime areas, whereas individuals who cannot afford to live in such areas are forced to move to or to remain in high-crime areas. Moreover, individuals' ethnicity may put special restrictions on their moving. The moves affect the social structure. Thus, crime affects the social structure of the areas, but at the same time this structure affects crime. In this process of reciprocal influence, crime and poor social conditions may escalate in some areas, which therefore become crime-ridden and have miserable social conditions. An explanation of this type is often connected to the disorganization perspective of crime (see, for example, Bursik, 1988).

The empirical research on the reciprocal influence between crime and social structure in small urban areas is very limited. Recently, however, Hipp (2010) presented such a study of offenses committed in areas. Because of the scarcity of empirical research, I will discuss his study at some length. Hipp argues that there are reciprocal influences and that the influence from crime to structure has considerable strength, and he has tested these statements using data on about 2,500 census tracts from 13 cities. In this study, violent and property crime were separately measured. Several structural characteristics were considered, including concentrated disadvantage (described by a scale constructed by a principal component analysis of measures of family income, poverty, divorce rate and unemployment), the percentage of African Americans, ethnic heterogeneity and residential instability. All characteristics were measured for the years 1990 and 2000. Some characteristics were used in squared versions or were spatially lagged. Models for the prediction of crime and the prediction of structural characteristics were simultaneously estimated. Crime in 2000 was predicted by crime and all structural characteristics in 1990, and each of the structural characteristics in 2000 was predicted by the same factors.

The disorganization perspective with the assumption about reciprocity added constitutes the theoretical basis of the model built by Hipp for the prediction of crime. As to the influences on the structural characteristics used, Hipp has practically nothing to say that goes beyond the realm of this revised disorganization perspective. No other independent variables are used for the analyses of these characteristics. This seems strange. Reasonably, the characteristics must have been affected by other factors.

Hipp finds that the partial coefficients obtained for previous crime in predicting some structural characteristics are statistically significant (the significance levels of 0.01, 0.05 and 0.10 are used). For example, he maintains that neighborhoods with more crime tend to experience increasing levels of residential instability, more concentrated disadvantage, a diminishing retail environment, and more African Americans ten years later. These results, he claims, show that crime affects structural characteristics in a way that means that reciprocal influences must be considered when analyzing cross-sectional relationships.

There are reasons to be skeptical of these assertions, because the impression one gets of the relationships found by Hipp is not that of a strong influence of crime on social structure. In discussing this matter, I focus on the results for the central structural characteristics of concentrated disadvantage, ethnic heterogeneity and residential instability. It seems that neither violent nor property crime predicts general ethnic heterogeneity significantly. Violent crime predicts the percentage of African Americans significantly ($p < 0.05$), but property crime does not do the same. Property crime does not predict concentrated disadvantage significantly, but violent crime does this at the 0.01 level. Both types of crime predict residential instability significantly. For several of the other structural, less central characteristics significant relationships are reported. Most of the significant relationships are difficult to judge, because crime is used in these cases both in original and squared versions and the coefficients for these two variables have different signs.

A problem with the Hipp study is that the strength of the relationships, expressed as the contribution to the explained proportion of variance, is not reported. Only the significance of the relationships is reported, but figures of the contribution to explained variance would have been helpful. The statistical significance of relationships in a sample of about 2,500 cases is of limited interest, since very weak relationships are statistically significant in such a large sample (for example, it may be mentioned that, assuming randomness and bivariate normality and using the F test, a correlation of 0.052 – that is, an explained proportion of variance of 0.0027 – would be significant at the 0.01 level in such a sample). However, reported coefficient values and other facts indicate that the relationships discussed are very weak. In most or all cases it can hardly be the question of an explained proportion of considerable magnitude. Rather, it might be questioned whether the results do not actually support the idea that crime has no influence of any greater importance on social structure.

Turning to the results of the prediction of crime in 2000 using all characteristics in 1990, skepticism remains. In these analyses, much of the variance in crime in 2000 is explained, mainly by crime in 1990. However, some of the coefficients obtained for the characteristics seem dubious. For example, interpreting coefficients causally, a higher percentage of African Americans and a higher residential instability have caused decreases in crime. Another questionable finding is the very high positive coefficients found for previous crime. Previous property crime has got the coefficient 0.88 in predicting later property crime, and for violent crime the corresponding coefficient is 0.78 (it may be noted that the standard deviations of previous and later crime of each type are about the same). This means that previous crime predominates totally as a cause of crime ten years later. This does not seem realistic.

It may be doubted that Hipp has succeeded in selecting adequate independent factors. The factors used are chosen to fit the disorganization perspective, but this perspective can be called into question and is hardly sufficient for explaining the structural characteristics. Combining control and resources factors into one single measure of concentrated disadvantage is also questionable. It would probably have been better to use these factors separately. Moreover, there are other factors that could have been used, for example age and sex factors. The problem with the lack of factors is that the obtained coefficients of previous crime may have absorbed effects of them, and it seems possible that this could explain the relationships obtained between previous crime and later social structure.

Thus, I do not think that the Hipp study shows that crime influences social structure so strongly that reciprocity must be considered in cross-sectional analysis. As far as I know, no other study does this either.

The above-mentioned hypothesis that crime influences the social structure of urban areas presupposes that crime influences individuals' moves and that these moves transform the structure. Thus, a crucial assumption is that crime influences mobility. Such an influence is a necessary but not a sufficient condition for the influence of crime on social structure to arise, and it is therefore of interest to examine what empirical support there is for it. South and Messner (2000) have reviewed several studies of the matter. They think that these suggest that exposure to crime and violence has an important influence on migration and residential mobility, but they also maintain, somewhat surprisingly, that there are troubling inconsistencies across studies in various respects that make it difficult to propose sweeping conclusions regarding this relationship, and they point out that victimization experience and aggregate crime rates are just two of many factors that shape population movements.

It seems that South and Messner (2000) and other researchers (for example, Hipp et al., 2009b) believe that crime influences mobility positively. I think that this view is too simple. Reasonably, both increases and decreases in crime in an area may affect the attractiveness and prices of dwellings so that residents prefer to live somewhere else. Moreover, mobility may of course be influenced by a lot of other circumstances as well, for example authorities' housing control, the frequency of privately owned dwellings, new buildings, and many other things.

Much of the discussion above refers primarily to the crimes committed in areas, but results of such studies on reciprocal influence are probably not fully applicable to studies of the crimes that are committed by the areas' residents, since the two types of crimes differ. To be sure, residents may commit many crimes outside their own area (this seems relatively often to have been the case in Sweden, see below).

It is hard to know what role the type of crime studied in this book has played for people's judgment of the attractiveness of areas in Stockholm. Some people may have been interested in knowing what offenders there were in an area, for example if they considered moving to this area but did not wish their children to get into bad company. However, it must have been difficult for the general public to get information about the offender rates of the areas. There were no published official statistics of this kind (or of the rates of offenses). Presumably, people had to consider the social structure of the residents in the areas in order to get an idea of the offenders or the offenses. In Sweden it is a well-known fact, constantly repeated in mass media, that foreign citizens tend to be more criminal than native citizens, and no doubt it is a common view among the general public in this country that individuals with poorer social backgrounds tend to be more criminal. Perhaps people used such views of the relationship between social factors and the criminality of individuals when they judged the attractiveness of an area, a judgment that may have affected their moves. However, such judgment meant that influence went from (perceived) social factors to crime, and it does not contradict the assumption made in this study about non-reciprocity of influences.

I have now discussed what significance people's perception of and reaction to properties of areas have for the direction of the causal relationship between crime and social structure. Another aspect of the problem of direction has to do with how the commission of crimes influences characteristics of the perpetrators or of people in the perpetrators' environment. Committing crimes of traditional types (thefts and violent crimes) may change the social conditions of the perpetrator. As a rule, committing such crimes breeds misery – and it may therefore be asked if this individual-level influence of criminality on social conditions, when aggregated up to the area level, implies that crime influences social structure in a way that must be considered in analyses.

As regards crime as measured in the study presented in this book, the answer to this question is no. The reason is that the perpetrators only constitute a small minority of the population of an area, and that only some of them are subjected to sanctions of any greater importance from authorities. Most perpetrators are leniently treated. For example, in 1990 about 86 per cent of all individuals found guilty in Sweden of criminal offenses could get off by paying fines. Only five per cent were deprived of their liberty. Of all individuals in the country who were 15 years of age or older only 0.25 per cent were imprisoned in this year (all types of crimes considered, also types not considered in the crime measure used in this study). This figure refers to the whole country, and the figure of the imprisonment of Stockholm residents must have been higher, but it cannot have been so high that it meant a considerable influence of area crime on social properties.

The assumption in this study that the crime factor has had no considerable influences on the social properties does not imply that there cannot have been any such influence at all. What is assumed is only that such influences were so unimportant when set in relation to influences in the opposite direction that they can be disregarded. Reviewing the evidence found in empirical research and considering the significance of the type of crime measure used in this study, there is support for this assumption: 1) There seems to be no study in the research on urban area crime that demonstrates the existence of an influence of considerable strength of crime on social structure. 2) By using data on suspects, it is possible to avoid some of the problems of causal interpretation that appear when using data on crimes committed by all types of persons. Furthermore, more support for the assumption is found when considering the social and economic-political conditions in Stockholm. 3) There were no slum areas in Stockholm that ordinary people can be assumed to have kept away from because they were afraid of being the victim of crime there. The levels of area crime were probably lower than was the case in many other big cities. 4) The market process, which has been assumed to produce reciprocal influences, was to a rather great extent limited in Stockholm because of authorities' housing control. 5) There are no findings in the present study that contradict the assumption. Rather, results indicate that the assumption is true. For example, in a multivariate regression analysis that has been performed of the changes 1985–1990 in the social control and social resources properties using the changes 1980–1985 in crime and in a set of independent properties (those listed in Table 4.4) as regressors, no findings indicate that the change in crime had any influence of notable strength on these control or resources factors (figures not shown). Moreover, if previous crime affected social structure, which in turn affected later crime, it seems likely that previous crime would have affected later crime and that there would therefore be a positive relationship between previous and later changes in crime. But that is not what is found – as described above the relationship between previous and later changes in crime is slightly negative.

**Macro-Level Product Models**

In this study, an important question is whether crime in an area should be explained by considering interaction between macro-level properties. Models characterized by such interaction can be of different formal types. For example, crime can be assumed to be a linear function of both basic area properties and interaction properties, or it can be assumed to be a product of linear functions of basic area properties. The latter and more complicated type – single-equation models constructed as products of functions – is used in this study and will now be discussed. It follows principles discussed elsewhere (Dahlbäck, 2001, 1998a, 1998b; see also Dahlbäck, 2003, pp. 163–173).

Thus, in the product-of-functions models the dependent variable is the product of factors that are linear functions of independent variables. Let the dependent variable at time point $t$ be denoted by $T_t$, the factor $j$ ($j = 1, \ldots, m$) at $t$ by $F_{jt}$. Then it holds true that

$$T_t = F_{1t}F_{2t}\cdots F_{jt}\cdots F_{mt}. \tag{7}$$

It is assumed that the factors $F$ have only positive values. Now, let $F_{jt}$ be a linear function of contemporary and earlier values on independent characteristics $x_i$ ($i = 1, \ldots, n$) and a constant $c_j$ according to

$$F_{jt} = \sum_{i=1}^{n} \left( b_{jit} x_{it} + b_{ji,t-1} x_{i,t-1} + b_{ji,t-2} x_{i,t-2} + \ldots \right) + c_j. \tag{8}$$

The independent variables describing characteristics $x_i$ pertain to adjacent, equally spaced points in time: $t$, $t-1$, $t-2$, ... . Using (7) and (8), $T_t$ and the change in $T$, $T_t - T_{t-1}$, can be given as functions of the independent variables. However, in order that these models be identifiable, $c_j$ must have a fixed value, otherwise all coefficients in one given factor can be multiplied by an arbitrary constant and all coefficients in another, arbitrarily selected factor can be divided by this constant without changing the value of $T$.

Since the factors $F_j$ assume only positive values, standardization of the independent variables implies that the constants $c_j$ have positive values other than 0. This means that the value of $T_t$ is not altered if each factor $j$ is multiplied by $1/c_j$ and the total factor product is multiplied by $c_1 c_2 \cdots c_j \cdots c_m$. After such multiplications, $T_t$ can be written as

$$T_t = d F_{1t} F_{2t} \cdots F_{jt} \cdots F_{mt}, \tag{9}$$

where $d$ is greater than 0 and equal to $c_1 c_2 \cdots c_j \cdots c_m$, and where, after redefining the $b$ coefficients,

$$F_{jt} = \sum_{i=1}^{n} \left( b_{jit} x_{it} + b_{ji,t-1} x_{i,t-1} + b_{ji,t-2} x_{i,t-2} + \ldots \right) + 1. \tag{10}$$

Thus, the constant $c_j$ has been given the value 1 in all $F$ factors. A model of the (9)-(10) type can be assumed to be identifiable except for special cases (for example, due to collinearity among variables within a factor).

Standardization of the independent variables in this study implies that these variables lose their original intertemporal comparability quality. However, standardization is not the only way of forming independent variables that are appropriate for product models. Normalized variables of the type described above can also be assumed to be appropriate, since they come close to being standardized, at least in most cases. A product model using standardized variables and the corresponding model using variables in normalized form are, if the latter model allows of positive constants in the linear expressions, transformable into each other and they will produce exactly the same explanation of crime. This is so because when the standardized and normalized variables are transformed into each other the model value is kept unchanged by multiplying the terms in the expressions by numbers so that the constants are still 1 and by multiplying the *d* coefficient by the product of the inverted values of these numbers.

Models of the desired product-of-functions type are advantageous to use in many contexts, because they can capture a nested structure of influences on the dependent variable. However, not unexpectedly, using these models empirically is made complicated by their nonlinearity, which may make it difficult to find the set of coefficients that minimizes the deviations of the actual values from the modeled values of the crime factor. No proof is given that the product models obtained in this study give global minima.

In a product model of the type discussed here, the crime factor at a point *t* of reference time is assumed to be the product of four independent factors $A_t$, $S_t$, $R_t$, and $H_t$ and the constant $d_t$. All the independent factors and, if applicable, their sub-factors, are assumed to be positive numbers that describe stimulating effects on crime. The *A* factor measures aspects of the age and sex distribution of the residents, the *S* factor measures the lack of social control of the residents, the *R* factor measures the lack of social resources, while the *H* factor measures aspects of the dwelling and housing environment. The factors *A*, *S*, *R*, and *H* are assumed to be ratio scale measures of influences, and the constant *d* calibrates the product of the values of these ratio scale measures. Thus, the influence of the factors on crime at *t*, denoted $C_t$, is a product of the factors as follows:

$$C_t = d_t A_t S_t R_t H_t. \tag{11}$$

Obviously, the higher the value of an independent factor, the stronger the influence of this factor on crime, other things being equal. If an independent factor has the value 1, it has a neutral effect on the other factors' influence on crime.

The factors *A*, *S*, *R* and *H* are assumed to affect the residents' motivation and proneness to commit crime. No factor is explicitly designed to describe the effects of basic circumstantial determinants of crime, that is, such basic circumstances that make crime possible at all. For example, for property crime such a determinant is the fact that there are objects that can be stolen and for violent crime such a determinant is the fact that there are conflicts between individuals that may trigger violent reactions (as to the latter determinant, see Dahlbäck, 1996b).

Circumstantial determinants of crime are focused in the routine activity theory (Cohen and Felson, 1979; Felson and Cohen, 1980; see also Cohen et al., 1981). According to this theory, crime occurs when the three elements of motivated offenders, suitable targets (victims of violence or goods to be stolen) and absence of capable guardians of these targets converge in space and time, something that often occurs in connection with people's routine activities (I find it somewhat strange to speak of victims of violence as "targets" in the routine activity perspective, since this seems to indicate that people have an intent of committing violent crime that they carry out when they find an opportunity to do so in their routine activities, something that I do not think is an adequate description of how the behavior is caused in most cases). This theory does not explain how the motivation of offenders is caused, and one may therefore believe that it is irrelevant for the study presented in this book. The theory seems to fit better for studying the crimes committed in areas than for studying the criminality of the residents. Nevertheless, since residents in big cities tend to commit many of their crimes near their homes, it could be thought that the idea of the routine activity theory about the significance of the occurrence of unguarded "targets" still is of interest. However, it seems that the distance between offenders' residence and the place where they commit crime tends to be rather long in Stockholm, longer than in cities in the USA. Wikström found that most of the crimes – excluding those committed in private – committed by Stockholm inhabitants occurred quite a distance away from the place where the offenders resided (Wikström, 1991, p. 220).

Furthermore, it seems that there is not much empirical support in the study presented in this book for the idea that the occurrence of unguarded targets affects the rate of residents' crime. The circumstantial determinants of violent and property crime can, as discussed below, be assumed to differ from each other, and if they do the violent and property types of crime can also be assumed to differ, that is, to be different dimensions. However, in this study crime of the residents is found to be a one-dimensional construct, comprising both violent and property crimes of traditional types.

Some circumstantial determinants of crime can be assumed to be measured to some degree by factors included in the study. Conflicts between individuals that cause violent crime may arise for several reasons – for example, sexual, political, or economic ones. Sexual and some other types of conflict can probably be measured with DIVOR, but this property is certainly no perfect measure of all conflicts. The supply of suitable targets for property crime may be described by the affluence in the area, which perhaps could be measured with INCMULT. The lack of guardiance of targets is often said to be a function of people's employment outside the home – people who are at home can guard their belongings better than people who are at their working place. Guardiance can therefore be approximately measured with UNEMPL. The lack of guardiance could perhaps also be measured with MULTHS – in and around multi-family houses there are often easily accessible public or half-public spaces, for example in the form of basements, attics, and parking places.

It turns out that DIVOR does not correlate very strongly with either INCMULT or UNEMPL. For the 1990 data these correlations are −0.28 and −0.07, that is, there is no indication that there is a positive relationship of substantial strength between the assumed circumstantial determinants for violent and property crimes, which should be the case if the residents' violent and property crimes are affected by the determinants and they form a one-dimensional construct. However, for the 1990 data it turns out that DIVOR correlates 0.88 with MULTHS, and this seems to be consistent with an influence of circumstantial determinants and the one-dimensionality of the crime construct.

The possibility that some of the measured properties may describe circumstantial determinants means a complication of the analyses. For example, this is the case with MULTHS, which may describe both a lack of guardianship due to poor physical control and a lack of social control due to the anonymity of the residents living in multi-family houses.

If circumstantial determinants of the type discussed above affect crime, they can be assumed to do so in an interactive fashion. These determinants describe the amount of occasions that are constituted so that crime is an attractive action alternative, while the properties focused in the study describe primarily the tendency of residents to commit crime at one such occasion. Formally, these two types of factors should therefore be multiplied with each other in a model of crime.

For cross-sectional analyses of $C_t$, the factors $A$, $S$, $R$ and $H$ are assumed to be functions of properties at $t$. In order to have operational models of (11), the factors have been formulated in two versions. In Version I, the factors are linear functions of basic properties of the four mentioned categories. In Version II, the factors are products of linear functions of each property, except the age/sex factor, which is a linear function of all age/sex properties. The two model versions are identifiable in ordinary cases. In Version I, the factors have the following form:

$$
\begin{aligned}
A_t &= b_{11}\text{YNGMALE}_t + b_{12}\text{YNGFEML}_t + b_{13}\text{MDLMALE}_t \\
&\quad + b_{14}\text{MDLFEML}_t + b_{15}\text{OLDMALE}_t + b_{16}\text{OLDFEML}_t + 1; \\
S_t &= b_{21}\text{FORGN}_t + b_{22}\text{SINGLE}_t + b_{23}\text{DIVOR}_t + b_{24}\text{MOVES}_t + 1; \\
R_t &= b_{31}\text{INCMULT}_t + b_{32}\text{INCDICH}_t + b_{33}\text{INCSTD}_t + b_{34}\text{UNEMPL}_t \\
&\quad + b_{35}\text{SOCAID}_t + b_{36}\text{OCCMULT}_t + b_{37}\text{OCCDICH}_t + 1; \\
H_t &= b_{41}\text{MULTHS}_t + b_{42}\text{PUBLIC}_t + b_{43}\text{OVERCR}_t + 1 .
\end{aligned}
\tag{12}
$$

All interaction between properties is here assumed to exist between the factors. In Version II, the following factors are used:

$$
\begin{aligned}
A_t &= b_{11}\text{YNGMALE}_t + b_{12}\text{YNGFEML}_t + b_{13}\text{MDLMALE}_t \\
&\quad + b_{14}\text{MDLFEML}_t + b_{15}\text{OLDMALE}_t + b_{16}\text{OLDFEML}_t + 1; \\
S_t &= (b_{21}\text{FORGN}_t + 1)(b_{22}\text{SINGLE}_t + 1)(b_{23}\text{DIVOR}_t + 1) \\
&\quad (b_{24}\text{MOVES}_t + 1); \\
R_t &= (b_{31}\text{INCMULT}_t + 1)(b_{32}\text{INCDICH}_t + 1)(b_{33}\text{INCSTD}_t + 1) \\
&\quad (b_{34}\text{UNEMPL}_t + 1)(b_{35}\text{SOCAID}_t + 1)(b_{36}\text{OCCMULT}_t + 1) \\
&\quad (b_{37}\text{OCCDICH}_t + 1); \\
H_t &= (b_{41}\text{MULTHS}_t + 1)(b_{42}\text{PUBLIC}_t + 1)(b_{43}\text{OVERCR}_t + 1) .
\end{aligned}
\tag{13}
$$

Here there is also interaction between properties within the same factor.

The interaction described by macro-level product models may be due to micro-level interaction within or between individuals. In the former case, the macro-level model (11) can be derived from an individual-level model of a particular kind. This individual-level model implies that the impact on area crime of an individual $i$ at time point $t$, $y_{it}$, is seen as a product of the constant $d_t$ and four individual-level factors, corresponding to the four macro-level factors just discussed: an age/sex factor (denoted $a_{it}$), a lack-of-social-control factor ($s_{it}$), a lack-of-social-resources factor ($r_{it}$), and a dwelling and housing environmental factor ($h_{it}$). Again, all the four factors are assumed to be positive numbers that describe stimulating effects on crime, these factors are assumed to be ratio scale measures of influences, and the constant $d_t$, which is also positive, is used to calibrate the product of these scale values. Thus, $y_{it}$ is a product of the factors and the constant as follows:

$$y_{it} = d_t \, a_{it} \, s_{it} \, r_{it} \, h_{it} \, . \tag{14}$$

The total number of crimes is assumed to be the aggregate of all $n$ residents' impacts, and the rate of crime is then

$$C_t = \frac{\sum y_{it}}{n} = \frac{\sum d_t \, a_{it} \, s_{it} \, r_{it} \, h_{it}}{n} \, . \tag{15}$$

If the correlations between the individual-level factors $a_{it}$, $s_{it}$, $r_{it}$, and $h_{it}$ are 0, and if $A_t$, $S_t$, $R_t$, and $H_t$ are the means of $a_{it}$, $s_{it}$, $r_{it}$, and $h_{it}$, then, in line with what has been shown above, $d_t A_t S_t R_t H_t$ will be equal to the right side of (15). But it is of course extremely unlikely that the correlations are 0. However, $d_t A_t S_t R_t H_t$ may also be seen as the result of interaction between the factors among different individuals in accordance with what has been said above about the extension of formula (6) to more than two independent variables.

The macro model in its two versions has been used in empirical analyses, and its structure has then been determined by nonlinear regression technique. Parameters are estimated by the least-squares method using Gauss-Newton iterations. In doing so, 0 has been used as initial values of the $b$ coefficients. Due to the homogeneous form of the model, this gives all these coefficients the same possibilities for growing in absolute value in the iterative process of finding a minimum. The initial value of the $d$ coefficient is the mean of the crime rate.

Chapter 4

# Results I. Cross-Sectional Relationships

Of the results of the study, those pertaining to cross-sectional relationships will be discussed first. The focus is on the relationships for the years of 1990 and 1985, since data on important independent properties of social resources exist for these years only. The results for 1990 are particularly interesting, since the validity of the crime measure is probably highest for this year.

**Relationships for Single Independent Dimensions**

Correlation and regression coefficients for the bivariate linear relationships between the independent variables in normalized versions and the crime factor for the years 1980, 1985 and 1990 are shown in Table 4.1. Many of the correlations reported for the social control, social resources and dwelling environment properties are strong. For example, looking at the figures for 1990, we find that crime correlates 0.90 with OCCDICH, −0.87 with OCCMULT, 0.80 with PUBLIC, −0.72 with INCMULT, 0.71 with SOCAID, 0.65 with FORGN, 0.64 with SINGLE, and 0.56 with DIVOR. For the previous years most corresponding correlations are also strong. On the other hand, most of the correlations for the age/sex properties are very weak. INCSTD has negative correlations with crime – not positive ones as might have been expected. UNEMPL correlates positively and rather strongly with crime in 1990 and positively and weakly with crime in 1985. MULTHS and OVERCR correlate positively and strongly or rather strongly with crime in all three years. The regression coefficients for all properties for which there is information for all three reference years except MOVES, INCSTD and the age/sex properties increase steadily in their absolute values when going from 1980 to 1990. The regression coefficients for UNEMPL, SOCAID, OCCMULT and OCCDICH increase their absolute values when going from 1985 to 1990. It should be noted that the regression coefficients – except the ones for 1980 – cannot be compared between properties, but should only be used in comparisons for the same property.

The fact that most of the correlations between the age/sex properties and the crime factor are very weak might seem puzzling. For example, it might be expected that there would be a relationship of substantial strength between crime and YNGMALE implying that the higher the value of YNGMALE, the higher the incidence of crime, since young males tend to be especially prone to commit crime and prone to stimulate other young men to do the same. But this is not the case for 1985 and 1990. What is the reason for these weak correlations for young males and for the weak correlations for other age/sex properties? One reason for the weak

**Table 4.1** **Linear cross-sectional relationships between the crime factor and single basic independent variables and sets of power versions of such variables. For all 83 areas. Independent variables normalized**

| Independent prop. | C80 | C85 | | C90 | |
|---|---|---|---|---|---|
| | Regr./Corr. | Regr. | Corr. | Regr. | Corr. |
| *Age and sex* | | | | | |
| YNGMALE | .29 | .08 | .04 | −.00 | −.00 |
| YNGFEML | .45 | .22 | .15 | .06 | .03 |
| MDLMALE | .07 | .07 | .06 | .02 | .01 |
| MDLFEML | .01 | −.21 | −.15 | −.24 | −.16 |
| OLDMALE | .01 | .15 | .10 | −.03 | −.02 |
| OLDFEML | −.11 | .02 | .01 | −.03 | −.02 |
| *Social control* | | | | | |
| FORGN | .41 | .56 | .47 | .84 | .65 |
| Power versions[a] | .48 | - | .59 | - | .75 |
| SINGLE | .60 | .66 | .51 | 1.12 | .64 |
| DIVOR | .54 | .78 | .61 | .81 | .56 |
| MOVES | .01 | .13 | .07 | .10 | .05 |
| *Social resources* | | | | | |
| INCMULT | −.72 | −.91 | −.72 | −1.01 | −.72 |
| INCDICH | .25 | .44 | .39 | .47 | .31 |
| Power vers. of INC vars.[b] | .80 | - | .79 | - | .84 |
| INCSTD | −.54 | −.46 | −.47 | −.24 | −.38 |
| UNEMPL | - | .28 | .22 | .54 | .44 |
| SOCAID | - | .89 | .69 | 1.26 | .71 |
| Power versions[c] | - | - | .78 | - | .77 |
| OCCMULT | - | −1.08 | −.84 | −1.20 | −.87 |
| OCCDICH | - | 1.06 | .83 | 1.24 | .90 |
| Power vers. of OCC vars.[d] | - | - | .85 | - | .90 |
| *Dwelling environment* | | | | | |
| MULTHS | .48 | .66 | .49 | .78 | .46 |
| PUBLIC | .80 | 1.01 | .79 | 1.22 | .80 |
| OVERCR | .42 | .60 | .38 | 1.12 | .50 |

[a] FORGN, FORGN**2, FORGN**3.
[b] INCMULT, INCMULT**2, INCMULT**3, INCDICH, INCDICH**2.
[c] SOCAID, SOCAID**2, SOCAID**3.
[d] OCCMULT, OCCMULT**2, OCCDICH.

correlations for young males 1985 and 1990 is probably the fact that the percentage of these residents varied only little among the areas (for 1990, the mean value of the percentage in original version is 0.052 and the standard deviation is only 0.011). A reason for the general weakness of correlations for the age/sex properties may be the fact that there are relationships between these properties and other independent properties that work against the emergence of strong correlations. For example, if there are relatively many males in the ages of 15–24 years, there also tend to be many individuals who are younger than 15 years of age and who have not been considered in the construction of the crime rate measure. Another reason is possibly the fact that the different types of crime that are factor analyzed vary with respect to how old the perpetrators tend to be and that the first factor describes what is common to them all. Thus, due to the construction, the factor may to some extent be rather weakly related to age/sex properties of the area.

For some independent properties, their nonlinear relationships with the crime factor are much stronger than their linear relationships. For example, crime increases at a slower rate for higher values of FORGN and SOCAID (hence, the second derivates are negative). INCMULT has a decreasing relationship with crime for which the second derivative is negative at lower values, but positive at higher values. One simple way of formalizing these and other nonlinear relationships is to use polynomials of the second or third degree, and this has also been done, using the power versions of independent properties that give a substantial increase in the explained variance in crime. Thus, crime has then been explained in a linear regression analysis using the independent variable as well as this variable squared and/or this variable raised to its third power as regressors. Table 4.1 shows the estimated correlations between crime and explanatory linear combinations of such power versions for some of the properties – that is, the square roots of the explained proportions of variance obtained using these power versions.

The figures of explained variance obtained in these analyses and used for the estimation of the correlations shown in Table 4.1 are corrected for lost degrees of freedom using the formula $1-[((n-1)(1-R^2))/(n-p)]$, where $n$ is the number of observations and $p$ the number of parameters including the intercept (the same formula is used throughout this book). Considering these figures and focusing again on the year 1990, it is found that FORGN explains 56 per cent of the variance in the nonlinear case, whereas the corresponding figure for the linear case is 42 per cent. For the simultaneous use of INCMULT and INCDICH, the corresponding figures are 71 vs. 53 per cent and for SOCAID 59 vs. 50 per cent. For the earlier years, similar results are obtained. For the simultaneous use of OCCDICH and OCCMULT, the same type of analysis yields no or only slight increase in the variance explained.

Of the independent properties, OCCDICH and OCCMULT stand out in explanatory power. Using these two properties and their power versions, 81 per cent of the variance in the 1990 crime factor is explained. For 1985, the corresponding figure is 72 per cent. The relationship for 1990 is remarkable (for this year, the correlation between OCCDICH and the crime factor is 0.90). It means that using the occupational status dimension explains the overwhelming majority of the information in a measure of crime that explains the overwhelming majority of the information in various rates of traditional crime in the areas. The relationship is all the more remarkable given that the obtained explained proportion of variance surely is but a minimum value of the true proportion. This is so because the measure of occupational status cannot be assumed to give a perfect description of this status or of the aspects of the status that influence crime.

The nonlinear relationships can be explained in a variety of ways. For example, the relationship found for FORGN might be attributable to the fact that foreign citizens who form a very large part of the population in their area tend to have many close contacts with other foreign residents. This means that they live less anonymously and therefore are subjected to relatively stronger social control. Another possible explanation could be that these foreign citizens have lived longer in their area and therefore have adapted better to the local society than those foreigners who make up a small part of the population. For INCMULT and INCDICH, it may be that very low and very high incomes are relatively poor measures of the actual resources of the residents. However, what should be the explanation of the relationship found for SOCAID seems more unclear.

Several of the properties that are particularly strongly related to the crime factor are also strongly related to the social rank factor. Not surprisingly, then, this factor is strongly related to the crime factor. This is true for all three reference years (for 1980, the correlation is 0.66, for 1985 0.76, and for 1990 0.82). A factor that describes the middle-aged, active population stands out clearly in the 1985 and 1990 data, and it is negatively related to crime (the correlation is −0.33 for 1985 and −0.38 for 1990). For the other factors for 1985 and 1990, the relationships with crime are much weaker.

The simple bivariate relationships found between independent properties and the crime factor do not differ much from results in previous research as to what properties are related to crime in urban areas, but they are in some cases stronger than what has hitherto been found to be the case. As to their bearing on suggested theories about environmental causes of crime, they seem to be fairly compatible with several such theories, and they also seem compatible with the view that crime in urban areas is primary the result of geographical selection of individuals.

It has been found that the crime factor value increases at a slower rate for higher values of SOCAID and that the nonlinear relationship between the crime factor and the measures of occupational status is not much stronger than the corresponding linear relationship. These results go to the question of how to approach the housing situation of problem and low-status families. The results give no indication that a concentration of these families in certain areas would increase total crime in the city.

**Multivariate Linear Relationships**

The strong relationships that exist between several independent properties cause problems in analyzing the multivariate linear relationship between the crime factor and these properties. This is true for all the reference years of 1980, 1985 and 1990. Particularly strong relationships exist, of course, between INCMULT and INCDICH and between OCCMULT and OCCDICH, respectively, since they are properties that describe similar things and are constructed on the basis of the same original data. The following analyses therefore make use of only one property in each pair. I have chosen to use OCCDICH since it is based on dichotomous individual-level data and since the occurrence of the lowest occupational status can be assumed to be especially important for crime. It would have been desirable to use INCDICH for about the same reason, but this property seems not to be of very high validity, possibly due to the fact that some persons with low registered incomes may be rather well-to-do. I therefore use the property INCMULT. The exclusion of INCDICH and OCCMULT does not reduce appreciably the proportion of the variance of the crime factor that is explained by the independent properties, particularly not when correcting this proportion for lost degrees of freedom.

Furthermore, it turns out that most power versions of independent properties do not contribute much to the explanation of the crime factor in multivariate analysis. For example, considering the 1990 data, when all basic independent properties in the reduced set are used without power versions, 90 per cent of the variance in crime is explained after correction for lost degrees of freedom, whereas 91 per cent is explained with these versions included. From a theoretical point of view, it does not appear that the solutions obtained without the power versions are substantially inferior to those including these versions, and since the inclusion means considerable complications with respect to interpretations of relationships, the power versions will not, as a rule, be used. The power versions of SOCAID, which are the power variables that contribute most to the explanation of crime, are included in an analysis reported below, but in ordinary cases only basic properties, excluding INCDICH and OCCMULT, are used.

Below, I discuss rather summarily results from multivariate analyses of data for the reference years of 1980, 1985 and 1990, and I then show more in detail some problems for the 1990 data. Thus, I have made multiple linear regression analyses of the crime factors using the reduced set of basic independent variables as regressors. In all of the analyses reported in this section, all variables are standardized. Hence, the partial regression coefficients obtained are beta weights. The explained proportions of the variance in the crime factor are corrected for lost degrees of freedom. The results of some of the analyses are reported in Table 4.2.

The results of the regression analyses of C80, C85 and C90, using all basic variables of the reduced set as regressors, are reported in Columns 1 – 3 in the table. In several respects, the figures for the different years show similarities. For all years, the DIVOR property has high positive beta weights, while OVERCR has positive weights with values that are not particularly high. For 1985 and 1990, OCCDICH has high positive weights. SOCAID has positive weights, of which one has a rather low and one a rather high value, whereas UNEMPL has negative weights with rather similar absolute values. These relationships, except the ones for UNEMPL, go in the expected direction. Furthermore, it is found that all weights for FORGN,

**Table 4.2     Results of multiple regression analyses of the crime factor. Variables standardized. For all 83 areas**

| Independent prop. | C80 | C85 | ------------- C90 ------------- | | | |
| | (1) | (2) | (3) | (4) | (5) | (6) |
| --- | --- | --- | --- | --- | --- | --- |
| *Age and sex* | | | | | | |
| YNGMALE | .03 | .04 | −.10 | −.04 | .08 | −.13 |
| YNGFEML | .00 | −.19 | −.17 | −.12 | −.09 | −.20 |
| MDLMALE | .13 | −.04 | −.51 | −.34 | −.17 | −.27 |
| MDLFEML | −.25 | −.39 | −.43 | −.63 | −.42 | −.42 |
| OLDMALE | .10 | −.01 | −.05 | .01 | .20 | −.07 |
| OLDFEML | −.42 | −.43 | −.80 | −.70 | −.59 | −.49 |
| *Social control* | | | | | | |
| FORGN | .02 | −.13 | −.10 | .21 | .18 | - |
| SINGLE | .40 | .18 | −.10 | .03 | .16 | - |
| DIVOR | .49 | .46 | .53 | .67 | .74 | - |
| MOVES | −.16 | .00 | .09 | .15 | .17 | - |
| *Social resources* | | | | | | |
| INCMULT | .09 | .11 | −.04 | −.16 | - | .03 |
| INCSTD | −.13 | .02 | .04 | .08 | - | .04 |
| UNEMPL | - | −.23 | −.32 | −.25 | - | −.45 |
| SOCAID | - | .21 | .34 | - | - | .26 |
| OCCDICH | - | .39 | .52 | - | - | .74 |
| *Dwelling environment* | | | | | | |
| MULTHS | −.17 | −.26 | −.01 | −.03 | −.14 | .17 |
| PUBLIC | .32 | .25 | .01 | .18 | .10 | .12 |
| OVERCR | .27 | .31 | .17 | .30 | .33 | .09 |
| *Explained proportion of variance* | | | | | | |
| Uncorrected | .87 | .85 | .92 | .90 | .89 | .90 |
| Corrected | .84 | .81 | .90 | .87 | .87 | .88 |

MOVES, INCMULT, and INCSTD have low or rather low absolute values, that the weights for the female age properties tend to be negative and to have lower values than the weights for the corresponding male properties (eight of nine female age properties have negative weights, and for eight of the nine properties the weight is lower than the weight for the corresponding male property).

Thus, there are clear similarities between the findings of the three analyses. However, the findings differ in some respects. For example, the beta weights for SINGLE and PUBLIC and for several of the age/sex properties, particularly MDLMALE, differ a great deal between years. Some properties have beta weights with different signs for different years.

As to the explained proportions of the variance in crime, it is found that relatively little is explained for the year of 1985, particularly when considering the high reliability of the crime measure of this year. What is the reason for this? It is difficult to say. One reason may be that there are more areas with very small populations for 1985 than for 1980 and 1990 and that this has impaired the quality of measurements. However, this is hardly the only reason.

The difference in explained variance between 1985 and 1990 notwithstanding, using the weights obtained for these two years produces rather similar results. This is made evident if the weights for one year are applied to the data of the other year. If the beta weights obtained for the 1985 independent variables are applied to the 1990 independent variables, the weighted sum of the latter variables explains 89 per cent of the variance in C90 – when used in ordinary multiple regression analysis, the variables explain 92 per cent of the variance (the explained proportions of variances discussed in this paragraph are uncorrected for lost degrees of freedom). If the beta weights obtained for the 1990 independent variables are applied to the 1985 independent variables, the weighted sum of these latter variables explains 81 per cent of the variance in C85 – a figure to be compared to the 85 per cent that these variables explain in ordinary regression analysis.

The evaluation of the differences between the years in the weights found is made difficult due to the strong relationships that exist between properties (for a discussion of the problems with such strong relationships in empirical studies of crime in urban areas, see Land et al., 1990). Obviously, there is a great deal of overlap between properties in their ability to explain the crime factor linearly. These collinearity problems imply that the weights for the properties can be much changed without any great change in the explained proportion of variance.

This is seen clearly from the results of regression analyses performed to construct models that include a fixed number of regressors selected from the above-mentioned set of independent variables. For example, such an analysis has been performed using the 1990 data. It turns out that the corrected explained proportion of variance for the 20 different best models comprising 10 variables goes from 90.20 to 90.87 per cent. Thus, there is very little difference in explained variance between these models.

The collinearity problems can be further explored by using subsets of the independent variables in regression analyses of the crime factor. Again using the 1990 data, we find that each of the social control, social resources and dwelling environment groups of variables, when used together with the age/sex variables, explain much of the variance in this factor. The social resources and age/sex variables explain a particularly large portion of the variance, 88 per cent. However, much is also explained when the control and dwelling environment variables are added to the age/sex variables (84 and 77 per cent, respectively). The age/sex variables themselves explain quite little of the variance (13 per cent). When all variables in the reduced set except for the social resources ones are used as regressors, 87 per cent of the variance is explained; when the social control variables are excluded, 88 per cent is explained (see Columns 5 and 6 in Table 4.2).

Which are the properties that are most troubled by collinearity problems? This may be analyzed by considering the tolerance values of the variables (the tolerance value of a variable is $1 - R^2$, where $R^2$ is the explained proportion of variance obtained from the regression of the variable on all other independent variables in the model used). Low tolerance values indicate collinearity problems. For the analysis of the 1990 data, it is found that tolerance is lowest for OLDFEML (the value is 0.02) and for MULTHS, SINGLE, MDLMALE and MDLFEML (for these properties the value is 0.04). For previous years as well, these properties have low tolerance values. Thus, results for these properties from multivariate analyses should be treated with particular caution.

The collinearity problems mean that the coefficient values obtained in regression analyses are very sensitive to errors in the data (errors that are thus assumed here not to be of sampling type). Small errors may lead to unrealistic coefficient values. How should this situation be handled? Is there any other way of analyzing the data? What about using the orthogonal factors obtained in the factor analyses of independent variables? Of course, in a technical sense, crime can be analyzed with the help of these factors. Taking the 1990 data as an example, it turns out that the first factor explains 67 per cent of the total variance in crime, and that the three other above-mentioned factors explain 14, 0 and 0 per cent each. Overall, 82 per cent of the variance is explained by these four factors. However, there are serious problems in analyzing crime in this way. First, the factors are difficult to use in an analysis of crime, since they fail to correspond with the theoretical perspectives used. Thus, it is difficult to interpret the relationships they have with crime. Second, substantially more of the variance in crime can be explained by using independent variables than by using the factors. Third, the factor approach is inappropriate to use longitudinally, because it is difficult to construct factors that are comparable between years.

Clearly, there are problems with performing multivariate analyses of crime using the original independent variables. Nevertheless, useful insights can be gained by doing this. First, because collinearity is not total, one may have some confidence that strong relationships found indicate real matters, especially if they concern independent variables with relatively high tolerance. This is particularly true, of course, if such relationships are found for different reference points. Second, even if collinearity is strong, it may be possible to analyze the effects that changes in regression parameters have on crime. Such analyses are carried out below, with focus on the 1990 data. Of course, caution must be observed in interpreting the coefficients obtained.

In the solution that includes all basic variables except INCDICH and OCCMULT for the 1990 data, there are some beta weights with high absolute values (see Table 4.2). If we set the age/sex variables aside for a moment (they will be discussed later), the highest absolute values are obtained for DIVOR (the beta weight is 0.53), OCCDICH (0.52), SOCAID (0.34) and UNEMPL (−0.32). Thus, the higher the percentages of divorced residents, unskilled workers, and social aid recipients, and the lower the percentage of unemployed residents, the higher the value of the crime factor. These relationships, except the one for UNEMPL, point in expected direction. However, there is no other control or resources variable that has a beta weight with the expected sign and a high absolute value. The weight for FORGN, as well as for SINGLE, is −0.10. As to the dwelling environment variables, the weight for OVERCR is 0.17, and thus as expected positive, whereas MULTHS and PUBLIC have weights with very low absolute values.

The negative weight for UNEMPL deserves a comment. It is found that the higher the percentage of unemployed residents, the lower crime, not the opposite which is expected. What is the reason for this? Could it be that unemployed people tend to be inactive, or, as far as the property crime aspect is concerned, that they are relatively efficient in guarding their belongings (Cantor and Land, 1985; Rosenfeld and Fornango, 2007)? Or has the reason to do with their age – despite the fact that age has been crudely controlled for? It is difficult to say. However, it should be noted that unemployment in the time period studied probably, due to relatively generous compensation, did not necessarily mean any very serious economic hardship.

As compared to the simple correlations between the variables and the crime factor (which are bivariate beta weights), the beta weights for some variables in the multivariate analysis of the 1990 data mean radical changes. The absolute values of most coefficients have of course decreased, due to the fact that many variables are strongly related to each other. Some of these changes are particularly interesting. This is the case with the variables describing the INCMULT and PUBLIC properties. These properties probably play very important roles in the geographical selection processes that result in individuals with different social backgrounds landing in different areas.

INCMULT and PUBLIC are strongly correlated with crime in 1990 (the correlations are −0.72 and 0.80). Together they explain 69 per cent (corrected value) of the variance in crime, corresponding to a correlation and a beta weight of 0.83. This figure can be assumed to describe approximately the total of four components: 1) the effect of the two factors' indirect influences, caused by geographical selection, on crime, 2) the effect of their direct influences, 3) the effect of their indirect, non-selective influences, and 4) the spurious relationship between the factors and crime that is due to the fact that both are affected by the same factors of other types.

There is evidence that the effects 2) and 3) were weak. The effect of the direct influences can be described by the two factors' beta weights, and these are only −0.04 and 0.01, indicating very weak influences. The two factors' indirect, non-selective influences were probably also weak. The effect of these influences have been estimated by multiplying the direct influences of factors on crime, measured by beta weights, with the direct influences of INCMULT and PUBLIC on these factors, measured by the beta weights obtained in an analysis in which the various factors for 1990 are regressed on the set of factors for 1985 for the individuals who resided in the same area 1985 and 1990 (thus, this analysis is longitudinal). These data are used for the estimation, because the temporal relation between factors is clear and the influence of selection can be expected to have been relatively weak. It turns out that that the total of the beta weight products is 0.01 for INCMULT and 0.14 for PUBLIC. Thus, the indirect, non-selective effect seems to have been weak.

There is also evidence that the spurious relationship 4) was weak. This relationship has been estimated as the total of the products of various factors' influences, measured by beta weights, on INCMULT and PUBLIC, respectively, and on crime. The former beta weights were obtained in an analysis in which INCMULT in 1990 was regressed on the various independent factors including INCMULT in 1985 and in which a corresponding analysis was performed for PUBLIC. It turns out that the total of the beta weight products is –0.16 for INCMULT and –0.00 for PUBLIC.

The conclusion to be drawn from these facts is that the selection caused by INCMULT and PUBLIC was very important for crime in the short run. Moreover, selection may of course have been caused by other factors than INCMULT and PUBLIC, for example by FORGN and OCCDICH.

For 1985 and 1980, INCMULT and PUBLIC together explain 68 and 73 per cent of the variance in crime, which is about the same figure as for 1990. However, other conditions that must be considered in judging the strength of selection differ. For example, for 1985, the beta weight of PUBLIC does not have a very low value, which may be due to the fact that there is some direct cause of crime missing for this year. For 1980, the beta weight of PUBLIC has a relatively high value, which is probably to a great extent due to the fact that both OCCDICH and SOCAID data are missing.

While residents' means of living in high-status areas is probably rather well described by INCMULT, the ability to manage various social problems and the motive to commit crime due to strain are probably better described by SOCAID and OCCDICH. The relatively high absolute values of the beta weights of these variables can be interpreted accordingly.

As shown in Table 4.2 for the 1990 data, the absolute values of beta weights rise for several variables when SOCAID and OCCDICH are removed (see Columns 3 and 4). The beta weight for FORGN increases from –0.10 to 0.21. Causally, this can be interpreted to mean that there is something in SOCAID and OCCDICH that is also found in FORGN and that affects crime. Closer inspection shows that this quality is found in OCCDICH. The individual-level correlation between Forgn and Occdich is 0.17, indicating some tendency for foreign citizens to be unskilled workers (the corresponding area-level correlation is 0.72). Thus, it seems reasonable to interpret the increase in the beta weight for FORGN when

SOCAID and OCCDICH are removed to be due, at least to a large extent, to the fact that foreigners often have low occupational status and that this means that an influence goes from FORGN to crime when the two variables are removed.

When the power versions of SOCAID are included in the analysis they take on beta weights that do not mean that the value of the crime factor increases at a faster rate for higher proportions of social aid recipients. Thus, there is no indication that a concentration of such recipients in certain areas would increase total crime in the city.

What about the beta weights for the age/sex variables? For the 1990 data (see Column 3), these weights are all negative. Some of them have high absolute values and several of them differ considerably from the corresponding simple correlations. The weights for YNGFEML, MDLFEML and OLDFEML are −0.17, −0.43 and −0.80, that is, the more women and the older these women, the less the value of the crime factor. This is expected. But the weights for the male age categories are not as expected. For YNGMALE, MDLMALE and OLDMALE the weights are −0.10, −0.51 and −0.05. The strongly negative weight for MDLMALE is particularly puzzling. It does not seem realistic. And as can be seen in the table, the corresponding weights for 1985 and 1980 are quite different for this property.

In interpreting the coefficient values obtained for the age/sex variables, the strong relationships that exist between these variables should be duly noted. Had variables describing the percentages of male and female residents who were less than 15 years of age been included, there would have been perfect collinearity between all the age/sex variables, because these variables would have totaled 1 in original versions. Furthermore, there are strong relationships between age/sex variables and other independent variables. These strong relationships mean that the coefficients can be assumed to be very sensitive to errors in the data.

What is the reason for the very low coefficient value for MDLMALE in the 1990 data? Possibly that this negative value implies that the influence on crime of other independent variables are corrected for the occurrence of middle-aged male residents. Crime is probably most strongly affected by young male residents, and several of the social resources variables describe conditions for young and middle-aged male residents. Therefore, a negative coefficient of MDLMALE may mean that the values of these variables are balanced and that this makes the residuals of these variables better suited than the original values for describing conditions conducive to crime.

It can be seen from Columns 3, 5 and 6 in Table 4.2, which describe results for the 1990 data, that removing the social resources variables, some of which primarily describe conditions for males, from the set of regressors means that the value of the coefficient for MDLMALE becomes less negative, and that removing the social control variables from the set of regressors also means that this coefficient becomes less negative, although not as much as when the social resources variables are removed. This indicates that the suggested explanation may be true, at least for the 1990 data (for the 1980 and 1985 data, the regression coefficient for MDLMALE has low absolute values).

Regarding the analyses of the 1990 crime factor using basic independent variables, it must be said in summary that they surely have yielded suggestions about how crime is caused, but that it is difficult to elucidate, due to collinearity problems, how the most accurate linear model of crime is constituted. The same is true for the 1985 and 1980 crime factors and independent data, but I do not discuss the problems for these years in detail.

## Influences from Adjacent Areas

The question may be raised whether crime of the residents in an area is influenced by conditions in adjacent areas in such a way that it cannot be adequately analyzed without considering these influences. For example, such influences may exist if crime is directly or indirectly stimulated or hampered by social contacts across the boundaries of the target area – say by the residents' contacts with people living in other areas but going in the same school or belonging to the same peer group or the same sports club. The possibility that there are influences of these and other types from adjacent areas should, it may be thought, be considered in analyzing crime (see Sampson et al., 2002).

In order to accomplish such an analysis in an advanced way, a sophisticated measure of the power of adjacent areas to influence crime in the target area must be used, since this power may be affected in complicated ways by various properties of the adjacent areas. Geographical nearness is important, of course, but is not the only property of importance. A lot of other things may play a role, for example the sizes, locations and concentrations of populations, barriers to contacts like water, forests, factory areas, etc., and conditions conducive to contacts like streets and public transport facilities.

However, the analysis performed in this study of the influences on crime in an area exerted by adjacent areas is much simpler. I have analyzed the relationship between crime of the target area and a measure of crime of adjacent areas, controlling for the independent factors of the target area. By controlling for these independent factors, it can be determined whether the crime values of other areas contribute to the explanation of crime of the target area beyond what the conditions in the target area do. If the crime values of other areas do contribute in this way, this may be due to an influence.

The analysis refers only to crime in 1990 and consists of a comparison of the results of different linear regression analyses. First, the target area's crime in 1990 is regressed on the set of this area's basic independent factors for the same year, on the set of such independent factors for 1990 and 1985, and on the set of such factors for 1990, 1985 and 1980, respectively (thus, the latter of these regression analyses are longitudinal, and they anticipate to some extent analyses reported later on). Second, the same types of regression analyses are performed again, but now with a measure of the 1990 crime values of adjacent areas added to the regressors. Third, it is determined whether adding this measure as a regressor increases the explained variance in crime, and the regression weight of the measure is checked to see how the influence of the adjacent areas can be assumed be constituted.

The measure is constructed in the following way. Maps of the City of Stockholm, showing the boundaries of the studied areas, the built-up areas and several other things, have been used to select the areas that may have influenced the target area strongly (for the selected areas, see Appendix IV). In selecting these areas consideration has, by rules of thumb, been paid to the possible impact of various factors, like those mentioned above. Only adjacent areas within the Stockholm City Area have been considered. For each target area, the mean of the selected adjacent areas' 1990 crime values is computed. No weighting of the selected areas by geographical distance, by size of population or by any other factor is made. The mean is the measure.

Admittedly, this measure is very simple. Nevertheless, using it can be assumed to yield interesting information. Should it turn out that using the measure adds to the explanation of crime of the target area beyond what using the basic independent factors does, this must be taken as an indication that an influence from adjacent areas going beyond the influences of the considered factors exists. On the other hand, if it turns out that using the measure does not add anything to the explanation of crime beyond what using the basic independent factors does, this cannot be taken as a definite proof of the non-existence of such an influence, since there may be better measures of adjacent areas' crime-influencing capacity. However, if it is found that using the measure does not add anything to the explanation of crime, one is surely apt to consider this to be an indication that there is no very strong influence from adjacent areas, since it is hard to believe that a strong influence is consistent with this finding.

The results obtained are the following ones. In the 1990 data, the measure of crime of the adjacent areas is as expected positively and strongly related to target area crime. The correlation is 0.48. However, adding the measure to the basic independent factors does not increase the corrected explained proportion of the variance in crime. In fact, after correction for lost degrees of freedom, this proportion diminishes slightly in each of the three types of analyses. The measure's beta weights obtained in these analyses have no notable strength. When using the 1990 independent factors the beta weight is 0.02, when using the 1990 and 1985 factors the weight is 0.02 and when using the 1990, 1985 and 1980 factors the weight is −0.01. Thus, no indication is found of a notably strong influence on crime from adjacent areas.

In the empirical analyses that follow, I completely quit the issue of an influence from adjacent areas. These analyses are performed on the assumption that there is no important such influence.

## Considering Micro-Level Interaction

The analysis of the influences on area crime is rendered complicated by the possibility that micro-level factors interact within and between individuals. Previously, I have discussed how the effects of aggregated bivariate interaction may be modeled. As mentioned, it may be doubted that aggregated within-individual interaction can be expressed in terms of ordinary macro-level factors, whereas it is clear that aggregated homogeneous interaction between different factors for all combinations of different residents can be approximately so expressed, namely as products of the mean factor values. It would be interesting to know how the two types of aggregated micro-level interaction affect crime. In much research in this field such an analysis cannot be performed, because there is no adequate information about the micro-level factors. However, in this study such data is available, and I have analyzed the effects of interaction of the two types.

Measuring aggregated micro-level interaction with the means of factor products and the products of mean factor values is somewhat complicated by the fact that the factor values of some residents are inappropriate to use, as mentioned above. The mean-of-products measure for two factors is constructed for all individuals with non-deleted values of the factors, that is, it is constructed using pair-wise deletion. However, the corresponding product-of-means measure is not constructed using pair-wise deletion. Instead, the measure is the product of the two factor means, each of which refers to all acceptable individual-level data for the factor in question taken separately. Thus, in constructing each measure I have used all of the information that can be used.

This means that the relationship between the two types of measures may not capture precisely the relationship intended. However, the arguments previously presented about differences between the relationships of area crime with mean-of-products and product-of-means properties still can be assumed to have merit. Thus, an analysis of the crime factor's relationships with the two types of measures can be assumed to be interesting, because it may indicate whether and how micro-level interaction affects crime.

For the construction of the measures of aggregated micro-level interaction, I have, as previously mentioned, considered nine combinations of control and resources factors, three combinations of control factors, and three combinations of resources factors. These combinations involve the control factors Forgn, Single and Divor and the resources factors Incdich, Socaid and Occdich. I have used mean-of-products measures and product-of-means measures for 1985 and for 1990 by adding them in linear analysis as regressors in standardized form to the standardized basic factors used in analyses reported in Table 4.2 (INCDICH is not included in this set of basic factors in spite of the fact that Incdich and INCDICH have been used for the construction of measures of interaction, but INCMULT can be assumed to work as a substitute). The interaction effects in all these cases are expected to be positive.

The dichotomous micro-level factors of basic types that are combined in the measures are not necessarily very strongly correlated with each other. It turns out that most correlations on the individual level between social control and social resources factors are weak or rather weak, as are most correlations between control factors, whereas there are strong correlations between resources factors.

Of course, several of the interaction variables are very strongly related to each other and to basic variables. Consequently, the collinearity problems become formidable, and there is not much sense in considering single coefficient values for the interaction variables. Instead, average coefficient values and the improvement of the explained variance in the 1985 and the 1990 crime factor, respectively, when adding these variables are analyzed.

It turns out that adding both types of control-resources interaction variables means an increase of the corrected explained proportion of the variance in crime by about one and a half per cent in the 1990 case and by about one per cent in the 1985 case. Adding only the variables of mean-of-products type means a smaller increase of this proportion than adding only the variables of product-of-means type (in the 1990 case the increases were about one and one and a half per cent, and in the 1985 case about a half and one per cent).

When entering both types of control-resources interaction variables in the regression equation, rather many of the coefficients obtained are negative, which is unexpected. In the analysis of the 1990 crime factor, five of the 18 coefficients are negative, whereas nine are negative in the analysis of the 1985 crime factor. Only few interaction variables have gotten positive coefficients with high values for both years. The average values of the coefficients obtained for the mean-of-products and the product-of-means variables are 0.09 and −0.07 for 1990 and 0.01 and −0.02 for 1985. These results do not indicate that micro-level control-resources interaction plays any very important role.

When adding the mean-of-products and the product-of-means variables of the nine control-resources types of interaction, the three control-control types of interaction and the three resources-resources types of interaction (that is, in total 30 variables) to the 18 variables of the reduced set of basic properties (which thus means that there are 48 regressors in the analysis of the 83 areas), the findings are as follows. The corrected explained proportion of the variance in crime increases with slightly more than five per cent for the 1990 data and with slightly less than three per cent for the 1985 data. The average values of the coefficients obtained for the mean-of-products and the product-of-means control-resources interaction variables are −0.03 and −0.84 for 1990 and 0.05 and −0.53 for 1985. The average values of the coefficients obtained for the mean-of-products and the product-of-means control-control interaction variables are −0.03 and 0.36 for 1990 and −0.38 and 0.50 for 1985. For the resources-resources interaction variables, the corresponding average values of the coefficients are 0.19 and 2.18 for 1990 and 0.09 and 1.04 for 1985.

Thus, it is found that using this extended set of interaction variables does increase the corrected explained proportion of the variance in crime, that the mean-of-products control-resources interaction variables obtain a higher average coefficient value than the corresponding product-of-means variables, but that the product-of-means control-control and resources-resources interaction variables obtain higher average coefficient values than the corresponding mean-of-products variables. The average coefficient values of the product-of-means control-control and resources-resources interaction variables have high positive values, which could indicate that there is interaction between different individuals' control properties and between their resources properties in the influence on crime. A finding that seems to be difficult to explain is the negative average coefficient value for the product-of-means control-resources interaction variables (similar findings will be commented on later on).

The findings of the analyses suggest that using interaction variables may increase the explained proportion of the variance in crime. It seems that interaction of product-of-means type between various resources properties and between various control properties does increase crime, whereas corresponding interaction of mean-of-product type does not do this, at least not to the same degree. However, when it comes to interaction between control and resources properties, the results are different. Here indications are found that interaction of product-of-means type has a strongly negative effect, but this is not found for interaction of mean-of-products type.

However, on the whole it is, due to the identification problems caused by collinearity, difficult to state anything definite about these various influences. Therefore, it remains to explain more convincingly 1) how important the interaction properties, set in relation to basic properties, are for crime and 2) how important interaction of the mean-of-products type and interaction of product-of-means type are when compared with each other, and how their relationship with crime should be interpreted.

How should these problems be solved? One way of solving the first problem is to consider change data. The results obtained so far pertain to cross-sectional data, in which basic and interaction variables correlate extremely strongly with each other. In analyses of change data collinearity problems will not be as troublesome.

One way of solving the second problem is to analyze the relative influence on crime of the mean-of-products and the product-of-means properties for long-term residents and for residents who are newcomers. These two types of residents can be assumed to be differently involved in social processes, and the two types of interaction properties can therefore be assumed to affect crime differently for them.

Analyses of these two types will be performed later on. I think that the first type of suggested solution has a kind of primacy. It is difficult to clarify the role of interaction for crime without distinguishing the influence of interaction from the influence of basic properties, and I think that this can be done using change data. However, as will be seen there are technical problems in doing so.

**Product Models**

In previous section, regression analyses were performed to find out what role aggregated micro-level interaction plays in the explanation of the crime factor using a linear model. In this section, the explanatory power of macro-level interaction is analyzed using models with a pure product form, that is, product models of the types of (11)-(12) and (11)-(13). Results of various analyses using normalized variables have given rise to the suspicion that the model of crime should have product rather than linear form. For example, results of bivariate linear analyses can be interpreted to support this suspicion. In these analyses, coefficients for several variables have higher absolute values for later years (see Table 4.1), and since some of the most important variables changed so that they on average became more conducive to crime the reason for this change in coefficient values might be that crime was affected in a multiplicative fashion.

In order to find out whether the model of crime should have product rather than linear form, three analyses using a linear model and the two product models are carried out: 1) with the 1990 data only, 2) with the 1985 and 1990 data combined, and 3) with the 1980, 1985 and 1990 data combined. All independent variables are used in standardized form. The crime variables are not standardized, since the product models presuppose that they assume only positive values. The UNEMPL, SOCAID and OCCDICH variables enter in the first two analyses, but not in the third one. Temporally unique $d$ coefficients are used for the product models (they are denoted $d_{90}$, $d_{85}$ and $d_{80}$ for the reference years of 1990, 1985 and 1980). As mentioned, the mean values of the crime factors of these years are taken as initial values for these coefficients in the Gauss-Newton iterative process, and 0 is chosen as initial value for the $b$ coefficients. For the linear models, dummy variables are used to describe temporally unique constants (denoted $const_{90}$, $const_{85}$, $const_{80}$). Such a variable takes on the value 1 for a certain year and the value 0 for another year or for other years. Results are presented in Table 4.3.

The linear models show how much of the variance in crime that can be explained disregarding interaction. However, as mentioned the linear form may be unrealistic, and it may particularly be so for intertemporal analysis of crime. Crime as measured in this study may differ between years for several reasons. It may differ because true crime differs, but it may also differ because the measure does not describe true crime adequately and the error varies with time. The measure describes reported crime, but reported crime is not equal to true crime. For example, if the tendency to report detected crimes to the police differs between years, the measure will be affected by a factor that may have little to do with the independent properties discussed in this study. Such a differential tendency could hardly be adequately described by a temporally unique intercept in a linear model. Rather, since reported crime can be assumed to be the product of true crime and a factor that describes the reporting tendency, the modeled true value of crime should be multiplied by a temporally unique factor. If the true value is linearly modeled, reported crime should be modeled as follows:

**Table 4.3**     **Results of multiple regression analyses of the crime factor, using basic independent variables as regressors. For 1990, 1985/1990, and 1980/1985/1990 data. Independent variables standardized**

| Indep. property | 1990 (n=83) | | | 1985/1990 (n=166) | | | | 1980/1985/1990 (n=249) | | | |
|---|---|---|---|---|---|---|---|---|---|---|---|
| | Linear | Prod. I | Prod. II | Linear | Quasi-linear | Prod. I | Prod. II | Linear | Quasi-linear | Prod. I | Prod. II |
| *Age and sex* | | | | | | | | | | | |
| YNGMALE | −.13 | −.05 | −.04 | .01 | −.04 | −.02 | −.02 | .10 | .13 | .04 | .04 |
| YNGFEML | −.25 | −.03 | −.05 | −.32 | −.26 | −.05 | −.05 | −.12 | −.08 | .01 | .01 |
| MDLMALE | −.72 | −.07 | −.11 | −.31 | −.36 | −.02 | −.05 | −.05 | −.04 | .12 | .07 |
| MDLFEML | −.61 | −.10 | −.03 | −.71 | −.62 | −.15 | −.10 | −.46 | −.36 | −.16 | −.14 |
| OLDMALE | −.07 | .14 | .19 | −.11 | −.07 | .14 | .17 | .11 | .19 | .17 | .19 |
| OLDFEML | −1.12 | −.17 | −.23 | −.90 | −.85 | −.17 | −.20 | −.74 | −.60 | −.17 | −.18 |
| *Social control* | | | | | | | | | | | |
| FORGN | −.14 | .04 | .01 | −.07 | −.10 | .01 | .00 | .13 | .06 | −.01 | .01 |
| SINGLE | −.14 | .11 | .02 | .01 | .01 | .14 | .09 | .13 | .15 | .19 | .17 |
| DIVOR | .74 | .20 | .19 | .64 | .58 | .19 | .18 | .76 | .60 | .22 | .24 |
| MOVES | .13 | .01 | .03 | 09 | .08 | .01 | .02 | −.03 | .02 | −.04 | −.01 |
| *Social resources* | | | | | | | | | | | |
| INCMULT | −.06 | −.07 | −.12 | .10 | .04 | −.10 | −.12 | −.06 | −.07 | −.15 | −.14 |
| INCSTD | .06 | .04 | .05 | .02 | .04 | .05 | .06 | −.03 | .01 | .03 | .03 |
| UNEMPL | −.46 | −.14 | −.10 | −.35 | −.36 | −.14 | −.11 | - | - | - | - |
| SOCAID | .48 | .21 | .22 | .19 | .30 | .12 | .12 | - | - | - | - |
| OCCDICH | .73 | .20 | .23 | .61 | .53 | .15 | .18 | - | - | - | - |
| *Dwelling envir.* | | | | | | | | | | | |
| MULTHS | −.01 | −.17 | −.10 | −.08 | −.11 | −.11 | −.08 | −.06 | −.05 | −.01 | −.02 |
| PUBLIC | .02 | −.03 | −.04 | .24 | .17 | .03 | .02 | .34 | .25 | .07 | .06 |
| OVERCR | .24 | .08 | .07 | .36 | .32 | .14 | .14 | .26 | .28 | .12 | .12 |
| $const_{90}/g_{90}\,q/$ $d_{90}$ | 2.74 | 2.76 | 2.72 | 2.88 | 2.90 | 2.82 | 2.80 | 2.85 | 2.96 | 2.84 | 2.88 |
| $const_{85}/g_{85}\,q/$ $d_{85}$ | - | - | - | 2.37 | 2.38 | 2.29 | 2.28 | 2.45 | 2.47 | 2.32 | 2.34 |
| $const_{80}/g_{80}\,q/$ $d_{80}$ | - | - | - | - | - | - | - | 2.11 | 2.04 | 1.90 | 1.93 |
| Expl. proportion of variance (uncorrected) | .92 | .93 | .92 | .87 | .88 | .89 | .89 | .84 | .85 | .87 | .86 |

$$C_t = g_t(b_1\text{YNGMALE}_t + b_2\text{YNGFEML}_t + \ldots + b_{18}\text{OVERCR}_t + q), \quad (16)$$

where $g_t$ is the temporally unique factor and $q$ a constant.

This "quasi-linear" model can be identified in non-linear regression analysis if $g_t$ is set at a fixed value for some year. This has been done here by setting $g = 1$ for the earliest analyzed year. As initial values for the $b$ coefficients zeros have been used. The mean value of the earliest crime factor analyzed is used as initial value of $q$. The mean value of the crime factor at $t$ divided by the mean value of the earliest crime factor analyzed is used as initial value of $g_t$. Results from using this model are reported in Table 4.3. However, values of $g_t$ are not found in the table. Instead the value of $g_t q$ (the intercept of the linear function for each specific year) is reported, which means that the value of $g_t$ is easily calculated (for example, for the analysis of C80/C85/C90, $g_{90} = 2.96/2.04 = 1.45$).

As seen from the figures in Table 4.3, it turns out that the product models explain about the same proportion of the variance in the 1990 crime factor as does the linear model. Version I of the product factors $A$, $S$, $R$ and $H$ explains 93 per cent and Version II 92 per cent of the variance, whereas the linear model explains 92 per cent (these figures are not adjusted for lost degrees of freedom; the same number of parameters has been used in the different models; the same is true for the other analyses, including the ones carried out with the quasi-linear model).

However, when explaining the variance in the crime factor values for 1985/1990 and 1980/1985/1990, the overall picture is that the product models are somewhat better than the linear model. This is particularly evident for the 1980/1985/1990 data. For these data, Version I of the product factors explains about three per cent more of the variance than does the linear model. For both data sets, the quasi-linear model explains more of the variance in crime than does the linear model, but somewhat less than do the product models.

As to the temporally unique coefficient values, it is found that they are similar for different types of models and also for different sets of data. These coefficient values for the quasi-linear model and the product models are of particular interest, because in line with what has been said above they can be used for drawing conclusions about the impact on the crime factor of the tendency to report crimes to the police. Thus, this tendency can be expected to affect the $g$ values of the quasi-linear model, and the $d$ values of the product models. In the analysis of the 1980/1985/1990 data, it turns out as mentioned that $g_{90}/g_{80}$ is about 1.45, that is, according to the quasi-linear model the tendency in 1990 to report crime could be assumed to be about 45 per cent stronger than the tendency in 1980. The values for the corresponding relations for the 1985/1990 and the 1980/1985 data are about 1.20 and 1.21. For the product models similar relations between $d$ values are obtained. However, it may be questioned whether these values are realistic. Surely, the tendency to report crime may have increased during the period studied – due to better insurance coverage and a more formalistic treatment by victims of crime cases – but it seems doubtful whether the tendency to report crime could have changed so strongly in such short periods, and this fact indicates that the models may not be quite adequate.

As far as the values of the other obtained coefficients are concerned, it seems that they are fairly similar in a relative sense for many variables between models. However, the absolute values of the coefficients of the product models tend, of course, to be lower than the absolute values of the corresponding coefficients of the linear model.

Thus, it is very much the same variables that dominate in the different types of models. Among the social control variables, DIVOR has relatively high positive weights in all models. In the linear models, the weight of FORGN is positive for the 1980/1985/1990 data in which UNEMPL, SOCAID and OCCDICH are missing, but negative for the other data in which these properties are included (this type of change is commented on above). In the product models, the weights of the variable have very low absolute values. The weight of SINGLE varies relatively much between the linear models, and it has always a positive value in the product models. For the product models and the 1980/1985/1990 data this weight has relatively high positive values. The weights of MOVES have low or rather low absolute values.

Among the social resources variables, OCCDICH and SOCAID have weights that are positive and high or rather high throughout. Thus, it is found that a higher percentage of unskilled workers and social aid recipients, respectively, is followed by higher crime. The weights of INCMULT are mostly negative. For the product models, they are all negative and most of their absolute values are of at least medium size. The weights of UNEMPL are negative throughout and relatively high in many cases, which is unexpected. The weights of INCSTD seem to indicate that the variation in income is relatively unimportant.

Turning to the dwelling environment and age/sex variables, it is found that OVERCR has positive weights throughout and that these weights are rather high in a relative sense for the data that refer to more than one year. However, the absolute values of the weights of MULTHS are low or rather low in a relative sense in most cases for these data. All weights of MULTHS are negative, which is unexpected. In linear modeling, the value of the weight of PUBLIC is high or rather high for the data that refer to more than one year, but in the product models the weights of PUBLIC have absolute values that are low. Within the age categories, the percentage of females has a lower weight than is the case for the percentage of males in most cases (in 30 of 33 comparisons, this difference holds). For the linear models, most weights of the age/sex variables are negative, but for the product models negative and positive weights balance each other better. For the product models, the weights for old males are positive and much higher in a relative sense than is the case for the corresponding linear models. These high weights may surprise, since people tend to be less criminal the older they become (the weights for old women are strongly negative). However, they should probably not be taken very seriously, because OLDMALE and OLDFEML correlate positively with each other and both have very low tolerance values.

The overall picture obtained for the product models is rather similar to the picture previously discussed for linear models with regard to what variables are important and to the direction in which they seem to influence crime. Thus, it is found that DIVOR has a relatively strong positive relationship with crime. The same is true for SOCAID and OCCDICH. One difference found between product and linear models is the relationships for SINGLE. For the product models they are more positive and therefore more in line with what was hypothesized.

In a previous section, a discussion was carried on about the influence on crime of geographical selection forces. Using the 1990 data, it was found that variables describing such forces, above all INCMULT and PUBLIC, had strong cross-sectional relationship with crime. It was argued that the properties measured with these variables did not affect crime strongly in a direct way. Instead, they probably worked largely via a geographical selection of individual-level properties that affected crime more directly. When other independent factors that could have affected crime directly were controlled for in the analysis, INCMULT and PUBLIC as expected showed relatively weak relationships with crime. This type of explanation seems not to go as well for PUBLIC for the 1985/1990 data in a linear model including several independent variables, because then the absolute value of the partial coefficient of this factor is not very low. However, this absolute value is still much lower than the value of the coefficient of the bivariate relationship.

Despite the very different forms of the models used, the importance of the various independent variables and the direction in which these influence crime seem to be rather similar. Moreover, all types of models with their widely different forms explain a great deal of the variance in crime. This indicates that the true model has not been found. Since all the models tested explain a great deal of the variance, it seems likely that the true model has both linear and multiplicative traits. In all likelihood, then, the true model is rather complicated.

**The Significance of Moves**

One question raised in this study is to what extent the relationships between crime and independent properties of the areas are due to local social processes that extend beyond the individual and the family and that affect crime directly and to what extent the relationships are due to other processes, above all geographical selection processes. This issue will now be treated by analyzing how individuals who have lived in an area for different lengths of time have affected crime. As mentioned, the rationale behind this analysis is that several local, extra-family social processes take time to develop and that their effects therefore appear only after some time. Consequently, residents who have lived in an area for periods of time of different lengths, and who therefore have been involved to different extents in these processes, can be expected to have contributed differently to the effects. In general, individuals who have lived there longer can be expected to have been more involved in the processes and to have contributed more to the effects.

The effects on crime exerted by newcomers to the area, on the other hand, can be assumed to be relatively more the result of geographical selection processes.

There are two types of local, extra-family social processes that are particularly interesting in this context: integration processes and the development of groups of deviant people. Social integration processes are interesting because they affect social control. Individuals who live longer in an area can be assumed to develop stronger bonds to people and organizations there and therefore to come more firmly under the local web of social controls. The development of groups of deviant people is interesting because it may affect attitudes towards conventional society. When deviant individuals live longer in an area, they have a greater chance of meeting other similar individuals and to form social groups with them. In such groups there may be a strengthening of deviant attitudes, for example deviant attitudes towards the law.

What can be said in this context about the effects on crime exerted by social processes that pertain to resources? To the extent that the resources affect crime because they are connected to the capacity to solve social problems, a time effect can be expected. This is because problem-solving capacity can be expected to be a function of local social relations among individuals. Thus, for individuals who live longer in an area, the resources can be expected to have a stronger effect on crime. However, to the extent that the resources affect crime because individuals with low resources feel that they are unjustly treated, such a time effect is more doubtful. This is because individuals who compare their resources with the resources of others probably do not restrict these comparisons to the residents in their local area, and to the extent that they do compare particularly with local conditions, it is unclear how their feeling of being unjustly treated changes with time.

As discussed above, social resources can be assumed to affect strongly the geographical selection of individuals. Also other properties may affect this selection. If the resources and these other properties affect the generation of crime globally on the individual level, or if they are globally related on the individual level with factors that affect this generation, a relationship on the area level will appear between crime and these properties, and the properties will in this sense affect crime via the selection and the ensuing geographical social differentiation. The individual-level relationships between the properties and the generation of crime probably do not need to be strong for the area-level relationships to have substantial strength. These ideas about the impact of geographical selection/ differentiation may be applied in the analysis of the influences on crime for individuals with different patterns of moves. In order to investigate how living in an area for different lengths of time influences crime, residents who have lived in the area the last five years and residents who have relocated to the area in the course of this period of time have been compared as to how variables that describe them are related to the crime factor. Thus, for a particular temporal reference point the residents are split into two groups: those who lived in the area at the previous reference point (that is, five years earlier) and those who did not. The former group is called Group A, the latter Group B. These groups may differ much in size.

Group B tends to be somewhat smaller than Group A. On the average, Group B's relative size (that is, the number of the members of the group divided by the total population of the area) is 0.36 for 1980, 0.39 for 1985 and 0.38 for 1990.

For each group, independent variables have been calculated and used in the analysis. Such a variable is the mean of the members' values of a property multiplied by the group's relative size. The independent variables for both groups are used jointly in regression analyses of the crime factor. This means that the relation between the coefficient values obtained for the groups' variables that describe a property can be assumed to capture the relation between the influences of this property exerted by the groups' average members.

The groups' regression coefficients will now be compared in order to see what conclusions can be drawn about how social processes and geographical differentiation influence crime. The results of these analyses are presented below. It should be noted that the social processes in themselves are not analyzed. There is no information about how long-term residents or newcomers interacted with other residents. Instead, the analysis is made on the assumption that if certain social processes do exist, then individuals with certain characteristics tend to act in certain ways, and, consequently, that if the relationships that such tendencies give rise to do not exist, then the social processes can be assumed not to exist either. However, if the relationships do exist, this does not prove the existence of the processes, although the existence of the relationships together with other facts may be taken as an indication of that existence.

Such an analysis has obvious limitations. First, it is not solely the involvement in local extra-family processes that produces differences between the two groups of residents. For example, long-term and new residents may differ with respect to their involvement in non-local social processes in the city – the long-term residents may have been more involved than the new residents in such processes because they have lived there for a longer period of time. Long-term and new residents may also differ in many other respects, for example, in social background, in the involvement in global processes, or in the general propensity to act in various ways.

Second, the fundamental idea behind the method concerns longitudinal relationships, but the analysis is cross-sectional. This probably means that the method works only for such independent properties that have remained relatively constant during the years (another way of studying the significance of time is of course to use change data, which is done below).

Third, the method involves technical problems due to the facts that each independent property is described by two variables, one for each group of individuals, and that the two groups of individuals tend to have similar values of these variables. This means that many independent variables are strongly correlated with each other and that coefficient values therefore may be difficult to identify. Furthermore, the doubling of the number of independent variables means that several degrees of freedom are lost.

In order to address these technical problems, the INCSTD and UNEMPL properties and, as before, the INCDICH and OCCMULT properties are excluded.

INCSTD is excluded because it seems to be relatively unimportant and UNEMPL is excluded because it may not be a good measure of the intended type of social resources. Of course, MOVES is also excluded. Moreover, only combined data sets are analyzed, namely the 1985/1990 and 1980/1985/1990 sets. The types of models previously used – linear, quasi-linear and product types – are used again. The new models are constructed by substituting each independent variable in the models as hitherto used by the corresponding independent variables of the two groups, and these are weighted by unique coefficients. The group variables are constructed by using the means of individual-level values, normalized (with some previously mentioned exceptions) in the same way as the variables for the total population. The independent group variables are also used in standardized versions. The product model solutions obtained for the standardized and for the normalized versions of these variables give the same value of the crime factor.

Initial values of the coefficients in the product and quasi-linear models have been chosen as before. Results for these models, as well as for corresponding linear models, are presented in Table 4.4 for the 1985/1990 data (results for the 1980/1985/1990 data are not presented in tabular form). This table shows solutions for normalized variables. The solutions for the standardized versions of the variables are given in Table V.i (Appendix V). The reported explained proportions of the variance in crime are uncorrected for lost degrees of freedom. I remind of the fact that obtained solutions for the product models are not proven to be the best global ones.

It turns out that the linear and quasi-linear models explain about the same uncorrected proportion of the variance in crime and that the product models explain about two per cent more of this variance. Furthermore, doubling the number of independent variables by considering the two groups of residents seems not to have yielded much improvement in the explained variance considering the fact that many degrees of freedom have been lost. For example, for the linear model this improvement is only about one per cent for the 1985/1990 data, and the same degree of improvement is found for the 1980/1985/1990 data (MOVES is then included among the nonpartitioned properties).

Looking at the coefficients obtained for the different models in Table 4.4, we find that they are rather similar in a relative sense. Thus, several differences in relationships between the two groups of residents can be found, more or less, in all or most models. For example, disregarding the age/sex variables for a moment and looking at the control variables, we find, interpreting coefficients causally, that DIVOR has a much more positive effect on crime – that is, that an increase in the percentage of divorced persons increases crime much more – for the long-term residents than for the newcomers in three of the models (this marked difference does not exist for the quasi-linear model; however, for the standardized versions of DIVOR the difference is quite pronounced in this model as well).

Thus, much stronger positive relationships, described by partial regression coefficients, have been found between DIVOR and the crime factor for the long-term residents than for the newcomers in three of the four models. Could this be explained as

**Table 4.4**　　**Results of regression analyses using basic independent variables of long-term residents (Group A) and of newcomers (Group B). For 1985/1990 data (n=166). Independent variables normalized**

| Independent property | Linear model A | Linear model B | Quasi-lin. model A | Quasi-lin. model B | Product model I A | Product model I B | Product model II A | Product model II B |
|---|---|---|---|---|---|---|---|---|
| *Age and sex* | | | | | | | | |
| YNGMALE | .39 | −.31 | .42 | −.32 | .15 | −.05 | .14 | −.10 |
| YNGFEML | −.31 | −.19 | −.28 | −.16 | −.20 | −.02 | −.17 | −.00 |
| MDLMALE | −.02 | −.04 | −.02 | −.07 | −.01 | .21 | .05 | .17 |
| MDLFEML | −.82 | −.29 | −.75 | −.28 | −.16 | −.06 | −.17 | −.03 |
| OLDMALE | .05 | 1.31 | .07 | 1.22 | −.05 | 1.20 | .06 | 1.22 |
| OLDFEML | −.84 | −2.86 | −.71 | −2.88 | −.04 | −1.12 | −.11 | −1.14 |
| *Social control* | | | | | | | | |
| FORGN | −.06 | .20 | −.14 | .14 | .24 | −.12 | −.05 | .34 |
| SINGLE | .15 | .13 | .19 | .05 | 15 | .54 | .11 | .35 |
| DIVOR | .88 | .30 | .68 | .64 | .23 | .07 | .24 | −.00 |
| *Social resources* | | | | | | | | |
| INCMULT | −.17 | .30 | −.14 | .25 | .02 | −.16 | −.02 | −.35 |
| SOCAID | .48 | −.31 | .47 | −.17 | .02 | .24 | .14 | −.26 |
| OCCDICH | .11 | .80 | .14 | .72 | .02 | .45 | −.01 | .36 |
| *Dwelling envir.* | | | | | | | | |
| MULTHS | −.43 | .76 | −.38 | .68 | −.27 | .28 | −.23 | .44 |
| PUBLIC | .33 | −.29 | .31 | −.30 | .08 | −.25 | .04 | −.10 |
| OVERCR | .06 | .65 | .23 | .50 | .13 | .23 | .17 | .14 |
| $const_{90}/g_{90}\,q/d_{90}$ | 2.29 | | 2.39 | | 2.16 | | 2.20 | |
| $const_{85}/g_{85}\,q/d_{85}$ | 2.09 | | 2.11 | | 1.95 | | 2.08 | |
| Expl. proportion of variance (uncorrected) | .89 | | .89 | | .91 | | .91 | |

the result of reduced social control for the long-term residents due to their involvement in local social processes? Surely, it seems natural to explain a positive relationship between DIVOR and crime with the help of social control theory, since divorces often result in divorcees and their children being less socially controlled, and since this could be due to or involved in some form of extra-family process. However, it seems doubtful whether the potential for such processes is greater for the long-term residents than for the newcomers. Is it really relevant to compare the long-term residents with the newcomers in this case? Why should not greater numbers of divorcees among newcomers be accompanied by more crime in the same way as for the long-term residents? This might seem puzzling, since divorced newcomers could be expected to be short of social bonds, both in terms of personal friends and neighbors. One explanation could possibly be that divorcees that move often do so when they have left their marital problems behind them and when their children are old enough to manage themselves, and that this lack of problems and of weakly controlled children reduces crime. If this is true, the difference in relationship between long-term residents and newcomers does not necessarily indicate that the relationships for the long-term residents are due to local social processes.

Thus, it seems questionable whether the differences between coefficients found for DIVOR could be reconcilable with social control theory as applied to the subject of urban area crime, but how is it with the differences between coefficients found for FORGN and SINGLE? All coefficients found for SINGLE are positive, which accords with the basic hypothesis made about the influence of single parent households. For the product models, the Group B coefficient has a much higher value than the Group A coefficient, which could be thought to be due to the fact that newcomers living in households with a single parent are particularly short of social bonds and social control. However, the same difference between coefficients of the two groups is not found for the linear and the quasi-linear models.

As to FORGN, the Group B coefficient has a higher value than the Group A coefficient for three of the models. Again, this may be reconcilable with social control theory, because it could be due to the fact that newly arrived foreigners are more poorly integrated socially and are therefore less controlled than foreigners who have lived in the area for a longer time. However, for Product Model I the sign of the coefficient difference is reversed, and the same is found for the linear model used for analyzing 1980/1985/1990 data.

A way of testing the social control explanation could be to compare the coefficients for FORGN that describe the relationships with crime for three parts of the area population: the long-term residents, the new residents who come from some other part of the city and the new residents who come from outside the city. Such an analysis has been made using the 1985/1990 data. This analysis is designed and carried through in the same way as the corresponding analyses using properties for Groups A and B. For both 1985 and 1990 the new residents who come from outside the city make up 22 per cent of the total population. Without correction for lost degrees of freedom Models I and II explain about 92 per cent of the variance in the crime factor, whereas the linear model explains about 90 per cent. Of course, the great number of variables describing the same properties for the three groups makes for extremely severe problems in identifying coefficients, so the results (not reported in figures) are only tentative. Interpreting coefficients causally, it is found for both product models and for unstandardized and standardized versions of the independent variables that the most positive effect on crime of the percentage of foreigners is exerted by the group of new residents from outside the city. This is in accordance with social control theory. For the linear models, findings are more mixed.

Returning to the analysis of the two groups of residents, and turning to the social resources variables and interpreting again the partial regression coefficients causally, it is found for all models in Table 4.4 that the percentage of unskilled workers has a much more positive effect on crime for the newcomers than for the long-term residents. Moreover, the coefficients for the standardized variables indicate that OCCDICH of the newcomers has a strong or rather strong effect on crime. This could perhaps be assumed solely to be the effect of geographical selection, while the effect of such selection could be counteracted by social processes for the long-term residents. However, similar differences in relationship are not found for the other resources variables. As to INCMULT and SOCAID, the results for the different models are mixed.

The relationships found for SOCAID are of interest for the question of whether deviant people form groups that influence the level of crime. SOCAID is probably the best measure of such social problems that contribute to the growth of deviant groups. As is seen from the table, it is found in linear modeling that this variable has a stronger positive effect on crime for the long-term residents than for the newcomers, and this finding is in agreement with what would be expected if such a process occurs. However, there is no corresponding difference in effect for Product Model I.

It is interesting to note the differences between the linear and quasi-linear models and Product Model I in the relationships between social resources and crime for the long-term residents. These relationships, which can be assumed to express the effects of extra-family social processes – if such processes do exist – to a relatively high degree, are totally different. For the linear and the quasi-linear models, they are all consistent with the existence of processes that imply that lack of resources causes crime, but for the product model most of them are practically non-existent (see also Table V.i).

Turning to the dwelling environment variables, it is in all cases found that the relationship between PUBLIC and crime for the long-term residents is positive, while the relationship is negative for the newcomers. For OVERCR, all coefficients for newcomers and long-term residents are positive and the coefficient for the newcomers has a higher value than the coefficient for the long-term residents in three of the models. Interpreting coefficients causally, it is found regarding MULTHS in all models that the percentage of residents living in multi-family houses has a strongly positive effect on crime for the newcomers, while the effect is negative for the long-term residents. This difference, it appears, can be easily explained in terms of social control. Of the residents in multi-family house dwellings, the newcomers live a more anonymous life than those who have lived there for at least five years. These dwellings do not stimulate early contacts with neighbors, and they are as a rule easy to leave. However, living there for some years results in less anonymity. This seems to be a reasonable explanation of the difference, which therefore lends support to the social control theory and also to the idea that local social processes affect crime.

As to the age/sex variables it is found again that the coefficients for women tend to have more negative values than the coefficients for men. The coefficient for the percentage of young men is positive for the long-term residents, but negative for the newcomers. One may speculate whether the positive relationship for the long-term young men is the result of social contacts within their age/sex group. However, it should be noted that very high correlations between variables make it difficult to identify the coefficients for YNGMALE and also the coefficients for other age/sex variables.

The results from the analysis of the 1980/1985/1990 data are rather similar to the just discussed results from the 1985/1990 data. For example, similar differences between Groups A and B in crime's relationships with DIVOR and MULTHS are found in them. However, I will not enter into details about these results.

The analysis of the influences on crime exerted by the two groups of residents has given some indications of how mobility may affect crime. As previously shown, multivariate analyses indicate that the influence of MOVES on crime is very weak. However, the influence of mobility – as this influence may be interpreted from cross-sectional relationships – stands out more clearly in the present analysis of the groups of long-term residents and newcomers. This analysis indicates that the very weak direct relationship found between moves and crime does not give a good picture of the importance of the dimension of moves, and that it is more interesting to analyze the influence of the moves by treating these as a contextual factor.

The results of the analyses seem to give some support for using the social control theory in explaining local social processes, although the picture cannot be said to be clear. The positive relationships found between crime on one hand and MULTHS among newcomers and FORGN among newcomers from outside the city on the other hand and the corresponding negative or weaker relationships found for the long-term residents stand out in this respect. These relationships are easy to interpret as the result of social control and social integration processes. However, for FORGN no consistent picture of the relationship with crime has been found for all types of models using the original two groups. The same is true for SINGLE. For DIVOR, similar relationships with crime have been found for the different models, although the findings do not give any very clear support for the social control theory. The problem is the relatively weak relationships found for newcomers in product models.

Regarding OCCDICH it has been found using both linear and product models that the percentage of unskilled workers has a much stronger positive relationship with crime for the newcomers than for the long-term residents. The reason could simply be that occupational status is important for the geographical differentiation and is globally associated with crime. Possibly, the difference could also to some extent be due to the fact that low occupational status means a poor ability to manage various sorts of social problems encountered when coming to live in a new place. As to SOCAID and INCMULT, no consistent picture of social processes can be found in the results for all models.

## Micro-Level Interaction and Moves

I now turn to an analysis of how aggregated micro-level interaction of the two mentioned types is related to crime in Groups A and B when considered together with basic properties. Thus, I have constructed measures of interaction of the mean-of-products and product-of-means types for each of the two groups. The measures for a group are based solely on the members of this group. Thus, there is no measure of interaction of any type between members of Group A and members of Group B.

Constructing separate mean-of-products measures for the two groups poses no particular technical problems, and it is also quite relevant to construct product-of-means measures for Group A, since the members of this group can be assumed to have had relatively much contact with each other. However, the members of Group B had only relatively little contact with each other and with other residents, and it may therefore seem curious to construct product-of-means measures for them. However, this type of measure will be used for Group B in order to balance the use of a similar measure for Group A.

How can interaction of the two types be assumed to have affected crime for the two groups of residents? In answering this question, consideration should be paid to the facts that the members of Group A lived in the area in at least five years and that they therefore could have been involved in social processes there, whereas the members of Group B, the newcomers, cannot have been involved in such processes to the same extent. Below, I discuss, in the light of these facts, how interaction of the two types may have affected crime in the two groups. I assume then that the individual-level factors $x$ and $z$ are dichotomous and that high values of them are conducive to crime.

*Mean of products in Group B.* For the members of Group B, the mean-of-products property describes the aggregated products of their own factors $x$ and $z$. If there is interaction between these factors within individuals when they do not have much contact with other residents, the coefficient for the influence of this property on crime will be positive.

*Product of means in Group B.* The product of the factors $x$ and $z$ for different members in Group B cannot be expected to have had any strong influence on area crime, since the individuals had relatively little contact with each other. Thus, the coefficient for the influence of the product-of-means property on crime will be about 0.

*Product of means in Group A.* The product of the factors $x$ and $z$ for different members in Group A can be expected to have had a positive influence on area crime, since some members had relatively much contact with each other and since these contacts of members with crime-conducive values of the factors can be expected to have generated crime. Possibly, social processes through the contacts neutralized this influence on crime to some degree. Nevertheless, it can be assumed that the neutralizing effect of such social processes did not balance the positive effect on crime. Thus, the coefficient for the influence of the product-of-means property on crime will be positive.

*Mean of products in Group A.* The product of values of $x$ and $z$ for members in Group A may have had effects of two types on area crime – those intraindividually caused and those socially caused. The latter effects are due to the fact that the individuals who had the value 1 on both $x$ and $z$ may have constituted a specific group and have been involved in social processes related to their group affiliation. The intraindividually caused effect can be assumed to be positive. The socially caused effect may be negative, for example due to integration processes, or positive, for example due to the development of deviant attitudes. Considering these facts, it is hard to say what value the coefficient for the influence of a mean-of-products property on crime will have.

These assumptions are tested using linear regression models for the 1985/1990 data (from now on, I do not report results from using the quasi-linear model, since this model has shown to give results similar to the results of the linear model). The basic independent variables are the same as the ones found in the previous section. All independent variables are weighted by group size and standardized. Again, I use the sets of nine control-resources, three control-control and three resources-resources interaction variables, and again I only report the average value of obtained coefficients for the variables in each set. Table 4.5 shows the obtained coefficients and the explained proportions of the variance in crime.

In the first model reported in table, weighted mean values in Groups A and B of all basic properties of the reduced set and of all mentioned interaction properties are used as regressors. Thus, 60 interaction variables are added to 30 basic variables, which means that many degrees of freedom are lost. In the second model only the variables that describe the control-resources interaction properties are added to the basic variables. The third model includes the same variables as the second model except the basic variables that describe the control and resources properties. Adding the interaction variables has meant a gain in explained proportion of the variance in crime, corrected for lost degrees of freedom, for the models obtained as compared with the model in which only the reduced set of basic variables is used. All models explain 89 per cent of the variance, which is a couple of percentages more than what is explained by the model using only the basic variables.

Practically the same corrected proportion of the variance, 88 per cent, is explained when adding only the product-of-means variables to the basic variables as when adding only the mean-of-products variables – that is, in both cases about one per cent less than what is explained when both types of interaction variables are added.

Taking a glance at the coefficients of the basic variables in the first model, we find that the coefficients for the age/sex variables are fairly similar to the ones obtained with the interaction variables excluded, while several of the coefficients for the other basic variables have changed much (see Table V.i). Very large changes are for example found for FORGN, SOCAID, OCCDICH and MULTHS. There

**Table 4.5**　Linear regression analyses using basic and interactional independent variables of long-term residents (Group A) and of newcomers (Group B). For 1985/1990 data (n=166). Independent variables standardized

| Indep. property | (1) A | (1) B | (2) A | (2) B | (3) A | (3) B |
|---|---|---|---|---|---|---|
| *Age and sex* | | | | | | |
| YNGMALE | .16 | .15 | .29 | .02 | .16 | .09 |
| YNGFEML | −.17 | −.26 | −.43 | −.25 | −.45 | −.27 |
| MDLMALE | −.12 | .09 | −.16 | .27 | −.20 | .23 |
| MDLFEML | −.73 | −.16 | −.72 | −.08 | −.69 | −.11 |
| OLDMALE | −.12 | .38 | −.10 | .31 | −.14 | .34 |
| OLDFEML | −.86 | −.46 | −.81 | −.29 | −1.04 | −.43 |
| *Social control* | | | | | | |
| FORGN | −1.57 | 2.76 | −1.20 | 1.17 | - | - |
| SINGLE | .46 | .20 | .82 | .14 | - | - |
| DIVOR | .77 | .29 | −.52 | .21 | - | - |
| *Social resources* | | | | | | |
| INCMULT | −.01 | −.07 | −.09 | .04 | - | - |
| SOCAID | −.72 | .04 | −.85 | 1.10 | - | - |
| OCCDICH | .17 | −.25 | .07 | −.03 | - | - |
| *Dwelling environment* | | | | | | |
| MULTHS | .01 | .13 | .19 | .01 | −.03 | .19 |
| PUBLIC | −.04 | −.02 | .18 | −.20 | .09 | −.03 |
| OVERCR | .14 | .25 | .25 | .21 | .23 | .15 |
| *Interaction* | | | | | | |
| M(Contr.*Res.) (9 vars.) | .05 | .07 | .01 | .01 | −.00 | .10 |
| CONTR.*RES. (9 vars.) | −.08 | −.55 | .17 | −.16 | .04 | −.03 |
| M(Contr.*Contr.) (3 vars.) | −.15 | −.08 | - | - | - | - |
| CONTR.*CONTR. (3 vars.) | .24 | −.01 | - | - | - | - |
| M(Res.*Res.) (3 vars.) | −.01 | −.02 | - | - | - | - |
| RES.*RES. (3 vars.) | .30 | 1.10 | - | - | - | - |
| $const_{90}$ | | 2.66 | | 2.85 | | 2.82 |
| $const_{85}$ | | 2.58 | | 2.40 | | 2.43 |
| Expl. prop. of var.: uncorr. | | .95 | | .94 | | .92 |
| corr. | | .89 | | .89 | | .89 |

are also large changes with respect to the second model. Large changes are not surprising, of course, since much of the information in the basic variables is found in the interaction variables.

Obviously, the linear analyses whose results are reported in Table 4.5 are hampered by very severe collinearity problems. As has been discussed above, there are severe collinearity problems when the interaction variables are not included, and including these variables naturally makes the problems worse, which makes interpretation of obtained coefficients very difficult. I therefore focus on the results of the third model, in which the collinearity problems can be assumed to be least serious.

These results accord fairly well with what can be expected. Of the average coefficient values for the control-resources interaction variables, the one for the mean-of-products variables in Group B is 0.10. A positive value is expected. The average coefficient value for the product-of-means variables in Group B is −0.03. A value of about 0 is expected. The average coefficient value for the product-of-means variables in Group A is 0.04, and here a positive value is expected. The average coefficient value of the mean-of-products variables in Group A is −0.00. Since this coefficient can be assumed to express the total of the intraindividual and social effects on crime, and since the intraindividual effect can be assumed to be positive, this indicates that there have been social processes affecting crime negatively in Group A. These processes may have been of integration type.

In the analyses just discussed, unique coefficients for the age/sex variables are used for the each group of residents. Alternatively, the coefficients of these variables could be assumed to be the same for the two groups, since the influences on crime of age and sex can be assumed to be of global type. The results obtained for such a revised model (not shown in tabular form) show that reducing the number of age/sex variables has not appreciably reduced the explained proportion of the variance in crime. However, the differences between the Group A and Group B coefficients found for several independent variables have increased.

Adding the interaction variables has only produced a small increase in the explained proportion of the variance in crime, but it has given an opportunity of testing ideas about different types of interaction and their causes. The obtained coefficient values give some support for the idea of connections between intraindividual and social processes and aggregated interaction within and between individuals. However, due to the methodological problems, above all the problems with collinearity, these results are only tentative.


## Discussion

The cross-sectional, bivariate analyses carried out in this study paint an interesting picture of the relationships between the crime factor and independent properties. Strong bivariate relationships have been found for properties describing social resources, social control and the dwelling environment. These findings concur with central theories presented in this field of research. However, some of the relationships are unusually strong in comparison with what has previously been found. There is no reason to believe that this is due to the fact that the residential differentiation with respect to the properties entering such relationships was greater in Stockholm than in other Western cities. Instead, these findings are probably due to the high quality of the data. Swedish official registers provide unusually good opportunities for collecting comprehensive, high-quality data. In particular, the strength of the relationships is probably to a great extent due to the high quality of the crime measure. This measure is better than most crime measures previously used, not only because of the very high quality of the data upon which it is based, but also because of its construction. The measure has a very high reliability and, one might surmise, a high validity in comparison with most measures based on official conviction data. Admittedly, criticisms of measuring crime with official register data have been lodged by advocates of the self-declaration measurement method, motivated by the belief that such data are biased due to discrimination against certain groups of residents. This hypothesis is difficult to test with the data of this study. However, the findings do not indicate that such discrimination means any severe problem, as noted above and further discussed below.

A striking result of the multivariate cross-sectional analyses is that much of the variance in the crime factor is explained by the independent properties. For the reference year 1990, an extraordinarily large proportion of the variance can be explained in this manner. In fact, the crime factor can be explained to a very high degree by using quite different sets of independent properties. Thus, it is found in linear multivariate analyses that models comprising different sets of independent variables explain about the same proportion of the variance in the crime factor and that it is difficult to make a choice between them. Furthermore, it is difficult to decide what role should be played by power versions of the basic properties, and by interaction of different types. The problem of finding the perfect model is all the more intricate since it is found that different macro-level product models and linear models explain the variance about equally well, although with some advantage for the product models.

Results of the analyses provide some support for the idea that micro-level interaction does affect the crime factor. When adding aggregated micro-level interaction variables to basic variables in linear regression analysis of crime, there is some improvement of the corrected explained proportion of the variance in the crime factor. There are also some results on the coefficients of these interaction variables that seem to indicate that the idea of micro-level interaction is relevant. However, very strong relationships among basic and interaction variables hamper the analysis. When using macro-level product models, findings indicate that there may be interaction between different macro-level properties, for example, between social control and social resources.

While many of the findings of the cross-sectional analyses are unsurprising and will not be commented on, some deserve further discussion. I take up four issues: 1) the character of the relationship between the crime factor and the social aid property,

2) the conclusions that can be drawn about discrimination bias of the crime measure, 3) the conclusions that can be drawn about the influences on the crime factor that come from the environment and from geographical selection, and 4) the evidence found for the validity of the social control and social resources perspectives.

The relationship between the crime factor and the percentage of the population that belongs to households that have received social aid is rather strong for the reference years of 1990 and 1985. However, there is no sign of any nonlinear relationship constituted so that the crime factor grows at an increasing rate as the percentage of such households increases. Instead the derivative is slightly negative. Causally interpreted, this finding suggests that total crime will not increase if households with social aid are concentrated to certain areas.

Could the crime measure be biased due to discrimination, meaning that it gives certain groups of residents higher values than what is justified by their actual criminality? As mentioned, foreigners and individuals with low social status have been assumed to be discriminated against in this way in Sweden, and considering results of the study presented here this hypothesis may seem reasonable, because the cross-sectional relationships found between the crime factor and the percentages of foreigners and social resources factors are strong and go in expected directions. However, the hypothesis is difficult to test in a sophisticated way in the data. Only tentative tests can be made. Findings of multivariate cross-sectional analyses do not give much support for the hypothesis for foreigners. The relationship between the crime factor and the percentage of foreign citizens is greatly weakened in several multivariate analyses, in fact to the extent that much of it disappears or even that it becomes negative. There is more support, it seems, for the existence of discrimination against low status individuals. Strong bivariate relationships have been found between crime and the OCCDICH property, and the relationships between crime and this property are still strong or have at least notable strength in multivariate analyses. But it has also been found in analyses of the 1985/1990 data that the relationship between OCCDICH and crime is positive and strong for the newcomers, while the corresponding relationship for the long-term residents is very weak, and this is difficult to reconcile with the discrimination hypothesis. However, this evidence is hardly enough to dismiss the hypothesis.

Since the perfect model has not been established, it is impossible to say with absolute certainty how crime is influenced by the environment and by geographical selection. Nevertheless, the results of the cross-sectional analyses performed offer some suggestions or indications of how these influences are constituted.

The results of the cross-sectional analyses of the 1990 data suggest an answer to the question of the relative strength of the influence of geographical selection on the crime factor. These results are particularly interesting, since the crime measure probably has the highest quality for this year. Geographical selection can be assumed to influence crime indirectly via properties that exert a direct influence. The INCMULT and PUBLIC variables describe properties that can be assumed to be strongly related to the selection, and they have strong bivariate cross-sectional relationships with crime. These relationships have the expected signs, and the two variables together explain much of the variance in crime. This figure of explained variance can be assumed to be the total of four components: 1) the effect of the factors' indirect influences on crime due to selection, 2) the effect of the factors' indirect non-selective influences, 3) the effect of the factors' direct influences, and 4) the non-causal relationship between crime and the factors that is due to the fact that both are affected by other independent factors. Because the components 2) – 4) seem to be of small significance, we might conclude that the influence of the selection on crime is very strong. Corresponding results for the 1990/85 data suggest the same, although the conclusion is not as clear-cut for these data.

There are indications that social control influences crime. In all analyses conducted in data for the total area population and for all models used, DIVOR has proven to have a positive relationship with crime. Other indications of an influence of social control are differences in the relationships found for MULTHS and to some extent FORGN for long-term residents and for newcomers, differences that are most simply explained as a result of social integration among the long-term residents – residents living in multifamily houses and foreigners are more anonymous and less socially integrated and therefore less socially controlled when they arrive in an area than when they have lived there for several years.

Social integration may concern the neighborhood, the city as a whole or the greater social or cultural setting. It may well be that foreigners' integration is more the question of an adjustment to the city as a whole or to Swedish culture than to local conditions. The results of a tentative analysis performed of the influence on crime exerted by different groups of newcomers support this idea.

As to the social resources properties, indications have been found that SOCAID and OCCDICH influence crime positively. For example, in multivariate analyses of the total population these properties have relationships of the expected sign with crime. For INCMULT results are more mixed. The results for these resources properties differ for long-term residents and newcomers. For INCSTD, which is assumed to measure the dispersion in economic resources on the local level, no strong relationship with crime has been found. If Agnew's theory is true and if inequality on the local level affects individuals' strain, one might think that there should be such a relationship. However, strain is perhaps more the result of the individual's comparison of his own resources with global rather than local conditions.

The results obtained are interesting, but since the perfect model of the crime factor has not been found many of them remain uncertain. Of course, the problem of finding the perfect model is mainly a problem of identifying the causes of crime, but doing this is very difficult in cross-sectioned analysis. The great strength of many cross-sectional relationships is surely due to the fact that selective forces have worked during a very long period of time, and since these forces have a feedback character the analysis is complicated. However, if consideration is paid to limited time periods, causal structure is more easily analyzed. I now turn to that type of analysis.

# Chapter 5
# Results II. Longitudinal Relationships

Do historical values of independent properties add something to the explanation of crime – and if they do, what do they add? In order to find out, this study analyzes longitudinal relationships expressed in linear models using point-of-time (here simply "point") and change data and expressed in product models using point data. The linear models will be of ordinary type – the quasi-linear models have shown to give explanations of crime that are not much better than the explanations given by ordinary linear models, and they will therefore not be used.

One drawback of using point data in these analyses is that for several properties the values for different points of time are strongly related to one another, and that this may cause problems in identifying model structure. Another drawback of using these data is that the coefficients obtained for independent properties of the most remote point in time can be assumed to absorb part of unanalyzed relationships that pertain to even more remote points in time of these properties. As a consequence of this, the comparability between coefficients may be impaired.

These problems vanish when using change data, but others appear. First, the influences on crime may be dependent on the length of the period of time during which changes have occurred, and it may therefore be wise to study periods of time of different lengths. Second, whereas linear models of crime are easy to apply to change data in many cases – if these models have no complicating error terms (or if they have no error terms at all), the difference between two crime values could simply be modeled as the linear function of the differences in the independent properties – there is no such easy application of the types of product models presented above. It should be noted that because some important properties have changed relatively much, it is inappropriate to take the differential of such product functions as an approximate model for change data.

**Linear Models Using Point Data**

It has been shown previously that the values for different years of various independent properties are strongly correlated to each other. It has also been shown that all independent properties explain a great deal of the variance in crime linearly and cross-sectionally. It can therefore be expected that there is not much to be gained in the linear explanation of the variance in a crime factor by adding historical data of these properties. This also turns out to be the case, for example, regarding the 1990 measure of crime. As mentioned above, all basic independent properties explain about 90 per cent of the variance in this measure in a linear cross-sectional analysis when correction is made for lost degrees of freedom. When all basic independent properties of 1985 are added, the corrected explained proportion of the variance increases, but only by about one and a half per cent. When the 1980 basic independent properties are further added in the same way, the corrected explained variance does not increase. Thus, adding data for previous years does not increase the explained proportion of the variance in the 1990 crime measure much. The same is true for corresponding analyses of the 1985 and 1980 measures of crime (figures not shown).

Furthermore, previous crime does not seem to contribute much to the linear explanation of later crime. When, in the analysis of the 1990 crime factor, the 1985 crime factor is added to the 1990 and 1985 basic independent properties, the corrected explained proportion of the variance does not increase. The regression coefficient obtained for the previous crime factor has a very low absolute value (it is 0.05). When, in the analysis of the 1985 crime factor, the 1980 crime factor is added to the independent variables of 1985 and 1980, the explained variance does increase (with about two per cent) and the factor gets a high absolute value (0.55), but then there are problems with lacking information on important social resources in 1980, whose relationship with crime in 1985 can be assumed to be taken over to a great extent by the 1980 crime measure. I do not think, therefore, that there is any strong evidence that previous crime affects later crime directly to a great extent. This conclusion is supported by the found relationships between the changes in crime 1980–1985 and 1985–1990, commented on above. Consequently, I do not consider previous crime in my analyses.

Evidently, adding historical independent data of the types analyzed in this study results in little increase of the explained proportion of variance in the crime factor. Nevertheless, this does not imply that insights into the causes of this factor could not be gained by performing analyses using point data for more than one year. However, it is a warning that when historical data are added, coefficients obtained in such analyses may be very sensitive to various disturbances, due to the strong relationships between independent variables. Therefore, these analyses are designed so that such relationships and ensuing identification problems are avoided as far as possible.

Most of the longitudinal linear models for point data used in this study are constructed in the following ways. Only the influences on the dependent variable that come directly from independent variables, that is, that do not go via other independent variables, are analyzed. The dependent variable is the crime factor for one or more reference years. The independent variables are values on basic properties for the same reference year as the crime factor and one or more previous reference years. When a five-year interval between measurement points is used, values pertaining to the current and to the previous year are analyzed. When a ten-year interval is used, values pertaining to the current and to the two previous reference points are analyzed, because the relationships between independent variables are then weaker. However, as described below, some independent properties are only represented by crime-synchronous values or by data reduced in other ways.

In all analyses, INCDICH, INCSTD, UNEMPL, OCCMULT and MOVES are excluded. As before, the income and occupational status dimensions are described by INCMULT and OCCDICH. PUBLIC and MULTHS are in some cases only represented by crime-synchronous values, because these properties have changed very little. Basic independent variables are used in normalized versions and the explained proportions of variances are corrected for lost degrees of freedom. When crime data for different reference years are analyzed simultaneously, one or more dummy variables are used so that there is a unique constant for each year. The analyses are also carried out using standardized variables. All variables including crime but excluding the dummy variables are then standardized. For a reference year, standardization is made for all areas for which there are data. In analyses of data sets including data for 1970 or 1975 (for these years areas are missing), variables pertaining to later years may therefore not be exactly standardized. However, the deviations are small.

The age/sex properties pose a particular problem. It would have been desirable to measure these properties in a simpler way than is the case, but this is difficult to do. Considering the sex distribution is necessary, of course, and measuring the age distribution more simply, for example by using the average, is inappropriate, because the influence on crime of age can probably not be expressed as a linear function. A problem with the six age/sex proportions used is, as mentioned above, that they are strongly linearly related to each other. Naturally, even more severe problems arise if the age/sex properties for different years are used together. Single such properties for one year can in some cases almost be constructed as linear functions of the other properties. This is particularly the case with the OLDMALE and OLDFEML properties. For example, when regressing OLDMALE for 1990 on all the age/sex properties of 1990, 1985 and 1980, 98 per cent (uncorrected value) of the variance is explained. If the values of some other properties are added as regressors, the explained variance may rise still more. For example, if the values of SINGLE for the three years are added to the regressors, 99 per cent is explained. Of course, when using such sets of data identification problems become formidable. Therefore, only crime-synchronous values of the age/sex properties will, as a rule, be used.

A property that is problematic due to strong correlations between values of different years is INCMULT. For example, for the 1980/1985/1990 data, the correlation between the values of the current and the previous year is 0.984 and the correlation between the values of the current year and the year ten years before is 0.962. Therefore, caution must be observed when interpreting the coefficients obtained for this property.

Results of four analyses using normalized independent variables are shown in Table 5.1 (results for standardized variables are shown in Table V.ii). In the first analysis, the dependent variable is the crime factor for 1990 and the independent variables refer at most to 1990 and 1985, that is, data going back only five years in time are used. This is the only linear analysis of point data in which social resources properties are considered with respect to all possible points in time.

**Table 5.1**  **Explaining crime with simultaneous and earlier values of independent properties. Linear regression analysis. Independent variables normalized**

| Independent property | 1990 (n=83) | | 1990 (n=80) | | | 1985/90 (n=166) | | 1980/ 85/90 (n=248) | |
|---|---|---|---|---|---|---|---|---|---|
| | 1990 | 1985 | 1990 | 1980 | 1970 | 1 | 2 | 1 | 2 |
| *Age and sex* | | | | | | | | | |
| YNGMALE | −.11 | - | −.02 | - | - | .12 | - | .14 | - |
| YNGFEML | −.40 | - | −.32 | - | - | −.27 | - | −.14 | - |
| MDLMALE | −.57 | - | −.40 | - | - | −.23 | - | −.14 | - |
| MDLFEML | −.26 | - | .02 | - | - | −.36 | - | −.49 | - |
| OLDMALE | .07 | - | .45 | - | - | .28 | - | .05 | - |
| OLDFEML | −1.84 | - | −1.48 | - | - | −1.21 | - | −.87 | - |
| *Social control* | | | | | | | | | |
| FORGN | 1.34 | −1.63 | .75 | −.81 | −.29 | .71 | −.73 | .35 | −.17 |
| SINGLE | −.41 | −.12 | −.62 | .18 | .45 | −.11 | .08 | .14 | .01 |
| DIVOR | .06 | .67 | .28 | .64 | −.14 | −.29 | 1.12 | .15 | .72 |
| *Social resources* | | | | | | | | | |
| INCMULT | −.19 | .36 | −.02 | - | −.12 | .62 | −.57 | .48 | −.57 |
| SOCAID | −.23 | .71 | .30 | - | - | .16 | - | - | - |
| OCCDICH | .72 | .14 | .61 | - | - | .49 | - | - | - |
| *Dwelling envir.* | | | | | | | | | |
| MULTHS | .17 | - | .17 | - | −.13 | −.11 | - | −.12 | - |
| PUBLIC | −.05 | - | .09 | - | −.26 | .12 | - | .32 | - |
| OVERCR | .43 | −.07 | .41 | −.19 | −.03 | .28 | .02 | .15 | .07 |
| *Constants* | | | | | | | | | |
| *1990* | 2.60 | | 2.79 | | | 2.72 | | 2.84 | |
| *1985* | - | | - | | | 2.90 | | 2.69 | |
| *1980* | - | | - | | | - | | 2.45 | |
| Expl. proportion of variance (corr.) | .91 | | .89 | | | .87 | | .84 | |

The analysis has resulted in several coefficients with interesting values. For the social control properties, this is especially the case with FORGN. The coefficient for 1990 is here 1.34 and for 1985 −1.63. Causally interpreted, this means that an increase in the percentage of foreign citizens very quickly leads to an increase in crime. However, this effect does not remain intact, but is reversed into a decrease after five years – a decrease that is about as strong as the initial increase. This could be the result of an integration of the foreign citizens in the area. When these foreigners first come to the area they are probably in many cases poorly integrated in the local society and perhaps also in society at large (the latter is particularly the case for those who have just immigrated to Sweden), but after some years they have formed new social bonds, which has made them more integrated and therefore more reluctant to commit crime and less influential in generating crime among others. It may be noted that the difference between the quick and delayed relationships with the crime factor is more easily explained as the result of integration than as the result of discrimination.

As regards the DIVOR property, there are also interesting relationships. It turns out here that the coefficient for 1985 has a high value, while the coefficient for 1990 has a value near zero. Thus, it appears that an increase in the percentage of divorced residents increases the level of crime relatively strongly after some time. One reason could be that negative consequences, for example for the children, appear after some time due to a process of degradation of social contacts.

The SINGLE property is found to be negatively related to the crime factor. The coefficient for 1990 is −0.41. Thus, it seems that an increase in the percentage of residents living with a single parent quickly decreases crime, which is unexpected. The relationship could perhaps be due to the fact that many of these residents are younger than 15 years.

Turning to the social resources properties, the table shows interesting relationships for SOCAID and OCCDICH. For OCCDICH, the coefficient for 1990 is strongly positive and it has a much higher value than the coefficient for 1985. For SOCAID, the opposite is true. Thus, it seems that an increase in the percentage of unskilled workers very quickly leads to an increase in crime, whereas an increase in the percentage of recipients of social aid leads to a more delayed such increase. The coefficients for INCMULT, which have different signs, may also seem interesting, but should probably not be taken very seriously for reasons mentioned above.

As for the remaining relationships, those found for OVERCR indicate that an increase of the percentage of residents living in overcrowded households quickly leads to an increase in crime. Of the relationships for the age/sex properties, all but one are negative, indicating that increases in these properties decrease crime. These relationships are not easy to interpret in detail, and they are similar to the ones found in cross-sectional analysis (as to the explanation of these relationships, see above). It should be mentioned that adding the age/sex categories for 1985 does not improve the explained proportion of the variance much, only by about half a per cent.

In the second analysis, the dependent variable is the crime factor for 1990 and the independent variables describe properties for at most the years 1990, 1980 and 1970, that is, data going back twenty years is used. In this analysis, I have used values for the years 1990 and 1970 for the properties of INCMULT, MULTHS and PUBLIC to manage the problems with strong relationships between values of adjacent reference points.

The analysis has given results quite reminiscent of the results of the first analysis. Expanding the historical perspective by increasing the space between considered reference years has not improved the explained proportion of the variance in the crime factor (corrected for lost degrees of freedom, 89 per cent of the variance is now explained against 91 per cent in the previous analysis). Most coefficients for 1970 indicate weak or rather weak relative influences on crime. Several coefficients for 1980 and 1990 are rather similar to the corresponding coefficients for 1985 and 1990 found in the first analysis, and several of the conclusions about the influences on crime that were drawn in this analysis therefore still apply for 1980 and 1990. This is no surprise, since it can be assumed that the coefficients for 1985 that were found in the first analysis to some extent absorbed influences from earlier values of properties. One interesting finding is the trend in coefficients obtained for SINGLE. The coefficients go from strongly negative for 1990 (−0.62) to rather strongly positive for 1970 (0.45). The positive coefficient for 1970, meaning that an increase in the percentage of residents with a single parent produces an increase in crime after 20 years, differs from other results for this property obtained in linear analysis and may give a hint that the idea behind using this property as an indicator of social control wasn't so bad after all (after 20 years all of these residents must have been at least 15 years of age – that is, their crimes can be assumed to affect the dependent variable with full strength).

In the third analysis, the dependent variable is the crime factor for 1985 and 1990 and the independent variables describe properties for the current reference point and the reference point five years earlier. The important properties SOCAID and OCCDICH can only be described with crime-synchronous values, and this makes for problems when interpreting coefficients (the same is the case in the second analysis). SOCAID and to some extent also OCCDICH have previously been found to have a delayed positive relationship with crime, and properties that correlate strongly with these two variables can be assumed to have their coefficient values affected if the values of these variables are lacking for the earlier reference point (this is for example the case with INCMULT). It should be noted that the constant term for 1990 has a lower value than the constant term for 1985, which seems unrealistic and could be a result of the design with incomplete data for SOCAID and OCCDICH. However, the trend in coefficients for FORGN and DIVOR has the same character as in previous analyses.

In the fourth analysis reported in the table, in which the crime factor for 1980/1985/1990 is the dependent variable, there are no data for SOCAID and OCCDICH. The constants have now values with a realistic rank order. The results obtained are rather similar to the result from the third analysis, although the trends in coefficient values are not as clear. The reduction of the sharpness in the trend of coefficients for FORGN may be due to the absence of the two social resources properties. Again, DIVOR has a delayed positive relationship with crime.

The analyses of point data seem to show that there are interesting longitudinal relationships behind several of the cross-sectional relationships. The results of the analyses agree to a great extent with ideas about social control underlying this study. According to these results, there seem to be influences from the percentages of foreign citizens and divorcees that can be interpreted as influences of social control. Thus, interpreting the results causally, an increase of the number of foreign citizens has a relatively strong and positive quick effect on crime that does not remain intact but fades away after some time – presumably due to the fact that the foreigners are integrated in the local society or in society at large. An increase of the number of divorcees has a positive effect on crime, an effect that is to a large extent delayed. However, in some analyses the percentage of residents living in single-parent families has not proven to have the expected positive relationship with crime.

Thus, the longitudinal analyses have offered opportunities for testing the social control explanation of crime – opportunities that are much better than the opportunities provided by cross-sectional analyses – and the conclusion is that this explanation has received rather much support.

There also seem to be influences from social resources properties. A strong quick effect comes, it appears, from the percentage of unskilled workers. Furthermore, it is found that the percentage of residents living in overcrowded dwellings – a property that can be seen as an aspect of the social resources – has a quick positive effect on crime. These quick effects might to a great extent be the result of geographical selection. However, the strong delayed effect found for the percentage of social aid recipients must be given some other explanation. The mixed results for INCMULT are difficult to interpret.

The results of the longitudinal analyses prompt reflection about the nature of the social processes that influence crime. As mentioned, social processes beyond the family and founded on group mechanisms can be assumed to take time. Analyzing longitudinal relationships therefore provides opportunities for studying them. Clearly, some of the relationships found can be interpreted as the result of such processes. The relationships found for FORGN are easily interpreted to indicate an integration process, and the relationships for DIVOR may be due to a process of deteriorating social bonds. Perhaps the delayed relationship found for SOCAID could be the result of a social process according to which an increase of the percentage of individuals who receive social aid increases crime due to growth of groups of deviant persons. However, other, more individual/family-centered explanations, for example focusing on the effect of "stigmatization", could also be thought of.

## Linear Models Using Change Data

Change data has been analyzed longitudinally and linearly. Since the conditions for identifying coefficient values in these analyses are more favorable than are the corresponding conditions in analyzing point data, I have considered changes in independent properties during three periods of time, and I have also considered historical data on the age/sex properties when such data have improved substantially the explanation of the variance in crime.

Four analyses are made. In the first one, the change in the crime factor between 1985 and 1990 (higher values mean increases in crime) is seen as a function of simultaneous changes in age/sex properties and in SOCAID and OCCDICH, and simultaneous and two previous five-year changes in FORGN, SINGLE, DIVOR, INCMULT, MULTHS, PUBLIC and OVERCR. Thus, the same types of properties enter the function as were used in longitudinal analyses of point data. A problem with this model is the fact that data are not balanced. There are no data for previous periods on the changes in SOCAID and OCCDICH (and neither on the changes in the age/sex properties).

In the second analysis the changes in the crime factor between 1980 and 1985 and between 1985 and 1990 are simultaneously analyzed. The change in the crime factor is seen as a function of changes in the same properties as in the first model, except for changes in SOCAID and OCCDICH. The values of the age/sex properties for the period preceding the current period are considered. This analysis is of interest because it makes use of a large portion of the data covering the whole period of 1970–1990.

Another way of performing a temporally comprehensive analysis of the crime factor is to study the change in this factor between 1980 and 1990, and the changes in independent properties in the same period of time as well as the changes in the period between 1970 and 1980. This is done in the third and fourth analyses. In the third analysis the change in crime is seen as a function of changes in the same types of properties as in the second model, although these changes now refer to two ten-year periods. The fourth analysis is identical to the third one, except that only simultaneous changes in the age/sex properties are considered.

In these four analyses, the independent properties have been normalized in the ways reported above (standardized data has also been analyzed; see Table V.iii). Since there are only 80 areas for the reference year 1970 and 82 areas for the reference year 1975, the analyses are based on a reduced number of areas. Because it is assumed that the constant of the underlying cross-sectional model for crime has unique values for different years, separate constants have been used for the two periods of time in the second analysis. The periods of time used in the analyses are referred to in the following manner: the period for which the change in crime is measured is called Period 1, the equally long period preceding this period is called Period 2, and the equally long period preceding this second period is called Period 3. Results of the analyses are reported in Table 5.2.

**Table 5.2**  **Explaining change in crime with changes in independent properties. Linear regression analysis. Variables normalized**

| Independent property | C90 – C85 (n=82) | | | C90 – C85/ C85 – C80 (n=162) | | | C90 – C80 (n=80) | | | |
|---|---|---|---|---|---|---|---|---|---|---|
| Period | 1 | 2 | 3 | 1 | 2 | 3 | 1 | 2 | 1 | 2 |
| *Age and sex* | | | | | | | | | | |
| YNGMALE | .11 | - | - | .05 | -.00 | - | -.17 | -.26 | -.00 | - |
| YNGFEML | -.40 | - | - | -.04 | -.08 | - | -.05 | .33 | -.19 | - |
| MDLMALE | -.32 | - | - | -.00 | -.76 | - | -.89 | -.50 | -.46 | - |
| MDLFEML | .27 | - | - | .44 | -.30 | - | 1.15 | .33 | .95 | - |
| OLDMALE | .21 | - | - | .08 | -.00 | - | -.53 | .25 | -.00 | - |
| OLDFEML | -.24 | - | - | .61 | -1.32 | - | .88 | -.34 | .66 | - |
| *Social control* | | | | | | | | | | |
| FORGN | 1.20 | -.10 | -.15 | 1.11 | .16 | .06 | 1.14 | .17 | 1.22 | .04 |
| SINGLE | .47 | .04 | -.23 | -.13 | -.48 | -.30 | -.93 | -1.06 | -.61 | -.49 |
| DIVOR | .49 | 1.12 | .04 | -.19 | .51 | .02 | .86 | .48 | .71 | .45 |
| *Social resources* | | | | | | | | | | |
| INCMULT | -.38 | -.39 | -.04 | -.08 | -.41 | .24 | -.19 | -.59 | -.11 | -.12 |
| SOCAID | -.22 | - | - | - | - | - | - | - | - | - |
| OCCDICH | .08 | - | - | - | - | - | - | - | - | - |
| *Dwelling envir.* | | | | | | | | | | |
| MULTHS | -.24 | -.34 | -.36 | .64 | .67 | -.07 | .11 | -1.07 | .51 | -.80 |
| PUBLIC | -1.21 | .39 | .83 | -.49 | .01 | .34 | .39 | .84 | .16 | .29 |
| OVERCR | .33 | .35 | .51 | .16 | .04 | -.09 | .32 | .15 | .21 | .16 |
| *Constants* | | | | | | | | | | |
| C90 – C85 | | -.05 | | | .14 | | | - | | - |
| C85 – C80 | | - | | | .41 | | | - | | - |
| C90 – C80 | | - | | | - | | | .57 | | .09 |
| Expl. proportion of variance (corr.) | .20 | | | | .18 | | | .47 | | .42 |

The figures in the table show that the changes in several independent properties have rather interesting relationships, as indicated by the trends of the coefficient values, with the change in the crime factor in the analyses. However, the explained proportions, corrected for lost degrees of freedom, of the variance in the change in the crime factor are small in the first two analyses.

In the first analysis only 20 per cent of the variance is explained, but some trends in coefficients indicate interesting relationships. This is especially the case with the social control properties. The coefficient of the simultaneous change in FORGN has a high positive value, whereas the coefficients of previous changes in the property are negative with low absolute values. Thus, causally interpreted, an increase in FORGN quickly increases crime to a relatively large degree, but later effects on crime are negative and relatively weak. These relationships are to a rather large extent compatible with the ideas previously discussed: newly arrived foreigners are not subjected to the same social control as are foreigners who have lived in the area for longer time. However, the strong reversion in effect that was found when analyzing point data is not found when analyzing the change data, which may be due to the fact that there are no variables describing previous changes in SOCAID and OCCDICH.

The relationships found for the changes in FORGN are not very likely to be solely due to discrimination. It is true that being an easy target for discrimination can be expected to be affected to some extent by conditions that especially often pertain to newly arrived foreigners (for example, poor language skills and poor ability to manage in a Swedish cultural setting), but it seems strange that discrimination would not pertain at all to the foreigners who arrived in the area five years earlier. However, there is the possibility that both discrimination and integration have affected the relationships.

The relationships found between changes in DIVOR and the change in crime mean, again causally interpreted, that there is a delayed effect of the change in DIVOR – this effect is very strong in a relative sense after five years. Also this could, in about the way discussed above with respect to the analysis of point data, be given a social control explanation.

As to the SINGLE property, the regression weight for the change in the first period has a positive sign, indicating that an increase in the percentage of persons living in single households is followed by an increase in crime, whereas the coefficients for the remaining periods have low or rather low absolute values – something that could be given a social control explanation but that gives a quite different picture of the influence of SINGLE on crime than the one obtained when analyzing point data.

As to the resources properties, the figures in the table show that the coefficient for the simultaneous change in SOCAID has a negative value. This suggests that crime will diminish in the short run if more people get social aid, which is unexpected when SOCAID is taken as a measure of lack of social resources (as is the case here), but which is not unreasonable if SOCAID is taken as a measure of the improvement of such resources (see DeFronzo and Hannon, 1998; Chamlin et al., 2002; Savage et al., 2008). The changes in INCMULT all have negative relationships with the change in crime, which is expected. As compared to the relationships found between OCCDICH and crime for point data, the simultaneous change in OCCDICH has a very weak relationship with the change in crime (see also Table V.iii). This unexpected relationship may be due to the fact that there are no data for changes in OCCDICH in the second and third periods.

Some of the relationships found for the dwelling environment properties are puzzling. The relationships for all changes in MULTHS are negative and no one of them has, when the changes are standardized, substantial strength. The coefficient for the simultaneous change in PUBLIC is strongly negative. The coefficients for the changes in OVERCR have positive values, and the value of the coefficient for the change in the third period is higher than the values of the coefficients for the more recent changes in the property. Causally interpreted, these relationships would mean that increases in the first period in the percentages of residents who live in multifamily houses and who live in dwellings owned by public landlords, respectively, decrease crime, and that an increase in the third period in overcrowding has a stronger positive influence on crime than either an increase in the first or second period in this property. This is difficult to believe.

As to the age/sex properties, it is found that negative relationships do not predominate as strongly as they do in corresponding analyses of point data.

The coefficients obtained in the analysis of C90 − C85/C85 − C80 show important differences in comparison with the coefficients obtained in the analysis of C90 − C85. For example, interpreting coefficients causally, the changes in MULTHS during the first and second periods have now positive effects on the change in crime, the change in OVERCR during the third period a negative effect, and the changes in DIVOR and SINGLE during the first period negative effects. But there are also similarities. For example, the change in FORGN has again a rapid effect and the change in DIVOR a delayed effect that are positive and relatively strong. For the changes in the age/sex properties during the second period two coefficients have very high absolute values, namely those of the changes in MDLMALE and OLDFEML. However, the values of these two coefficients are not very interesting because of collinearity problems.

On the whole, the picture of the influences on the change in crime obtained in the second analysis seems more realistic than the picture obtained in the first analysis. It is of course problematic that the pictures are so very different in some respects. If the forms of the models are the true ones, the conclusion must be that the changes in crime in the periods 1980–1985 and 1985–1990 have different causes in important respects. This would be unfortunate, since it is the general causes that are sought. Another problem is the fact that in both analyses only a small proportion of the variance in the dependent factor is explained after correction for lost degrees of freedom.

The question this raises is what should be done. Can change data be analyzed at all using linear models? There is much to argue that they can, and that one way of tackling the problem is to use longer time periods – that is, the periods of 1970–1980 and 1980–1990. Momentary influences on crime will then cancel each other out to a greater extent, and the more permanent influences, which are the influences sought, will dominate.

As can be seen from Table 5.2, the third analysis, which is thus based on ten-year periods, has resulted in more of the variance in the dependent variable, 47 per cent, being explained. The coefficients obtained provide a picture of the influences on crime that, considering the modifications that must be made due to the changed time perspective, agrees to a rather great extent with previously discussed ideas. The change in FORGN has a rapid positive effect that is relatively strong on the change in crime. The change in DIVOR has positive effects, both rapid and delayed. The change in SINGLE has negative effects. The effects of the change in INCMULT are negative. These effects, except for those of SINGLE, accord with assumptions made.

For the changes in the dwelling environment properties, the coefficients obtained in the third analysis provide a picture of influences that are slightly consistent with previously discussed ideas. The change in MULTHS seems to have practically no rapid effect on the change in crime, and a delayed effect that is negative and much stronger. The change in PUBLIC has positive effects, and the delayed effect is much stronger than the rapid one. The change in OVERCR has positive effects.

In the third analysis, the coefficients for the changes in the age/sex properties paint a different picture of influences on crime than what has previously been obtained in analyses of point data and, although less clearly, of change data for five-year periods. Previously, results were obtained that indicated that the females tended to have a more negative influence on crime than the males in most age categories. However, in the third model, this is not the case in five out of the six comparisons that can be made. Instead, the females tend to have a more positive influence. Is this unrealistic? Not necessarily, considering the changed time perspective. During later decades there have been substantial changes in the behavior of the sexes, with females tending to exhibit more of what have been considered male behaviors. Thus, when studying the ten-year periods of differences, an increased female tendency to influence the crime rate positively may, it seems, well appear.

In the fourth analysis, only age/sex variables pertaining to the first period are used when modeling the change in crime between 1980 and 1990. It can be seen from the table that this has caused some considerable changes in results obtained. For example, the explained proportion of variance has decreased rather much, from 47 to 42 per cent, and the quick effect of MULTHS is now more strongly positive. However, the previously found effects of FORGN and DIVOR remain.

The conclusion to be drawn from the results obtained from the different analyses presented of change data is, I think, that relying on the result of the analysis of C90 – C80 is safest. There is a price to be paid: the five-year perspective has to be abandoned, which means that very rapid influences of changes cannot be determined, and that changes in SOCAID and OCCDICH cannot be considered. However, the results of the analysis made of changes in ten-year periods are rather interesting. As to the FORGN and DIVOR properties, they offer support for the social control theory. For the SINGLE property, however, the results contradict this theory.

## Considering Micro-Level Interaction

The effect of adding variables pertaining to micro-level interaction as regressors in linear models will now be studied longitudinally using change data. The change in crime C90 – C85 will be analyzed with changes in basic and interactional properties. The same sets of mean-of-products and product-of-means properties are used as before, but in some analyses one or two other such properties are used as well. In most cases only changes in interaction for the first period of time are considered, since data on social aid and occupational status only exist for this period. All variables are standardized. All explained proportions of variance are corrected for lost degrees of freedom. Some main results are presented in Table 5.3.

As shown in the first column in the table, using data on the changes during the first period of time in basic properties but no data on corresponding changes in interaction properties results in 19 per cent being explained of the variance in the change in crime. Aside from the changes in a couple of age/sex variables, only the changes in FORGN and OVERCR obtain regression (that is, beta) weights that indicate any stronger influence on crime. Thus, as expected, increases of the percentages of foreigners and residents living in overcrowded households (or rather less decreases in the latter percentage, because overcrowding was a diminishing problem) are accompanied by an increase in crime. It may also be noted that all the changes in the age/sex variables indicate that an increase in the percentage of men is more conducive to crime than an increase in the percentage of women.

When adding the changes in the mean-of-products and product-of-means types of control-resources, control-control and resources-resources interaction properties – 30 variables that describe changes in interaction properties are added to 15 variables that describe basic properties – the explained proportion of the variance in the change in crime increases to 32 per cent (see the second column in Table 5.3). The values of the coefficients for the changes in several basic properties change. For example, the coefficient for the change in FORGN obtains a much

**Table 5.3     Explaining C90 – C85 with changes in independent properties, including interaction properties. Linear regression analysis. All variables standardized. For all 83 areas**

| Independent prop. | (1) | (2) | (3) | (4) | (5) |
|---|---|---|---|---|---|
| *Age and sex* | | | | | |
| YNGMALE | .11 | .37 | −.22 | −.06 | −.05 |
| YNGFEML | −.21 | −.36 | −.11 | −.26 | −.18 |
| MDLMALE | .16 | .23 | .16 | .14 | .04 |
| MDLFEML | −.03 | .20 | .62 | .27 | .07 |
| OLDMALE | .31 | .40 | .46 | .30 | .33 |
| OLDFEML | −.15 | .41 | .33 | −.01 | .00 |
| | | | | | |
| *Social control* | | | | | |
| FORGN | .24 | 1.36 | .49 | .32 | 1.00 |
| SINGLE | −.03 | −.17 | .46 | −.28 | .09 |
| DIVOR | −.03 | −.06 | −.23 | −.23 | .02 |
| | | | | | |
| *Social resources* | | | | | |
| INCMULT | −.10 | −.02 | .14 | .07 | −.10 |
| SOCAID | −.10 | .13 | .58 | .22 | −.23 |
| OCCDICH | .09 | −1.36 | −.65 | .05 | −1.35 |
| | | | | | |
| *Dwelling environment* | | | | | |
| MULTHS | .03 | .16 | −.02 | .08 | .03 |
| PUBLIC | −.08 | −.14 | −.13 | −.09 | −.09 |
| OVERCR | .29 | .31 | .42 | .30 | .34 |
| | | | | | |
| *Interaction* | | | | | |
| Contr.*Res. (9 vars.) | - | .11 | .02 | .05 | - |
| CONTR.*RES. (9 vars.) | - | −.15 | −.10 | - | −.02 |
| Contr.*Contr. (3 vars.) | - | −.02 | .01 | .04 | - |
| CONTR.*CONTR. (3 vars.) | - | −.10 | −.20 | - | −.43 |
| Res.*Res. (3 vars) | - | −.09 | −.03 | −.16 | - |
| RES.*RES. (3 vars.) | - | .51 | .10 | - | .46 |
| Forgn*Yngmale | - | - | 1.05 | .89 | - |
| FORGN*YNGMALE | - | - | .08 | - | .17 |
| | | | | | |
| Expl. proportion of variance (corr.) | .19 | .32 | .53 | .45 | .31 |

higher value, while the coefficient for the change in OCCDICH obtains a much lower value. However, the absolute values of the weights for these two variables are unrealistically high.

The average value of the coefficients for the changes in the control-resources mean-of-products properties is 0.11 in the second model, and this indicates that this type of interaction on the average had, as expected, a positive effect on crime. This contrasts with the coefficient values obtained for the control-resources product-of-means variables, for which the average is –0.15, which unexpectedly indicates that this type of interaction on the average had a negative effect on crime.

The average coefficient values found in the second column for the control-control and resources-resources mean-of-products variables are negative. Of the average coefficient values found for the corresponding product-of-means variables, the one for control-control interaction is negative, while the one for resources-resources interaction has a positive, very high value.

The second model has given indications that it is more likely that crime is influenced in an expected way by mean-of-products than by product-of-means interaction between control and resources, and it has also given indications that there is interaction of product-of-means type between different social resources. However, the coefficients obtained for the changes in a couple of basic properties are unrealistic.

The analysis of the influence of changes in the sets of interaction properties has given some interesting but tentative results, and one may ask whether changes in the interaction between other properties than the ones considered so far have explanatory power. It seems that this is the case with the interaction between a control and an age/sex property. It is the question of the property of being a foreign citizen (Forgn) and the property of being a young male (Yngmale). The changes in the two types of aggregated interaction between these properties will now be included in the analysis. These kinds of interaction, which were not used in cross-sectional analysis, are particularly interesting to use in an analysis of change data, since the percentage of foreigners increased much in many areas during the period of time studied (it may be mentioned here that the increase of the percentage of foreigners and the influence on crime exercised by young male foreigners are issues that have been much discussed in Sweden). Interaction between the two properties may arise for several reasons, for example due to the fact that young male foreigners are particularly inclined to feel that they are unjustly treated in society because they are discriminated against and because they have poor resources.

The changes during the first period of time in the two interaction properties M(Forgn*Yngmale) and FORGN*YNGMALE have been added as regressors to the previously used change variables. Results of the analyses are shown in the third column in Table 5.3. It is clear from the figures of the second and third columns that adding the two new variables has meant a radical change for the explanation of the change in crime. The new model explains 53 per cent of the variance in this change, that is, 21 percentages more than does the former model. The change in M(Forgn*Yngmale) has got the surprisingly high coefficient value of 1.05, while the coefficient of the change in FORGN*YNGMALE has got the much lower value of 0.08. The addition of the two new variables has changed the coefficient values of several of the other variables. For example, it has reduced the absolute values of the averages of the coefficients of the changes in mean-of-products properties so strongly that these are almost zero. Furthermore, it has reduced the average value of the coefficients of the changes in the product-of-means properties for resources-resources interaction so that it now has the more modest value of .10, and it has reduced the absolute values of the coefficients of the changes in the FORGN and OCCDICH properties so that they have become more realistic. However, the average coefficient values of the changes in product-of-means properties for control-resources and control-control interaction are still negative, giving no indication of an influence of interaction of hypothesized types.

The facts that the change in M(Forgn*Yngmale) obtains a high coefficient value and that using it strongly reduces the absolute values of the averages of the coefficients of the changes in other mean-of-products properties indicate, of course, that this variable is important. This importance is further supported by the following facts. Adding only the change in M(Forgn*Yngmale) and the changes in the other mean-of-products properties as regressors increases the explained proportion of the variance in the change in crime much more than adding only the changes in the corresponding product-of-means properties (the increases are 26 and 12 per cent; see the first, fourth and fifth columns in Table 5.3). However, when not including the changes in the two Forgn-Yngmale interaction properties, adding the changes in the other mean-of-products properties increases the explained proportion of the variance in the change in crime less than adding the changes in the other product-of-means properties (8 versus 13 per cent; not shown in tabular form). Thus, the mean-of-products Forgn-Yngmale property seems to have great importance for the explanation of the change in crime.

This does not mean, however, that adding only the change in the M(Forgn*Yngmale) property to the changes in the basic properties improves the explanation of the change in crime in a similarly substantial way. It turns out that doing so only increases the explained proportion of the variance in the change in crime by six per cent to about 25 per cent. Thus, it is when the change in the Forgn-Yngmale mean-of-products property is used together with the changes in other mean-of-products properties that the explanation is extraordinarily improved.

So far, I have shown what happens when variables that describe changes in interaction properties are added as regressors to variables that describe changes in basic properties. Obviously, changes in interaction properties have unique explanatory power. But how unique is this power? Could we manage with these properties alone? How well could we explain the change in crime if we only use the variables that describe changes in interaction properties as regressors?

Rather well is the answer. Using the changes in all mentioned interaction variables of mean-of-products and product-of-means types – thus including the changes in M(Forgn*Yngmale) and FORGN*YNGMALE – 47 per cent of the variance in the change in crime is explained. Again, the average coefficient of the changes in the control-resources mean-of-products variables is positive, while the average coefficient of the changes in the corresponding product-of-means variables is negative. The coefficient of the change in the Forgn-Yngmale mean-of-products variable has a high positive value. Furthermore, using as regressors the changes in all the mean-of-products properties, thus again including the change in the Forgn-Yngmale interaction property, but not considering changes in any basic property, yields the explained proportion of 34 per cent of the variance in the change in crime. When doing correspondingly with the changes in all the product-of-means properties, the explained proportion of the variance in the change in crime is 31 per cent. Thus, all these models comprising various sets of changes in interaction properties as regressors explain more of the variance in the change in crime than what is explained by the changes in basic properties.

In the analyses just described, no changes in basic properties are used as possible regressors. However, the interaction properties concern the social control and the social resources properties, and it may therefore be asked what will happen if only the variables that describe the changes in the basic properties of these two types are replaced as regressors by the variables that describe the changes in the interaction properties. It turns out that such a substitution, using all the changes in the mentioned interaction properties, works well. Of the variance in the change in crime, the new set of independent variables explains 56 per cent, which is thus 9 percentages more than what is explained using only the changes in the interaction variables. Again, the average coefficient value obtained for the changes in the control-resources mean-of-products properties accords fairly well with what could be expected – this value is 0.12. The average coefficient value obtained for the changes in the corresponding product-of-means properties is –0.07. The coefficient value obtained for the Forgn-Yngmale mean-of-products property is 1.01. Of the coefficients obtained for the changes in basic properties, the one pertaining to OVERCR stands out, having the value of 0.41. It may also be mentioned that when only the changes in the mean-of-products properties are substituted as regressors, 45 per cent of the variance in the change in crime is explained, whereas 27 per cent is explained when the corresponding product-of-means variables are used in this way. Also these results indicate that the changes in interaction properties are important for the change in crime, more important than are the changes in many basic properties.

Another way of examining the relative importance of the interaction properties for the explanation of crime is to perform a step-wise regression analysis of the change in crime, using the changes in all basic and in all interaction properties as possible regressors, thereby letting these variables compete with each other. This method has been applied, and the results are remarkable. Let us focus on the solution for a specific number of regressors, say the solution obtained for 10 regressors. It turns out that this solution explains 52 per cent of the variance in the change in crime. Of the regressors, only two describe changes in basic properties, six describe changes in mean-of-products properties, and two describe changes in product-of-means properties. The two regressors that describe changes in basic properties pertain to YNGFEML and OVERCR, and they have coefficients with expected signs. Of the six regressors that describe changes in mean-of-products properties, four pertain to interaction between social control and social resources (Forgn-Incdich, Single-Incdich, Single-Socaid, Single-Occdich), and the two regressors that describe changes in product-of-means properties both pertain to this type of interaction (SINGLE-SOCAID, DIVOR-SOCAID). The change in the Forgn-Yngmale mean-of-products property is one of the regressors, and its coefficient has the value of 0.66. The average value of the coefficients for the regressors that pertain to interaction of the mean-of-products type is 0.14, whereas the average value of the coefficients for the two regressors that pertain to interaction of product-of-means type is −0.04.

Thus, it is found that variables that describe changes in interaction properties play a very important role as regressors in the explanation of the change in crime, that variables that describe changes in interaction of the mean-of-products type predominate, that variables that describe interaction between social control and social resources play a very important role among these, and that the coefficient values for the regressors that describe interaction of mean-of-products type are on the average higher than the coefficient values for the regressors that describe interaction of the product-of-means type. Consequently, the results support the idea that crime is strongly affected by interaction of the mean-of-products type in which social control and/or social resources properties are involved, but they do not give equally much support for the idea that interaction of the product-of-means type involving these properties affects crime. These conclusions are based on results that pertain to only one solution obtained in a step-wise regression analysis. However, other solutions from the analysis have been examined, and the conclusions to be drawn from them are largely the same.

The analyses hitherto made refer only to data of the first period. Since interaction properties that are based on data on social aid or on occupational status can only be constructed for this period, no temporally extended analyses using a full set of interaction properties can be made. However, for the other mentioned interaction properties values for the second and higher periods can be constructed. This is the case with the M(Forgn*Yngmale) property, and I have used such values in order to get some indication of how the changes in this property effect crime. I have analyzed the change in crime 1985–1990 using the changes during three five-year periods (at most) in basic properties and the changes during the same periods in the interaction property. It turns out that the coefficients obtained indicate that the current change in the interaction property has a very strong, positive effect on the change in crime, whereas previous changes in this property have only very weak effects (figures not shown). Admittedly, however, the conditions for this analysis are not very advantageous.

The reason that interaction of the mean-of-products type between the foreign and young-male statuses is important in the short but not in the long run could be that young foreigners are only transitorily poorly controlled – being young implies that this is the case.

To summarize the results of the analyses discussed in this section, it must first be said that they have limited scope. They only concern the linearly analyzed changes in some interaction properties of the mean-of-products and product-of-means types, and almost all of them pertain only to the period of 1985–1990. Nevertheless, the results obtained are interesting because they suggest that crime is affected by micro-level interaction of a type that cannot be expressed in common macro-level terms often used in criminological research, but must be expressed as means of micro-level products. As shown – and this is no surprise of course – including changes in such means in the analysis can affect radically the found effects of changes in basic properties.

Thus, causally interpreted, the analyses using interaction variables indicate that interaction of the mean-of-products type tends to have a more positive effect on crime than has corresponding interaction of the product-of-means type. Furthermore, there are indications that interaction of the product-of-means type between different social resources properties tends to have a more positive effect on crime than has corresponding interaction of mean-of-products type, while the opposite relation is found between the effects of corresponding types of interaction between social control properties. One may speculate about the reason for these latter different relations. Could it be that the resources generally play a more important role in social relations of extra-family type than do the control properties? Anyhow, the most striking result is the very strong positive effect found for the change in M(Forgn*Yngmale), a finding that seems possible to reconcile with the theoretical perspective applied in this study, which emphasizes the influence on crime exerted by social control factors in particular but also by social resources.

The possibility that there may be micro-level interaction that cannot be expressed in the type of macro-level terms often used in criminological research is of great interest when evaluating the attempts made in this study to model crime and the change in crime. It is possible that in order to model crime perfectly small segments of the residential population must be considered separately. The effects found for various types of mean-of-products interaction properties imply that individuals who have particular combinations of values of such properties and who therefore form segments of the population, in several cases very small segments, affect crime particularly strongly when the size of their segment is considered. However, this does not necessarily mean that the basic ideas upon which this study is founded – the ideas about the significance of social control and of social resources – are wrong, only that they should be applied in an individualistic fashion to small segments of the population, and that these segmental applications are then to be aggregated in order to yield a complete explanation of crime. Thus, the difficulties to explain crime perfectly could, to a great extent at least, be due to within-individual interaction.

One rationale for the analyses reported in this section was the problem with analyzing the relative influence on crime of basic properties and of interaction properties using cross-sectional data. In such data, these properties are so strongly correlated that it is difficult or impossible to separate the influences. It was argued that this problem might be managed in two ways: 1) to use change data on the properties, because correlations would then be weaker, and 2) to analyze the influences for long-term residents and for newcomers, because the conditions for social interaction differ for these two groups of residents. The first method has now been used, and the findings indicate that micro-level interaction of the within-individual type matters much. However, the second method remains to be used. Before I do that, however, I will turn to another task – to analyze crime longitudinally using product models.

**Product Models of Point Data on Crime**

Point data on crime will now be analyzed longitudinally with product models (later, changes in crime will be analyzed with such models). Crime is then seen as a function of independent properties at the current point and an earlier point in time. Still earlier points will not be considered because of the identification problems that will then arise.

When constructing the longitudinal product models, the question of whether there is interaction between values of independent properties at different points in time must be addressed. I assume that interaction works only between properties of the same point. Therefore, in constructing these models, expressions including properties of different points will be added to one another. The general product model of the crime factor at the current point $t$ in time, which is a function of properties at $t$ and the previous point $t-1$, is formalized as follows:

$$C_t = d_t(A_t S_t R_t H_t + A_{t-1} S_{t-1} R_{t-1} H_{t-1} - 1). \qquad (17)$$

The parameter $d_t$ is unique for each reference year (and is as before denoted $d_{90}$ and $d_{85}$, respectively, for the two reference years of 1990 and 1985). As mentioned, it is affected by the relation between actual and registered/measured crime. This relation may vary with time due to the activities of the legal authorities and the general public. On the right-hand side of (17), $-1$ is entered in order to balance for the fact that the other terms within the parenthesis add to 2 when there is no influence on crime.

Product models constructed according to (17) do not have a pure product form, and this means that carrying out analyses with standardized independent variables cannot be expected to yield exactly the same explanation of crime as carrying out these analyses with normalized independent variables. In the analyses performed, normalized independent variables are used.

Below, I describe two versions of (17), corresponding to Product Models I and II. In these versions it is assumed that there are properties SOCAID and OCCDICH that can be used for both points in time, and that the factors $A_t$ and $A_{t-1}$ are unique. However, in empirical analyses described below the current value of the age/sex factor will be used for the previous point of time of this factor, unless it turns out that using unique factors increases the explained variance in crime substantially.

In Model I, factors are functions of properties according to:

$$
\begin{aligned}
A_t &= b_{11}\text{YNGMALE}_t + b_{12}\text{YNGFEML}_t + b_{13}\text{MDLMALE}_t \\
&\quad + b_{14}\text{MDLFEML}_t + b_{15}\text{OLDMALE}_t + b_{16}\text{OLDFEML}_t + 1; \\
S_t &= b_{21}\text{FORGN}_t + b_{22}\text{SINGLE}_t + b_{23}\text{DIVOR}_t + 1; \\
R_t &= b_{31}\text{INCMULT}_t + b_{32}\text{SOCAID}_t + b_{33}\text{OCCDICH}_t + 1; \\
H_t &= b_{41}\text{MULTHS}_t + b_{42}\text{PUBLIC}_t + b_{43}\text{OVERCR}_t + 1; \\
A_{t-1} &= b_{51}\text{YNGMALE}_{t-1} + b_{52}\text{YNGFEML}_{t-1} + b_{53}\text{MDLMALE}_{t-1} \\
&\quad + b_{54}\text{MDLFEML}_{t-1} + b_{55}\text{OLDMALE}_{t-1} + b_{56}\text{OLDFEML}_{t-1} + 1; \\
S_{t-1} &= b_{61}\text{FORGN}_{t-1} + b_{62}\text{SINGLE}_{t-1} + b_{63}\text{DIVOR}_{t-1} + 1; \\
R_{t-1} &= b_{71}\text{INCMULT}_{t-1} + b_{72}\text{SOCAID}_{t-1} + b_{73}\text{OCCDICH}_{t-1} + 1; \\
H_{t-1} &= b_{81}\text{MULTHS}_{t-1} + b_{82}\text{PUBLIC}_{t-1} + b_{83}\text{OVERCR}_{t-1} + 1 .
\end{aligned}
\tag{18}
$$

In Model II:

$$
\begin{aligned}
A_t &= b_{11}\text{YNGMALE}_t + b_{12}\text{YNGFEML}_t + b_{13}\text{MDLMALE}_t \\
&\quad + b_{14}\text{MDLFEML}_t + b_{15}\text{OLDMALE}_t + b_{16}\text{OLDFEML}_t + 1; \\
S_t &= (b_{21}\text{FORGN}_t + 1)(b_{22}\text{SINGLE}_t + 1)(b_{23}\text{DIVOR}_t + 1); \\
R_t &= (b_{31}\text{INCMULT}_t + 1)(b_{32}\text{SOCAID}_t + 1)(b_{33}\text{OCCDICH}_t + 1); \\
H_t &= (b_{41}\text{MULTHS}_t + 1)(b_{42}\text{PUBLIC}_t + 1)(b_{43}\text{OVERCR}_t + 1); \\
A_{t-1} &= b_{51}\text{YNGMALE}_{t-1} + b_{52}\text{YNGFEML}_{t-1} + b_{53}\text{MDLMALE}_{t-1} \\
&\quad + b_{54}\text{MDLFEML}_{t-1} + b_{55}\text{OLDMALE}_{t-1} + b_{56}\text{OLDFEML}_{t-1} + 1; \\
S_{t-1} &= (b_{61}\text{FORGN}_{t-1} + 1)(b_{62}\text{SINGLE}_{t-1} + 1)(b_{63}\text{DIVOR}_{t-1} + 1); \\
R_{t-1} &= (b_{71}\text{INCMULT}_{t-1} + 1)(b_{72}\text{SOCAID}_{t-1} + 1)(b_{73}\text{OCCDICH}_{t-1} + 1); \\
H_{t-1} &= (b_{81}\text{MULTHS}_{t-1} + 1)(b_{82}\text{PUBLIC}_{t-1} + 1)(b_{83}\text{OVERCR}_{t-1} + 1) .
\end{aligned}
\tag{19}
$$

The two types of models have been used for analyzing C90 and C90/C85. No simultaneous analysis is made of C90, C85 and C80, since data are then too much lacking on the independent properties SOCAID and OCCDICH.

The lack of data on SOCAID and OCCDICH for 1980 and earlier points in time is a problem in the longitudinal analyses using product models, because in these models other independent properties can be assumed to interact with these two properties. If data on SOCAID and OCCDICH are not used for some year or years, the influences from different years are not modeled in the same way, and coefficients are difficult to interpret. This problem does not exist for the analysis of C90 using data on independent properties for 1990 and 1985, but it does exist for all other longitudinal analyses. It has been handled by substituting lacking data with data on the properties for the latest possible year. It should be noted that when filling data are used in a product model, more coefficients are used than in the corresponding linear model. Coefficients for filling data are written in italic in the tables.

Results from the analyses of C90 are shown in Table 5.4, and results from the analyses of C90/C85 are shown in Table 5.5. As in the corresponding analyses of cross-sectional data, zeros have been used as initial values of all coefficients except $d_{90}$ and $d_{85}$, which have been given the mean values of the crime factor as initial values. The reported explained proportions of variance are uncorrected for lost degrees of freedom. Also shown are the explained proportions of variance for corresponding linear models (when C90/C85 is analyzed, a dummy variable indicating the reference year is used in the linear analysis). Of course, no guarantee can be given that the product models obtained are the ones that explain most of the variance in crime. The large number of coefficients and the strong relationships between independent properties can be expected to make it difficult to identify these models. However, the models obtained are interesting, since they say something about the explanatory power of specified causal structures of product types.

Table 5.4 reports results from analyses of C90 using independent properties for 1990 and 1985 and for 1990 and 1980. In both cases, figures for Model I and Model II are reported. Looking at the figures of the models built on independent data for 1990 and 1985, we find that the two product models explain about the same proportion of the variance in crime and that they explain slightly more of this variance than what is explained by the corresponding linear model. Several of the coefficient values obtained are rather similar in a relative sense to the coefficient values obtained in the linear analysis (as to an approximately corresponding linear analysis, see Table 5.1). This is the case, for example, with the social control properties of FORGN and DIVOR. Interpreting coefficients causally, according to the product models FORGN seems to have a positive quick effect and a negative delayed effect on crime. DIVOR has a relatively strong delayed effect that is positive. Similar effects are found in the linear analysis. Also when it comes to the social resources variables there are similarities. It has been found again that SOCAID has a delayed and OCCDICH a quick positive effect. As to the age/sex variables, it has been found again for most of the age categories that the coefficient for the women is more negative than the coefficient for the men.

However, there are also differences when comparing the coefficients obtained for the product models built on independent data for 1990 and 1985 with the coefficients obtained for the corresponding linear model. For example, the coefficients for most of the age/sex properties have gotten values that are much smaller in absolute and relative senses in the product models than in the linear model. This makes them more realistic, one may think. Also with respect to the values of other independent properties, the coefficients in the product models seem to be more realistic.

**Table 5.4** **Explaining C90 with product models and point data on independent properties (n=83). Independent variables normalized**

| Independent property | Model I | | Model II | | Model I | | Model II | |
|---|---|---|---|---|---|---|---|---|
| | 1990 | 1985 | 1990 | 1985 | 1990 | 1980 | 1990 | 1980 |
| *Age and sex* | | | | | | | | |
| YNGMALE | .02 | - | .02 | - | .03 | - | .03 | - |
| YNGFEML | −.03 | - | −.06 | - | −.03 | - | −.04 | - |
| MDLMALE | −.01 | - | −.04 | - | −.02 | - | −.04 | - |
| MDLFEML | −.03 | - | −.01 | - | −.00 | - | −.01 | - |
| OLDMALE | .07 | - | .08 | - | .07 | - | .04 | - |
| OLDFEML | −.16 | - | −.17 | - | −.14 | - | −.15 | - |
| *Social control* | | | | | | | | |
| FORGN | .26 | −.47 | .29 | −.28 | .16 | −.28 | .21 | −.33 |
| SINGLE | −.12 | .06 | .12 | −.13 | −.18 | .05 | −.16 | −.09 |
| DIVOR | −.04 | .23 | −.04 | .25 | .11 | .09 | .13 | .18 |
| *Social resources* | | | | | | | | |
| INCMULT | −.20 | .17 | .09 | .01 | .03 | −.06 | .10 | −.07 |
| SOCAID | −.01 | .30 | .06 | .26 | −.03 | *.23* | .03 | *.19* |
| OCCDICH | .18 | .08 | .16 | .14 | .27 | *−.09* | .32 | *−.11* |
| *Dwelling envir.* | | | | | | | | |
| MULTHS | .01 | −.07 | −.23 | .10 | .22 | −.17 | .19 | −.10 |
| PUBLIC | .04 | −.06 | .10 | −.08 | −.13 | .12 | −.09 | .08 |
| OVERCR | .06 | −.01 | .03 | .00 | .18 | −.05 | .18 | −.07 |
| $d_{90}$ | 2.74 | | 2.48 | | 3.11 | | 3.07 | |
| Expl. proportion of variance (uncorr.), figure for lin. model within parenthesis | .94 (.93) | | .94 (.93) | | .94 (.93) | | .95 (.93) | |

Turning next to the coefficient values obtained when applying Models I and II to the independent data for 1990 and 1980, we find some differences compared to what was found in the previous analysis of the data for 1990 and 1985. One difference is that DIVOR now has a positive quick effect, that the difference between the quick and delayed effects of OCCDICH is now more pronounced and that MULTHS now has a quick effect that is positive and relatively strong. However, the coefficients of FORGN and SOCAID are rather similar to what was found in the previous analysis.

In analyzing C90 and C85 simultaneously, age/sex properties for two points in time have been considered – the current point and the point five years earlier. In this analysis, many of the findings obtained when analyzing C90 recur, as can be seen in Table 5.5. Again, the two product models explain about the same amount of the variance in crime and slightly more than what is explained by the corresponding linear model. Below, I comment briefly on the coefficient values obtained, interpreting them causally.

Regarding the control properties, coefficient values indicate that FORGN has a quick positive effect on crime and a delayed negative effect that is almost as strong. DIVOR has a delayed effect after five years that is positive and relatively strong. The quick effect of SINGLE is negative and the delayed effect positive. As to the social resources properties, OCCDICH has a positive quick effect, INCMULT a positive quick effect and a negative delayed effect, and SOCAID a positive delayed effect. For the dwelling environment properties, the differences between the quick and the delayed effects are small. All effects of OVERCR are positive. The quick and delayed effects of the separate age/sex properties do not differ much in most cases, the quick effect of OLDFEML being an exception. The effects of the proportions of females in the population are consistently more negative/less positive than the effects of the corresponding proportions of males. It is found that $d_{90}$ has a somewhat higher value than $d_{85}$ for both models.

Summarizing and interpreting the results obtained when analyzing point data on crime with product models and using independent data for two points in time, it can be said 1) that it has been found without exception that FORGN has a positive quick effect and a delayed negative effect and that these effects differ much, 2) that no consistent picture of the influences from SINGLE has been found, 3) that it has been found without exception that DIVOR has a delayed positive effect, and that this effect is relatively strong when the independent data refer to the current point in time and the point five years earlier, 4) that no consistent picture of the influences from INCMULT has been found, 5) that SOCAID has a delayed positive effect, 6) that OCCDICH has a positive quick effect, 7) that no consistent picture of the influences from MULTHS and PUBLIC has been found, 8) that the quick effect of OVERCR has in all cases been found to be positive, and 9) that the influences from the age/sex properties are mostly weak and that the influences from the proportion of women in the various

**Table 5.5**    **Explaining C90/C85 with product models and point data on independent properties (n=166). Independent variables normalized**

| Independent property | Model I | | Model II | |
|---|---|---|---|---|
| | $t$ | $t{-}1$ | $t$ | $t{-}1$ |
| *Age and sex* | | | | |
| YNGMALE | .05 | .05 | .01 | .08 |
| YNGFEML | −.13 | .04 | −.13 | .04 |
| MDLMALE | .01 | −.03 | −.03 | −.02 |
| MDLFEML | −.04 | −.11 | −.13 | −.06 |
| OLDMALE | .10 | .05 | −.01 | .09 |
| OLDFEML | −.36 | −.02 | −.54 | .06 |
| *Social control* | | | | |
| FORGN | .34 | −.28 | .34 | −.29 |
| SINGLE | −.09 | .13 | −.06 | .06 |
| DIVOR | .00 | .29 | .09 | .20 |
| *Social resources* | | | | |
| INCMULT | .09 | −.13 | .09 | −.08 |
| SOCAID | −.06 | *.20* | −.06 | *.18* |
| OCCDICH | .16 | −.08 | .14 | −.05 |
| *Dwelling environment* | | | | |
| MULTHS | .01 | −.06 | −.04 | .01 |
| PUBLIC | −.03 | .04 | −.02 | .04 |
| OVERCR | .03 | .08 | .06 | .07 |
| $d_{90}$ | 2.56 | | 2.67 | |
| $d_{85}$ | 2.42 | | 2.40 | |
| Expl. proportion of variance (uncorr.), figure for linear model within parenthesis | .91 (.89) | | .91 (.89) | |

age categories as a rule are more negative/less positive than the influences from the proportion of men of corresponding ages. These conclusions are rather similar to the conclusions drawn from the linear analyses.

## Product Models of the Change in Crime

As discussed above, conditions are inappropriate for analyzing changes in crime using product models and change data for independent properties. Nevertheless, it is possible to analyze changes in crime with product models if point data for independent properties is used. The change in crime between two points in time may be modeled as follows with data on independent factors for the current and the previous point in time:

$$C_t - C_{t-1} = d_t (A_t S_t R_t H_t + A_{t-1} S_{t-1} R_{t-1} H_{t-1} - 1)$$
$$- d_{t-1} (A_{t-1} S_{t-1} R_{t-1} H_{t-1} + A_{t-2} S_{t-2} R_{t-2} H_{t-2} - 1), \tag{20}$$

where the parameters $d_t$ and $d_{t-1}$ are unique for each reference year. However, finding the structure for such models of the change in crime is more difficult than finding the structure for product models of point data on crime. One reason for this is that the models of the change in crime are more complicated formally. Another reason is that non-valid components play a greater role for the change in crime than for crime at a point in time. Taking the difference between strongly correlated crime values at two points in time means that much of the valid components of the crime measurements vanishes, and that non-valid components therefore play an important role for the difference.

When analyzing the change in crime under these conditions, it may of course be difficult to find an adequate product model. This has also turned out to be the case when analyzing the changes C90−C85 and C90−C85/C85−C80, using Models I and II and data on independent properties for two points in time. These analyses have not been very successful. The analyses of the change C90−C85 may be taken as an example. In these analyses only current values of age/sex properties have been used. For SOCAID and OCCDICH, the lacking data of 1980 have been substituted by the 1985 values. Various types of initial values have been used, including the same ones as before. The models obtained explain relatively much of the variance in the dependent variable, much more than what is explained by the corresponding linear model. However, for both Models I and II, the solutions obtained include extreme, unrealistic coefficient values (figures not shown).

The difficulties in finding an adequate product model can be expected to be due to some extent to the fact that this type of model does not describe aggregated effects of within-individual interaction. Thus, if mean-of-products properties were included in the analysis, they could be expected to improve the explanation of the change in crime. This idea has been tested, by adding to the product models a linear expression of the standardized versions of the changes in the nine previously used control-resources interaction properties of mean-of-products type and the standardized version of the change in the Forgn-Yngmale interaction property of the same type. Zeros have been used as initial values of the coefficients of the terms of this expression as well as of the other coefficients except the $d$ coefficients for which the mean crime values have been used.

Admittedly, the new models then obtained have an unsophisticated character. In these models interaction of multivariate macro-level type is combined with aggregated micro-level interaction of bivariate mean-of-products type, which does not fit the product multivariate form very well. Furthermore, the mean-of-products variables describe changes, whereas the ordinary macro-level variables describe conditions at points in time (the changes in interaction properties are used in order to reduce the identification problems). Still further, the changes in the interaction variables only refer to the years of 1985 and 1990, while other variables refer to 1980 as well. However, despite these shortcomings, this analysis may still give an idea of whether mean-of-products interaction plays a role for the change in crime beyond the role played by macro-level multivariate interaction.

The results of the analyses performed seem to support the idea that micro-level interaction of within-individual type does play such a role (figures not shown). Solutions have been obtained that yield high explained proportions of the variance in the change in crime. The most striking results are obtained for the modified version of Model I. This solution explains 79 per cent of the variance in the dependent variable (uncorrected value; for the modified version of Model II, the corresponding value is 74 per cent). The corresponding value when using the changes in the basic independent variables and in the interaction properties in a linear model is 68 per cent. In Model I, the value of the coefficient of the change in the Forgn-Yngmale mean-of-products property is 0.74, which is very high considering that the change in crime has the standard deviation of 0.72. The average coefficient value for the nine control-resources mean-of-products variables is 0.06. However, the average coefficient value of the changes in the six control-resources mean-of-products properties that do not pertain to Forgn and that are thus not very similar to the variable that describes the change in the Forgn-Yngmale mean-of-products property is 0.22, indicating a substantial positive influence on crime. The coefficients of the variables in the product part of the model have values that are not quite realistic. However, despite this and other shortcomings, the conclusion to be drawn from the analysis seems to be that the results indicate that interaction of mean-of-products type plays a role for the change in crime that goes beyond the role played by macro-level multivariate interaction. The results of the analyses using a modified version of Model II are of a similar kind.

The methods of analyzing the change in crime discussed above pertain to periods of time of five years. However, if periods of time of ten years are used instead, the change in crime can be assumed to be less affected by temporally unique factors, and it can be expected to be easier to find the model structure of the change. This method has been applied. Thus, the changes $C90 - C80$ has been analyzed with product models of the two types. As before, zeros have been used as initial values of the coefficients for the independent properties, and the mean values of C90 and C80 have been used as initial values of the $d$ coefficients. Results are presented in Table 5.6.

The explained proportions of the variance in crime that are obtained in the analyses using the two models – these proportions are 58 and 57 per cent – may be compared to the explained proportion of variance for a corresponding linear model, which is 57 per cent. The independent variables used in the linear model then refer to change data (in the linear function one constant has been used; thus, the linear model uses one parameter less than do the product models).

Looking at the figures of the two models in the table, we find that they are very similar to each other. In fact, they are so similar that it is unnecessary to make a distinction between them when interpreting the results. We also find that the coefficients for the previous point in time have lower absolute values than the coefficients for the current point for all the properties that are measured for both points, except for OVERCR. The coefficient values for FORGN and DIVOR at the current point in time stand out, relatively speaking. Causally interpreted, they mean that these properties have positive quick effects. Moreover, FORGN has a relatively weak negative effect and DIVOR a relatively weak positive effect on crime after 10 years. The SINGLE and INCMULT properties have negative effects. OVERCR has positive effects. Both MULTHS and PUBLIC have negative quick effects. The effects of the age/sex properties for the middle aged and the old residents are more positive for women than for men.

Thus, it seems that conditions that are 10 years old affect crime relatively little, and – considering the changed time perspective, which means that finer temporal effects cannot be distinguished – that the relationships found are compatible with much of what has been found in previous analyses. For example, DIVOR and FORGN seem to play roles of the types discussed above. However, it should be noted that the relationships are obtained without consideration paid to the important social resources properties of SOCAID and OCCDICH.


**The Significance of Moves**

In order to find out whether and to what extent local social processes have affected crime, longitudinal analyses have been performed of the significance of moves for the influence of changes in various properties on the change in the crime factor. The purpose of these analyses is to elucidate and to compare the influences of groups of residents with different patterns of moves. The fundamental underlying idea is as before that living in an area is a prerequisite for an individual's partaking in social processes taking place there. The approach used raises high demands of a technical nature, since the influence model applied must be used simultaneously in different structural versions for the different groups. Problems can then be expected to arise, particularly if point data is used. For this reason, I have only used change data and linear models. The change in crime 1980–1985/1985–1990

**Table 5.6** **Explaining C90 – C80 with product models and point data on independent properties (n=80). Independent variables normalized**

| Independent property | Model I | | Model II | |
|---|---|---|---|---|
| | $t$ | $t{-}1$ | $t$ | $t{-}1$ |
| *Age and sex* | | | | |
| YNGMALE | −.02 | - | −.02 | - |
| YNGFEML | −.04 | - | −.04 | - |
| MDLMALE | −.06 | - | −.05 | - |
| MDLFEML | .15 | - | .14 | - |
| OLDMALE | −.05 | - | −.07 | - |
| OLDFEML | .14 | - | .16 | - |
| *Social control* | | | | |
| FORGN | .45 | −.07 | .31 | −.05 |
| SINGLE | −.13 | −.08 | −.09 | −.02 |
| DIVOR | .45 | .10 | .43 | .11 |
| *Social resources* | | | | |
| INCMULT | −.16 | −.07 | −.12 | −.07 |
| SOCAID | - | - | - | |
| OCCDICH | - | - | - | - |
| *Dwelling environment* | | | | |
| MULTHS | −.11 | −.08 | −.10 | .04 |
| PUBLIC | −.11 | .09 | −.11 | −.05 |
| OVERCR | .09 | .13 | .08 | .14 |
| $d_{90}$ | | 2.39 | | 2.30 |
| $d_{80}$ | | 2.10 | | 2.03 |
| Expl. proportion of variance (uncorr.) | | .58 | | .57 |

or 1985–1990 is used as the dependent variable. Independent variables are the changes in properties in the same period as is used for the change in crime (the current period) and in some analyses also changes in the previous period. The independent variables are constructed as changes in the mean property values of the groups of individuals who are analyzed. These mean property values are adjusted by being multiplied by relative group size unless unadjusted data yield a better explanation of the variance in the dependent variable.

Several analyses have been made. Since the first one of the analyses reported below has traits that also characterize later analyses, I will discuss it at some length. In this analysis, I have tried to explain the change in crime 1980–1985/1985–1990 using independent data for three groups of the residents in an area. For the change in crime between 1985 and 1990, these three groups are: 1) Group A, which contains the residents who lived in the area in 1990, 1985 and 1980, but who did not live there in 1975; 2) Group B, which contains the residents who lived in the area in 1995, 1990 and 1985, but who did not live there in 1980; and 3) Group C, which contains the residents who lived in the area in 1990 or 1985, but who do not belong to any of the first two groups. The total of the residents of the three groups is equal to the population of residents living in the area in 1990 and/or 1985. For the change in crime between 1980 and 1985, corresponding groups are formed. In the total data set, Groups A and B are on average about equally large and together they cover about 25 per cent of the total number of individuals living in the studied areas at the reference points of the current period.

The purpose of the analysis is to make clear how the change in crime was affected by the changes in independent properties in the previous period. The idea is that this can be accomplished by comparing the regression coefficients of changes in properties of Groups A and B. A basic difference between these two groups is that most of the residents in Group A lived in the area during the entire previous period, while the residents in Group B did not. If local social processes affected crime, this could therefore be expected to be manifested in differences between the two groups' regression coefficients for changes during the previous period in properties indicating such processes. For social control and social resources factors involved in integration processes and in the development of groups of deviant people, these coefficients can be expected to have higher absolute values for Group A than for Group B, since a prerequisite for taking part in these processes as mentioned was, as a rule, to be at the places where the processes were enacted. If, on the other hand, the coefficients of the changes in these factors for Group B, that is, for the individuals who did not live in the area during the entire previous period, are similar to the coefficients of the corresponding changes in Group A, this can be expected to be to a great extent the result of individual-level processes or non-local social processes. Of course, there may also be quicker effects of the changes, but analyzing the relationships between previous changes in independent factors and the later change in crime gives particular advantageous possibilities of determining causal relationships.

This is thus the logic behind the idea of comparing the coefficients of the changes in the control and resources factors for the two groups (for the change in MULTHS, things are different, as explained below). However, there are complications in comparing long-term residents (individuals who lived in the area during the entire previous period) with newcomers (individuals who arrived at the area at some point in time during the previous period). The problem is that individuals who moved may have been different from those who did not move – not only regarding where they lived and how they were influenced by conditions there and how they influenced these conditions, but also regarding how they were constituted personally. It is for example possible that individuals who recently moved to an area differed from those who had lived there for a long time regarding the family situation and the intention to live there in the future. Such differences could probably affect results of the analysis in various ways. In order to avoid this problem, I have tried to make Groups A and B similar with regard to the moving aspect, and therefore I have constructed these groups so that both have moved, although not at the same time, before they came to the area. The two groups are not perfectly equal in this respect (that is impossible to accomplish), but they are much more similar than they would have been if they were selected only with regard to the information about their place of residence in the reference years defining the current and previous periods.

As mentioned, the aim of the analysis is to compare the values of Group A's and Group B's regression coefficients for the changes in independent properties during the previous period. Other changes in independent properties for Group A and B and all changes in independent properties for Group C are included in the analysis because they may have affected the change in crime, but focus is not on the influences of these changes. It should be noted that both Group A and Group B only contain individuals who are assumed to have resided in the area during the entire current period, whereas the same is not the case with Group C. Group C is made up to a great extent, although not exclusively, of individuals who resided in the area in one of the years of 1985 and 1990 or in one of the years of 1980 and 1985, but who did not reside there both years. For the current period, the properties of Group C for these years are calculated only for the members who resided in the area, that is, data for the different years used to calculate a change refer to a great extent to different individuals. For the previous period, a change for Group C is constructed as a weighted mean of the changes of the same subgroup members.

The fact that the data for different points in time refer to the same individuals in each of Groups A and B, but do not do that for the current period in Group C implies that the measures of the changes during the current period in the independent properties must be used with care in comparisons between the groups. In the first analysis reported below, there is no comparison of regression coefficients for Group C and the matter is then of no interest. However, in a later analysis a corresponding comparison problem will turn up.

To explain the matter, let us take SOCAID as an example. The individual-level property Socaid measures the reception of social aid of the individual's household.

This factor is certainly strongly related to various historical background factors that may have affected the individual's influence on crime. People who belong to households that have received social aid tend to have another background than people who do not belong to such households. Socaid may therefore be seen as a function, assumably a linear function approximately, of this background and of other independent factors, for example the current economic situation. Suppose that we take the difference for an individual between the values on Socaid at two points in time. For this individual, there will be no difference in such social background between these points. However, the same is not true when taking the difference between Socaid at one point in time for one individual and Socaid at another point in time for another individual. Then, the difference in Socaid will to some extent also be accompanied by a difference in social background. These differences will turn up on the aggregate level. Hence, for Groups A and B, the change in SOCAID will not be accompanied by any change in background factors, while for Group C the change in SOCAID during the current period will be accompanied by a change in these factors – something that may make it difficult to compare the groups as to the causal relationship between the change in Socaid and the change in crime.

It should also be noted that for Groups A and B changes in some properties can only go in a certain direction, while the same is not true for Group C. This is the case for the age/sex properties and for FORGN. The residents of Groups A and B have only been older with time, not younger, and they may have changed from foreign to Swedish citizenship, but they have certainly almost never changed the other way around. However, the same is not true when changes are described for some residents at a certain point in time and some other residents at another point in time, as for Group C and the current period.

In analyzing the influence exerted by the three groups on the change in crime 1980–1985/1985–1990, the independent properties are used in normalized versions. A dummy variable indicating the time position of the data is included. Only changes in the current period are used for the age/sex properties. Many independent variables are used, 61 in total, which of course means an extraordinary consumption of the 165 degrees of freedom available. Data for the three groups have not been adjusted for relative group size, since analyzing non-adjusted data has turned out to explain more of the variance in the difference in crime. The explained proportion of this variance is only 17 per cent after correction for lost degrees of freedom (the uncorrected value is 48 per cent).

I do not report the coefficient values obtained in tabular form, but only discuss them in the running text. Before I do so, a word of caution regarding the credibility of these values is in place. Certainly, much confidence cannot be attached to single coefficient values obtained in a regression analysis involving 61 regressors, several of which describe the same types of properties for different subgroup of residents, an analysis which moreover is based on a model that only explain a minor part of the variance in the dependent variable and that cannot be expected to have the exactly true form. However, the total picture of how several of these coefficients for the two groups compare with each other can be more trusted and is therefore of some interest.

I discuss the coefficients for the social control properties, INCMULT (the only social resources property in this analysis) and the dwelling environment properties only. It is found that the coefficient for the change in FORGN during the previous period for the long-term residents is 0.23 (the value for standardized variables is 0.13), while it is −0.31 (−0.18) for the newcomers. This means that getting a Swedish citizenship in the previous period for foreigners who are long-term residents is negatively related to the change in crime, while getting such a citizenship for foreigners who are newcomers is positively related to the change in crime. The reason could perhaps be that social integration worked better for the long-term residents than for the newcomers, something that could be due to the fact that a local social process among long-term residents affected crime.

For the change in SINGLE during the previous period, the coefficient for the long-term residents is −0.17 (−0.09), while it is −0.03 (−0.04) for the newcomers. For the change in DIVOR the corresponding coefficient for the long-term residents is 0.21 (0.11), while it is −0.11 (−0.12) for the newcomers. The coefficient values for the change in SINGLE do not mean that living with a single parent meant a positive influence on crime, and comparing them may therefore be irrelevant. For the change in DIVOR the reason for the difference in coefficients could perhaps be that divorce due to local processes often meant a degradation of social relations for the long-term residents, while the divorced newcomers had left much of such problems behind them when moving to the new area. This explanation is compatible with the idea that a local social process affected crime.

For the change in INCMULT during the previous period the coefficient for the long-term residents is −0.00 (−0.00), while it is 0.03 (0.03) for the newcomers. Thus, there are practically no relationships. It might have been thought that long-term residents were more involved in processes in which economic resources decreased crime, which would have given rise to a difference between the relationships. Thus, the hypothesis that there was a local social process involving INCMULT is contradicted.

For the change in MULTHS during the previous period the coefficient for the long-term residents is 0.33 (0.04), while it is 0.54 (0.78) for the newcomers. For the change in PUBLIC the corresponding coefficients are 0.11 (0.03) and −0.23 (−0.30), while they are 0.27 (0.19) and 0.03 (0.06) for the change in OVERCR. Thus, it seems that moving to a multi-family house affected crime positively and more strongly for the newcomers than for the long-term residents (the difference in relationship is much larger for the standardized than for the normalized version of the MULTHS property, reflecting the fact that the change in MULTHS varied much more for the newcomers than for the long-term residents). An explanation of this could perhaps be that the newcomers kept their anonymity when moving to a multi-family house and therefore were less involved in social integration processes in the area. Thus, the finding could be due to the influence of local social processes. For PUBLIC and OVERCR the more positive relationships for the long-term residents could possibly to some extent be a result of local social processes, in which contacts between people who were poorly controlled or who had poor social resources led to more crime, although this is a more uncertain explanation.

It is not possible to draw any definite conclusion about the validity of the hypothesis about the influence of local social processes from the results of the comparison of the relationships for the two groups of residents. However, relatively many findings are compatible with the hypothesis. Clearly, the idea of the importance of local social processes among the long-term residents cannot be ruled out on the basis of these results.

In the analysis just described many residents were not considered in any comparison because they did not live in the studied area during the entire current period. Thus, there was a substantial flow of individuals into and out of areas. In analyzing the influences on the change in crime for different groups of residents, these individuals may be interesting to consider, because they cannot have been involved to any great degree in local social processes involving contacts with residents and taking some time. It was not possible to consider them separately in the previous analysis, because this would have required the use of more groups of residents, leading to absurd overparameterization of the explanatory model. However, I will now consider them by using another model, in which only two groups of residents are included.

These groups are defined with respect to whether their members lived in the area at the two reference points of time used for measuring the change in crime. One of the groups, Group D, contains those residents who lived in the area at both points of time, and the other group, Group E, contains the residents who lived in the area at only one of these points. Thus, these two groups have no member in common and the total of the residents of them is equal to the population of residents living in the area at the first and/or the second of the points of time. The aim is now to analyze how the changes in independent properties during the current period are related to the change in crime during the same period for residents of the two groups, that is, to compare what can be assumed to be the quick effects on crime in the groups. For Group E, the change in an independent property is then calculated as the difference between the mean of the property for the members living in the area at the latest point in time and the mean of the property for the members living in the area at the previous point in time.

For the members of Group D, the relationships between the changes in independent properties and the change in crime may have been affected by several kinds of mechanisms: social processes within the area, social processes outside the area, individual-level processes, and, to some extent, geographical selection processes (because the members may have been locked up in their areas). But how is it with the corresponding relationships for Group E? The members of this group moved to or out of the area and they were thus, it may be assumed, particularly strongly subjected to geographical selection processes. They were of course also affected by individual-level processes. But did these individuals affect crime through social processes?

The answer is that they can have done that to some extent, but that their possibilities of affecting crime through social processes that involve contacts with residents and that take some time were obviously more restricted than were the corresponding possibilities of the members of Group D. No doubt, the possibilities of taking part in such social processes in the area were much greater for individuals who lived there the whole considered period of time than for individuals who lived there only a part of the period. Also with respect to social processes involving people in other places in the city or outside the city, there may have been differences between the groups, since some members of Group E may have come from outside the city and since the fact that the members of this group relocated may have meant that they had social relations impaired. Therefore, the relationships for Group E should express the result of social processes of the mentioned types to a much less extent than the relationships for Group D, and it should express the result of immediate geographical selection and of moving to or out of areas to a higher extent, whereas the influence of several individual-level, nonsocial processes can be assumed to be similar for the two groups. Hence, by comparing the relationships for the two groups we may draw conclusions about the roles that social processes and geographical selection played.

As mentioned, this type of analysis pertains only to simultaneous changes – analyzing the influence of previous changes in independent properties for Group E hardly makes much sense, because this group is made up of different individuals at different points in time. Thus, the conditions for determining causal relationships between changes in independent properties and the change in crime are not as advantageous in this analysis as they were in the previous analysis. Furthermore, there is the problem that very few individuals in Group D changed with respect to certain properties.

Two linear regression analyses are made of the influence on crime of changes in basic properties. One analysis concerns the changes in crime 1985–1990, the other the changes in crime 1980–1985 and 1985–1990 (which are simultaneously analyzed). Data are weighted by relative group size, and a special constant is used for the 1985–1990 change data in the latter analysis. Results from using normalized independent properties are reported in Table 5.7, and from using standardized change variables in Table V.iv.

Before examining the results, it should be mentioned that the mean values of several of the independent variables differ much between the two groups. For example, the moving individuals became more middle-aged, more foreign and more often members of single-headed households than the long-term residents.

Looking at Table 5.7 and focusing first on the results of the analysis of $C90 - C85/C85 - C80$, we find that the model used explains only 14 per cent (the uncorrected value is 28 per cent) of the variance in the dependent variable. The intercept of the linear function is not 0, which indicates that crime is not a perfect linear function of the independent properties used. Of the variables, those of Group E explain more of crime than the Group D variables. Using only the Group E variables and correcting for lost degrees of freedom, 19 per cent of the variance in the change in crime is explained, whereas the Group D variables explain only 10 per cent. Thus, as far as the properties used are concerned, it seems that the in- and outflow of people meant more for the change in crime than did the long-term residents during a five-year period – despite the fact that the latter residents were more numerous than the former (on average, Group D contains 4,884 and Group E 2,998 individuals).

In evaluating the results, it should be noted that many individuals in Group D did not change their values on many properties and that this means that the variations in the variables are much less for Group D than for Group E. For example, for Group D the standard deviation of the change in FORGN is about 40 per cent of the corresponding standard deviation for Group E. For the change in MULTHS, the relation between the standard deviations of the groups is even more unbalanced, Group D's standard deviation being about 6 per cent of the standard deviation of Group E.

The figures in the table that pertain to the analysis of C90 – C85/C85 – C80 reveal some interesting things. What strikes first is the relatively strong positive relationship found for the change in FORGN in Group E. The regression coefficient of this relationship for the normalized version of FORGN has a much higher value than the corresponding coefficient for Group D. For the standardized versions of the variables the difference is even more marked. Thus, considering the results obtained for the combined data it would seem that a major portion of the positive relationship that can be assumed to have existed for the whole population between the change in FORGN and the change in crime during a five-year period (see Table 5.3) can be explained by geographical selection – when the proportion of foreigners among the residents increased due to migration, crime tended to increase – while only a minor portion was due to social processes among the long-term residents implying that foreigners getting Swedish citizenship became more integrated.

Another striking finding is the relationships obtained for the changes in PUBLIC. The coefficient for the normalized version of the change in this property is negative for Group D but positive for Group E, and the absolute coefficient value is much higher for Group D than for Group E. Thus, it seems that when the proportion of dwellers with public landlords increased due to migration, crime tended to increase – perhaps because individuals with such landlords tended to be conducive to crime – but that crime tended to be reduced when long-term residents moved to such dwellings. The latter finding does not seem very realistic.

The coefficient for the change in the normalized version of MULTHS has a high value for the long-term residents. For the moving individuals, the corresponding coefficient has a low absolute value (for the standardized variables, both relationships have very low values). This does not seem very realistic either. However, possibly the coefficient values should not be taken very seriously because there are problems of identifying the coefficients due to the fact that the changes in PUBLIC and MULTHS are strongly positively correlated to each other.

The relationships found for the change in DIVOR for the long-term residents and for the moving individuals are negative. Thus, it would seem that an increase

**Table 5.7**  **Explaining change in crime with simultaneous changes in basic properties for Groups D and E. Linear regression analysis. Data adjusted for relative group size. Independent properties normalized**

| Independent property | C90 − C85 (n=83) | | C90 − C85/ C85 − C80 (n=166) | |
|---|---|---|---|---|
| | D | E | D | E |
| *Age and sex* | | | | |
| YNGMALE | .27 | −.02 | .03 | .05 |
| YNGFEML | −.29 | .10 | −.01 | .13 |
| MDLMALE | .29 | −.23 | .68 | .36 |
| MDLFEML | −.55 | .55 | −.46 | .31 |
| OLDMALE | 1.46 | .60 | 1.41 | .11 |
| OLDFEML | −1.40 | −.47 | −1.58 | 1.13 |
| *Social control* | | | | |
| FORGN | 1.19 | .24 | .09 | 1.21 |
| SINGLE | .06 | −.61 | .03 | .03 |
| DIVOR | 2.20 | −.65 | −.39 | −.35 |
| *Social resources* | | | | |
| INCMULT | −.39 | −.40 | −.14 | −.02 |
| SOCAID | −.37 | .55 | - | - |
| OCCDICH | −1.53 | 3.36 | - | - |
| *Dwelling environment* | | | | |
| MULTHS | 2.62 | −.55 | .98 | .03 |
| PUBLIC | −4.63 | 1.17 | −1.37 | .27 |
| OVERCR | 2.10 | .03 | −.06 | .15 |
| *Constant* | .26 | | .16 | |
| *Dummy90−85* | - | | −.25 | |
| Expl. proportion of variance (corr.) | .34 | | .14 | |

in the proportion of divorced individuals tended to decrease crime in both groups. This does not seem very realistic either.

For the long-term residents, it is found that the relationship for the change in each age property is negative for the women and positive for the men. The same is not found for the moving individuals. For them, all coefficients are positive. Some of the differences between the coefficients of the two groups are large. How this should be explained is difficult to say.

Both for the long-term and for the moving individuals, the relationships for the changes in SINGLE, INCMULT and OVERCR are weak or relatively weak, whether pertaining to the normalized or to the standardized versions of the variables.

Considering the results from the analysis of C90−C85/C85−C80, the impression is that the model used has serious shortcomings. Only little of the variance in the change in crime is explained, and the fact that the found value of the intercept is not 0 indicates that the true model of crime for different years cannot be perfectly linear. The lack of data on social resources properties is a serious problem and is perhaps the reason that some coefficients have got unrealistic values.

In analyzing C90−C85 measures of changes in social resources may be used, and, as can be seen from Table 5.7 and Table V.iv, several large differences between regression coefficients for the two groups are then obtained. Above all, an extremly strong positive relationship is found between the change in crime and the change in OCCDICH for Group E, while the corresponding relationship for Group D is strongly negative – indicating that the unskilled worker status of people moving into or out of the area was relatively important for the change in crime (the beta weights are 0.46 and −0.24). In some cases coefficients are obtained that differ much from what was found when analyzing C90−C85/C85−C80. The relationship for the change in FORGN for the moving individuals, which was previously found to be very strong, is now much weaker, and there are stronger relationships for the changes in FORGN, DIVOR, MULTHS, PUBLIC and OVERCR for the long-term residents. For the changes in these properties there are large differences in relationship between the two groups. PUBLIC and MULTHS are examples of this. Again, the differences in relationship for the changes in these two properties go in opposite directions. For the changes in some age/sex properties there are also large differences in relationships. The corrected explained proportion of the variance in the change in crime has increased substantially, but still only a minor part of the variance is explained. Some variables seem to have unrealistic coefficient values, for example the changes in OCCDICH and SOCAID for Group D and the change in MULTHS for Group E (the coefficients for these variables could be expected to be positive but are negative). Again, the impression is that the model used has serious shortcomings.

One reason that the changes in OCCDICH and SOCAID have got coefficient values that seem unrealistic for Group D may be that these changes do not imply an increased lack of social resources for the individuals of this group. An increase in SOCAID for individuals in Group D may mean an increase in immediate economic resources, but no greater change in underlying social resources. For the different individuals in Group E, the same may not be true. As to the changes in OCCDICH it seems probable that many unskilled workers in Group D got higher occupational status as they grew older, which may have had other effects than corresponding changes in occupational status for the different individuals of Group E.

## Micro-Level Interaction and Moves

In order to elucidate the influence of micro-level interaction on area crime the changes in previously described mean-of-products and product-of-means properties will now be used as independent variables in an analysis of the change in crime in Groups D and E. Such an analysis may give insight into what role social processes played for crime. Again, the individuals in Group E cannot have been much involved in local social processes involving contacts between residents and taking some times, while the individuals in Group D may have been involved in such processes, and for much the same reasons as were brought forward for the cross-sectional analysis micro-level interaction between social control and social resources can therefore be assumed to have influenced crime differently in the two groups.

The changes in the mean-of-products properties can be assumed to have exerted positive influence on the change in crime for Group E, since crime in this group was probably relatively strongly affected by intraindividual and nonsocial causes and by geographical selection. The changes in the product-of-means properties can be assumed to have exerted positive influence on the change in crime for Group D, since crime in this group was probably more socially caused. However, the changes in the latter properties can be assumed to have exerted no strong influence on the change in crime for Group E, since the individuals in this group did not have much contact with other residents. It is difficult to say what influences the changes in the mean-of-products properties exerted on the change in crime in Group D, since in that case it may be the question of both social and nonsocial causes of crime.

These assumptions about relationships between the changes in interaction properties and the change in crime for the two groups have been tested. Admittedly, the validity problems mentioned above concerning the changes in OCCDICH and SOCAID for members in Group D complicates the analysis.

The assumptions are tested by using C90 – C85 as the dependent variable in a linear regression analysis with changes in independent properties of basic and interactional types as independent variables. Again, only changes in the independent properties that are synchronous with the change in crime are considered. In order to keep the number of consumed degrees of freedom down and to simplify the analysis, only the control-resources interaction properties as well as the young male-foreigner interaction properties are used. All variables are standardized (this facilitates the interpretation of the average coefficient values of the interaction properties). Three analyses have been made. In the first one, all variables that describe basic and interaction properties are used, which means that extremely many degrees of freedom are consumed (70 variables are used to analyze the changes in crime in 83 areas). In the latter analyses variables that describe basic properties are excluded – in the second analysis all control and resources properties and in the third analysis all properties.

Results of the analyses are shown in Table 5.8. It turns out that adding as regressors the mentioned variables that describe changes in interaction properties to the variables that describe changes in basic properties decreases the corrected explained proportion of the variance in the change in crime from 34 to 30 per cent. Moreover, the coefficient values obtained for some variables in the first analysis are quite unrealistic. However, the corrected explained proportion is increased to 53 per cent when the variables that describe changes in the basic control and resources properties are excluded. When only the interaction variables are used as regressors, the corrected explained proportion, 62 per cent, is much higher than when the changes in basic properties are used. Thus, it seems that the results of the second and the third analyses, particularly the results of the third analysis, are interesting. Below, I focus exclusively on the results of the third analysis.

As to the mean coefficient values for the changes in the control-resources interaction properties, the following results are obtained in the third analysis. For Group E, the average coefficient value for the changes in the nine mean-of-products properties has the remarkably high value of 0.18. For Group D, the average coefficient value for the changes in the nine product-of-means properties has the positive but low value of 0.09. These average coefficient values have the expected sign. However, for Group E the average coefficient value for the changes in the product-of-means properties is not, as expected, zero, but –0.07. For Group D, the average coefficient value for the changes in the mean-of-products properties is also –0.07.

Thus, the average coefficient value in Group D for the mean-of-products control-resources properties is negative. How this matter should be interpreted is not quite clear. It could be due to the fact that social processes that involved within-individual products of control and resources factors and that reduced crime were going on in the areas (or in the city outside the target areas) with the result that there were negative influences from within-individual products of these factors. This is an explanation that fits previous findings in this study and previous arguments about the significance of integration processes rather well. However, the matter could possibly also be due to the fact that the changes in resources properties for the members of Group D do not measure what they are intended to measure – that is, that increases in the measures of the interaction properties do not describe true increases but rather describe decreases in the products of control and true resources for these members.

The positive but low average coefficient found for the product-of-means control-resources properties in Group D indicates that local social processes involving control and resources factors of different individuals and increasing crime were going on in the areas.

**Table 5.8** Coefficients obtained in explaining C90 – C85 linearly with simultaneous changes in basic and interactional properties for Groups D and E. Data adjusted for relative group size. All variables standardized (n=83)

| Independent prop. | D | E | D | E | D | E |
|---|---|---|---|---|---|---|
| *Age and sex* | | | | | | |
| YNGMALE | −3.25 | −.85 | −.45 | −.45 | - | - |
| YNGFEML | .51 | −.25 | −.28 | −.29 | - | - |
| MDLMALE | .49 | −.30 | .94 | −.09 | - | - |
| MDLFEML | 1.02 | .05 | −.28 | .11 | - | - |
| OLDMALE | .69 | .21 | .58 | .13 | - | - |
| OLDFEML | .40 | −.31 | −.12 | −.15 | - | - |
| *Social control* | | | | | | |
| FORGN | 1.51 | −.68 | - | - | - | - |
| SINGLE | −1.45 | .65 | - | - | - | - |
| DIVOR | .54 | −1.19 | - | - | - | - |
| *Social resources* | | | | | | |
| INCMULT | −.12 | −.26 | - | - | - | - |
| SOCAID | .80 | −.76 | - | - | - | - |
| OCCDICH | 1.01 | −1.03 | - | - | - | - |
| *Dwelling environment* | | | | | | |
| MULTHS | −.19 | .18 | −.01 | .01 | - | - |
| PUBLIC | −.08 | .05 | −.15 | .03 | - | - |
| OVERCR | −.09 | .61 | .08 | .22 | - | - |
| *Interaction* | | | | | | |
| M(Contr.*Res.), 9 var. | −.16 | .16 | .01 | .14 | −.07 | .18 |
| CONTR.*RES., 9 var. | −.19 | .11 | −.01 | −.10 | .09 | −.07 |
| M(Yngmale*Forgn) | .25 | 1.31 | .09 | .56 | .20 | .32 |
| YNGMALE*FORGN | 1.41 | .33 | .84 | .26 | .18 | .01 |
| Expl. proportion of variance (corr.) | .30 | | .53 | | .62 | |

As regards the coefficient values for the changes in the young male-foreigner interaction properties in the two groups, it is found that they all have positive values. The coefficient value for the change in the mean-of-products property is 0.32 for Group E. The coefficient value for the change in the product-of-means property is 0.18 for Group D, and only 0.01 for Group E. These coefficient values are compatible with expectations.

Pursuing the analysis of the significance for change in crime of changes in the young male-foreigner interaction properties, we find that the coefficient value for the change in the mean-of-products property is 0.20 for Group D. This value is lower than the value of the corresponding coefficient for Group E. Again, the reason could be that there was an integration process in Group D implying that the positive influences on crime from within-individual products became weaker.

The positive coefficient found the product-of-means property in Group D indicates that interindividual combinations of the statuses of being a young male and of being a foreigner among the long-term residents affected crime positively, that is, that there were local social processes in the area that were conducive to crime.

On the whole, a reasonable interpretation of the results obtained is that changes in the interaction properties influenced the change in crime. The evidence supports the idea that interaction of mean-of-products type affected crime positively and strongly for moving individuals and that interaction of the product-of-means type affected crime positively for long-term residents. It seems that the changes in the mean-of-products properties were particularly important in affecting crime, and the relationships obtained for these properties for the moving individuals support the idea that geographical selection and intraindividual processes affected crime. The relationships obtained for the product-of-means properties support the idea that local social processes affected crime. However, the influence of these latter processes on crime seems to have been weak.


## Discussion

In order to explain crime, a variety of approaches for analyzing longitudinal relationships have been used in this study. Linear and product models, point and change data, interaction of micro- and macro-level types, periods of different lengths, and the influence of moves have been considered. These various approaches have not always given results that allow of clear explanations. In fact, in some respects the complexity of the results makes it rather difficult to discern a clear, coherent picture. Below, I offer some reflections on the matter. The discussion focuses on results that pertain to analyses in which the population of an area is treated as a whole and in which only basic properties are used – that is, analyses of conventional type – and on the problems that these results entail. The point made is that the relationships found are difficult to interpret and that other approaches – above all dealing with the influence of moves and with interaction of micro-level type – must be used to improve the understanding. Admittedly, new complications arise when doing so. I discuss these complications in the concluding section of this book.

Overall, the independent properties explain a very large portion of the variance in crime cross-sectionally, and therefore much more cannot be expected to be gained in explained variance by taking historical data into account. This is also what has been found to be the case. However, some additional explanatory leverage has been gained.

As to the longitudinal relationships between crime and point data of independent properties, patterns of coefficients for different periods of time have emerged that seem to be the results of causal processes affecting crime. When analyzing changes in basic properties and crime, the proportion of the variance in the change in crime that can be explained is naturally much less. Another complication is the fact that the same results have not always been obtained when using these different approaches. However, some patterns are fairly similar, and this offers a certain measure of confidence that they describe the effects of actual processes of general types. The question is how they should be interpreted.

Such patterns are obtained for FORGN and DIVOR, and their causal interpretation may seem to be rather straightforward, at least at a cursory glance. Thus, it seems that foreign citizens contribute strongly and quickly to crime in an area, but that the influence does not remain intact. This can be given a social control interpretation: newly arrived foreigners have few social bonds and are therefore poorly controlled, but after some time they are integrated in society and become better controlled. However, the question may be raised whether it is the neighborhood – the area investigated – or the city that is the society into which they are integrated. Divorced residents seem to have an increasing effect on crime after some time, whereas the immediate effect is not as strong. How this should be interpreted is not quite clear, but an interpretation of control type could be appropriate here as well, since divorces often mean losses of social bonds. The delayed effect could perhaps be due to a process of degradation of social relations. Thus, in both these cases the relationships found are difficult to interpret quite satisfactorily.

It has been difficult to analyze the relationships between crime and the social resources properties. This is among other things due to the problem of lacking data for SOCAID and OCCDICH. However, it seems that OCCDICH has a positive quick effect on crime, whereas SOCAID has a delayed such effect. For INCMULT the results are more mixed, but it seems that most of the interesting relationships found in multivariate analyses between this property and crime are negative, meaning that a higher income level tends to decrease crime. One question raised by these findings between social resources and crime is to what extent they are due to geographical selection processes and to what extent to direct influences in the area. This is difficult to explain quite satisfactorily if the population is treated as a whole and if only basic properties are used.

# Chapter 6
# Summary and Conclusions

This study was designed to answer important questions about crime among residents in urban areas. Among these questions are: How is crime of the residents in these areas constituted? How do different processes – the process of geographical differentiation of individuals and processes implying a direct influence from the local environment – affect crime? What roles do social control and social resources play in the latter context? I will now summarize and discuss results of this study that are relevant for answering these questions.

However, before I do, some words of caution regarding the possibilities of drawing general conclusions from the findings of the study are in place. Drawing such conclusions is made difficult for two reasons. First, the empirical phenomena studied have a limited scope geographically and temporally – they concern what has happened in one city in one country during a rather short period of time. Most of the results concern crime in two years, 1985 and 1990. Naturally, this restricts the possibilities of making generalizations. Secondly, establishing several of the results has been made difficult by various circumstances, above all the fact that many strongly correlated variables are simultaneously analyzed in many cases. Admittedly, the identification problems then encountered lower the credibility of relationships obtained, in many cases to the extent that the results must be considered tentative. In order to secure more certain conclusions, I will therefore, when this is possible and appropriate, evaluate combined findings from different approaches. Below, I present the main points of my evaluations and add some comments.

*Crime of the residents is adequately described by one single factor, and this factor has very strong bivariate relationships with certain independent properties.* Important findings of this study are the extremely strong predominance of the first factor extracted in a principal component analysis of various crime rates and the very strong cross-sectional bivariate relationships between this factor and certain independent properties. For example, for the year of 1990 – the year for which the measure of crime seems to have particularly high quality – the first factor explains the overwhelming part of the total reliable variance in the analyzed crime rates, and this factor correlates extremely strongly with the percentage of unskilled workers in the area. It is not surprising that a single factor explains much of the rates of traditional crimes and has strong relationships with various properties, but the degree of the predominance and the strengths of certain relationships found in this study are remarkable. They raise the question of whether the conditions of the studied areas differ from what is usually found for other Western cities and do so in a way that makes the results uninteresting in an international context. The answer to this question, I am convinced, is no. The results mentioned do not differ substantially from what has been found in many other studies of Western cities with respect to their qualitative character, even if they do differ with respect to their quantitative character. Several of the relationships identified are stronger than most of those that have been found previously. However, this is probably due to the fact that the data used in this study are of higher quality than the data of most other studies. There is, as far as I know, nothing unique about Stockholm urban areas that would point to any other explanation.

*Separating the effect of geographical differentiation of individuals and the effect of the direct influence of local environment constitutes a major challenge.* The crime factor has been found to be cross-sectionally and bivariately related to several independent properties in similar ways in the reference years of 1980, 1985 and 1990. Some very important independent properties changed very little during the period studied, that is, from 1970 through 1990. This indicates that the local social structure was reproduced in main respects so that areas retained much of their properties and that this structure affected crime in a relatively similar way in the different years. These facts make the cross-sectional relationships found between crime and independent properties interesting to analyze. The question is how this should be done in order to make clear how crime was caused. In the study, the analysis is performed using the assumption that crime was affected by two processes – indirectly by the geographical differentiation of individuals with respect to characteristics related to crime and directly by the influence of the local environment on individuals residing in the area. Separating the effects of these processes constitutes a major challenge.

*In multivariate cross-sectional analyses, certain independent properties have strong partial relationships with crime.* Several of the independent properties used in the study are strongly or rather strongly related to each other and to the crime factor, and this complicates the analysis of the relationship between crime and these properties. Using linear and product models, multivariate cross-sectional analyses have been performed for all residents. These analyses, which explain much of the variance in crime, show that certain independent properties have strong partial relationships with crime in the different years studied. Thus, the percentages of divorced individuals, social aid recipients and unskilled workers have strong positive such relationships with crime, while the percentage of residents living in overcrowded households has weak or rather weak positive relationships of this type. The percentage of foreigners has no strong partial relationship with crime when analyzed together with other independent properties including income and occupational status. The percentages of females in various age categories tend to have partial relationships with crime that are more negative/less positive than the partial relationships for the corresponding percentages of males. Thus, it is found that certain social structure factors have partial relationships with crime that are relatively stable over time. One aim of the study has been to explain the mechanisms underlying these conditions by analyzing longitudinal relationships between crime and the factors. These longitudinal relationships have been analyzed in various ways – by considering linear and product models, point and change data, different time periods, micro- and macro-level interaction, and data for individuals with different patterns of moves. The analyses have been complicated by various circumstances – by the fact that it is not known how the true model is constituted formally in detail, but also by the facts that some data are lacking and that the various methods used have their special merits and shortcomings.

*Findings indicate that geographical differentiation of individuals affected crime very strongly.* The effect on crime of the geographical differentiation of individuals has been analyzed in two ways. First, an analysis has been performed of the relationships between crime and two factors assumed to underlie the differentiation – the average income for men and the percentage of residents living in dwellings having a public landlord. These factors probably affected the differentiation very strongly. Together they explain much of the variance in crime cross-sectionally. This cross-sectional relationship can be assumed to describe the total of the relationships caused by their influences on crime and their non-causal relationship with crime. The factors' influences on crime can be assumed to have been of three kinds: indirect influences due to geographical differentiation and going via directly influencing or associated properties, indirect influences unrelated to this differentiation, and direct influences. In an analysis of crime in 1990, the latter two influences and the non-causal relationship have been estimated. They seem to have been weak, and therefore the conclusion can be drawn that the two factors affected crime very strongly via differentiation. Secondly, the indirect effect of differentiation and the direct effect of local environment have been analyzed by considering residents' patterns of moves. Relationships between independent factors and crime for long-term residents and for newcomers have been compared. It is then assumed that the direct influence from local environment was stronger for the long-term residents than for the newcomers. Findings, although rather complex, indicate that these two types of residents should be considered separately when modeling the influences on crime, that the influence of the newcomers was much stronger than the influence of the long-term residents, and that geographical differentiation therefore was very important. However, as further discussed below, there are also findings that indicate that crime was directly affected by factors in the environment.

*The form of the true model of crime is probably complicated.* Much of the efforts of this study concern various ways of formulating the model of crime, and key results pertain to this problem of form. Different forms have been tested, but finding the perfect one has proven to be difficult. Product and linear models for point data each explain much of the variance in the crime factor cross-sectionally and longitudinally. Moreover, they each explain about the same proportion of the variance in crime, although with some advantage for the product models, and they yield rather similar pictures of the influences on crime. However, neither of them can be assumed to be perfect. Since several complicated processes probably influence crime, the perfect model can also be assumed to be complicated. For example, both linear and product expressions may play a role in the perfect model. In this study, various ways of adding sophistication to the model form have been tried. One is to consider the aggregated effects of micro-level interaction.

*Two types of micro-level bivariate interaction have been analyzed – interaction within and between individuals.* In order to describe bivariate interaction within an individual, different factors of the individual have been multiplied with each other. In order to describe bivariate interaction between individuals, different factors of different individuals have been multiplied with each other. Only dichotomous micro-level factors are used empirically in this type of analysis. The aggregate for all residents of interaction within individuals, set in relation to area population, is described as the mean of the products of these factors. The aggregate for all residents of homogeneous interaction between two factors of different individuals, also seen as a relative property, can be proved algebraically to be approximately describable as the product of the means of the factors. Thus, the latter aggregate can be described in ordinary macro-level terms. However, the former aggregate cannot be described in such terms in a practically manageable way if the micro-level factors are correlated with each other. Mean-of-products properties are used for analyzing both social and nonsocial influences on crime, while product-of-means properties are only used for analyzing social influences. Since analyzing the influence on crime of aggregated micro-level interaction of the two types using cross-sectional data is very difficult due to the extremely strong relationships that exist among interactional and basic properties, I have principally relied on change data for this type of analysis. I have also used data for long-term residents and newcomers, who can be assumed to be differently involved in social processes.

*In analyses of change data, it is found that aggregated micro-level bivariate inter-action explains much more of crime than do macro-level factors of ordinary types and that aggregated within-individual interaction dominates in this explanation.* Linear analyses have been performed of the change in crime using changes in various independent factors as regressors, including changes in aggregated micro-level bivariate interaction within and between individuals, for the undivided area population as well as for the long-term residents and the newcomers. The analyses concern some selected types of interaction – those focused are interaction among social-control and social-resources properties and interaction between being a young male and being a foreign citizen. It is found that the explanation of the change in crime is improved by adding changes in the interaction properties to changes in basic ordinary properties as regressors. In fact, using only the changes in aggregated micro-level interaction of the mentioned types as independent factors explains much more of the variance in the change in crime than using changes in the ordinary factors. Furthermore, it is found that changes in aggre-gated within-individual interaction play a dominating role in the explanation of the change in crime. Thus, clear indications have been obtained that aggregated within-individual products of properties have unique explanatory power, and this raises the question of whether an adequate model of crime can really be constructed using only macro-level properties of ordinary types.

*It may be conjectured that the perfect model of crime includes a sum of expressions that describe the influences from small segments of the population.* The difficulties of finding the form of an adequate model of crime notwithstanding, a reasonable inference can be drawn from the results of this study about the form that must be used in order to explain crime in urban areas perfectly. This inference is that aggregated micro-level interaction of the mean-of-products type between various factors, particularly between social control and social resources factors, must be considered. This means that small segments of the residential population having within-individual combinations of such factor values that indicate conduciveness to crime should be considered especially, because these segments affect crime very strongly. Thus, the perfect form would probably to a great extent be a sum of expressions that describe the influence from such segments.

*Crime is affected indirectly – through the geographical differentiation of individuals – by social resources.* It seems clear that much of the cross-sectional relationship on the area level between social structure and crime is due to the geographical differentiation of individuals and the global relationships between the differentiating factors and crime. Of course, the differentiating process can be assumed to be governed to a great extent by social resources. However, the conditions for analyzing the relationships between these resources and crime have not been very advantageous in the study. Data on the important properties of occupational status and social aid exist only for 1985 and 1990, and for income there is no measure that can be directly compared between years in an absolute sense. Another complication is that some social resources properties may have affected crime both indirectly via the geographical differentiation and directly. The percentage of unskilled workers is an interesting resources property to consider in analyzing the influences on crime. Results of longitudinal analyses of the undivided population of residents indicate that this percentage had a quick influence on crime, and a linear regression analysis of the change in crime using change data on basic properties for residents with different patterns of moves as independent factors has given results that indicate that this relationship was to a large degree due to geographical differentiation. Cross-sectional analyses using independent factors for residents with different patterns of moves have given similar results. For the income measure, the results concerning its direct influence on crime are mixed. As mentioned above, however, comparing results obtained in bivariate and multivariate analyses of crime indicates that income affected crime mainly through geographical differentiation.

*When models with no reference to aggregated micro-level bivariate interaction are used, there is no clear evidence of a direct influence on crime from social resources in the environment, as measured by basic properties.* True, using these models in multivariate analyses of the undivided area population, the percentages of social aid recipients and unskilled workers have shown to have cross-sectional and longitudinal positive relationships with crime, and this is compatible with a direct influence of social resources in the environment on crime. However, the relationships between crime and social resources have also been studied particularly for the long-term residents using these models – for these residents the relationships found can be assumed to be largely due to direct influences from the environment – and here the results obtained are mixed. Thus, for models with basic properties no clear evidence has been found of a direct influence on crime from social resources in the environment (as to the evidence when considering aggregated bivariate micro-level interaction, see below).

*Findings indicate that the percentages of foreigners and divorcees, when analyzed as basic properties in models with no reference to aggregated micro-level bivariate interaction, directly affected crime, but this does not need to be due to influences from local environment.* Findings indicate that these two types of lacking social control of residents were conducive to crime. When analyzing crime longitudinally and multivariately with basic independent properties in models with no reference to aggregated micro-level bivariate interaction, it seems that robust or rather robust results support the existence of the following influences on crime: 1) a quick positive influence from the percentage of foreigners that is reversed into a later negative influence, 2) a five-year delayed positive influence from the percentage of divorced individuals. The quick and delayed influences of the percentage of foreigners can be interpreted as the result of an integration process. The delayed positive effect of the percentage of divorcees can possibly be interpreted as the result of deteriorating social bonds. Thus, in both cases social processes may have underlain the relationships found. However, there is no clear evidence that these processes were local. The relationship with crime that is found for the percentage of residents with a single parent – a third measure of social control – does not give the same support for an influence. This could possibly be due to the fact that many of these residents were too young to have any strong influence on crime.

*Some findings indicate that there were no very strong influences from local social processes on crime.* If local social processes affected crime, some of these processes can be assumed to have worked across the boundaries of the target area, which suggests that crime in this area was affected by crime in adjacent areas. However, no indication of such an influence is found. Moreover, if local social processes stimulated crime, one might expect that crime should have grown at an increasing rate when the percentage of residents of low social status, of foreign extraction, or with social problems increased – that is, that the derivatives of crime with respect to these properties should be increasing, but the evidence for such a growth is very weak. However, it is found that different resources and control properties have interacted positively between different residents in their influence on area crime, and this indicates that there have been local social processes involving these properties, but the influence of these processes seems to have been weak.

*As to the explanation of the direct influence of the environment on crime, the social control perspective, as ordinarily understood, has got some support, but the social resources perspective, as ordinarily understood, has got no clear support.* The two main sociological perspectives of crime that have been used in research to explain the direct influence of the environment on area crime and that are focused in this study – the social control and social resources perspectives – can be understood in different ways. As ordinarily understood, they seem to mean that control and resources factors, respectively, affect crime strongly and additively when considered together with other explanatory factors. Taken in this sense, it is clear that neither of them have got unequivocal support in this study. However, findings have been obtained that are compatible with the social control perspective, while the social resources perspective has got no clear support.

*The subcultural perspective is not directly tested in this study.* It has not been a very urgent task to test this perspective, since there are no criminal subcultures in the Swedish society. However, if the subcultural perspective is revised so that it refers to the influence on crime of groups of deviant or marginalized residents, application to Swedish conditions is more relevant. An important question that bears on the perspective may then be formulated as follows: do groups of deviant or marginalized residents exert a positive influence on crime so that crime increases at an increasing rate with a bigger group size? The answer is that the results of this study on the whole do not give any strong support for the existence of such an influence when single properties of deviance or marginalization are analyzed. Larger percentages of foreigners and of social aid recipients do not seem to have produced crime in excess of a linear effect. However, the data of the study are not very appropriate for testing this perspective.

*Important aspects of the disorganization perspective are not tested.* In evaluating the disorganization perspective, its complex structure should be considered. The support that may be found in this study for influences of the three elements in the perspective that are often mentioned in the research – economic resources, ethnic heterogeneity and mobility – is discussed above. However, the essence of the perspective is of course the direct influence on crime of local disorganization. If this influence is assumed to refer to the way residents from different families organize specifically to protect against crime, its occurrence cannot be tested in the study.

*Findings indicate that social control and social resources interacted on the micro level in their influence on crime. These findings are of interest for the evaluation of theoretical perspectives.* In explaining the direct influence of the environment on crime using only properties of ordinary types, the social control perspective has gained stronger support than the social resources perspective in the present study. This result is in broad agreement with what has been found in much previous research. However, I think that the results in the study that are of greatest interest for the evaluation of theoretical perspectives are the indications found about the interaction between social control and social resources on the micro level. These findings suggest how the two main sociological perspectives in criminological research may be united. The findings indicate that social resources and social control properties interacted within individuals in their influence on crime, and there are also some indications that these properties interacted between individuals. Thus, it seems that crime was caused in a more complicated way than has often been assumed in the research.

*It is unclear how a direct influence of social resources on crime, if such an influence existed, was constituted.* The interpretation of the social resources' relationships with crime is rendered complicated by the fact that it does not seem perfectly clear why resources would have had a direct influence. The reason most often suggested in modern research for an influence of individuals' resources on their criminality is that individuals with poor resources feel that they are unjustly treated and therefore have a motive for committing crime (strain explanation). Another reason for an influence could be that individuals with poor resources have lesser ability or capacity to avoid such problems that may lead to crime (problem-solving explanation). It is difficult to use the results of this study to determine the validity of these explanations. Possibly, it could be thought that the fact that social resources seem to have played an important role in interaction but not to have played an equally important role as basic properties in linear models indicates that they did not work as causes of their own, and that this gives the problem-solving explanation some precedence, but this is an uncertain inference. A condition that could be thought to make it possible to distinguish between the two explanations is that the problem-solving explanation implies that lack of social resources of others is conducive to crime, while this is not the case with the strain explanation. However, the assumption about this difference cannot be used for making a choice in the study between the explanations, because the influences on crime of individuals' own and of others' poor resources are not separated in the analysis.

*The results indicate that much previous research overstates the importance of the influence on crime of local social processes.* In much previous research on urban crime, it is argued that local social processes in neighborhoods affect crime with considerable strength. However, the picture of urban crime that can be painted on the basis of the findings of the present study does not support this view. Instead, these findings imply that geographical selection of residents and ensuing social differentiation played a quite dominating role. True, some evidence has been found of effects on crime of local social processes. True as well, the product-of-means measures used for analyzing the influence of social processes can be criticized for not being of very high quality, since they do not refer exclusively to the interaction between factors of individuals having contact with each other. However, on the whole the findings of the study – as to how crime was affected by the mean income and the occurrence of public landlords, how it was influenced by crime in adjacent areas, and how it and the change in it were affected by long-term residents and newcomers/moving individuals and by aggregated micro-level interaction – indicate that geographical selection dominated strongly. If this picture is true and generally valid, the aim and the direction of much previous research on the subject are not very adequate. In fact, in the light of the findings of this study, explaining urban area crime does not seem to be a very difficult problem. To a very large extent, the causes of this crime must be found in the geographical selection of individuals. However, surely there are still interesting questions about urban crime that are not treated in the present study – for example, the questions of how very serious crime arises and develops in urban neighborhoods and of how crime is influenced by the general metropolitan environment.

*Final comments.* Two findings in this study stand out when it comes to explaining crime among residents in urban areas – the findings of the significance of the influence of geographical differentiation and of the significance of the influence of aggregated micro-level interaction. I think that these results indicate the direction in which future research should proceed in order to be successful. Two suggestions can be made in this respect. The first one is that the influences of geographical differentiation must be separated from the direct influences of the environment. It is quite clear that it is very difficult to analyze the direct influences if the effects of the differentiation are not removed or controlled in some way. The second suggestion is that the micro-macro link should be considered more explicitly than has often been the case. One reason for this is that using a micro-level perspective is a way of building a total theory that unites ideas of the different theories that now predominate in the field. Another reason is that it has been found in the study presented in this book that aggregated micro-level interaction has effects on crime that cannot be expressed in ordinary macro-level terms in a practically manageable way. I think that this finding may be of great importance when considering how the crime of residents in urban areas should be explained. In fact, the finding may have relevance far beyond that question. It can be expected to be relevant for research on macro-level crime of many other types as well.

# References


Agnew, R. (1992). "Foundations for a general strain theory of crime and delinquency", *Criminology*, 30, 47–87.

Agnew, R. (1993). "Why do they do it? An examination of the intervening mechanisms between social control variables and delinquency", *Journal of Research in Crime and Delinquency,* 30, 245–266.

Agnew, R. (1999). "A general strain theory of community differences in crime rates", *Journal of Research in Crime and Delinquency,* 36, 123–155.

Agnew, R. (2001). "Building on the foundation of general strain theory: Specifying the types of strain most likely to lead to crime and delinquency", *Journal of Research in Crime and Delinquency,* 38, 319–361.

Agnew, R. (2005). *Why Do Criminals Offend? A General Theory of Crime and Delinquency*. Los Angeles, CA: Roxbury.

Agnew, R., S. K. Matthews, J. Bucher, A. N. Welcher, and C. Keyes (2008). "Socioeconomic status, economic problems, and delinquency", *Youth Society*, 40, 159–181.

Agnew, R. and H. R. White (1992). "An empirical test of general strain theory", *Criminology*, 30, 475–499.

Ahlberg, J. (1996). *Invandrares och invandrares barns brottslighet* (Criminality of Immigrants and of Children of Immigrants). The Swedish Council for Crime Prevention (Brottsförebyggande rådet), Report 1996:2.

Akers, R. L. (2000). *Criminological Theories. Introduction, Evaluation, and Application* (3rd ed.). Los Angeles, CA: Roxbury.

Andersson, R. and Å. Bråmå (2004). "Selective migration in Swedish distressed neighbourhoods: Can area-based urban policies counteract segregation processes?", *Housing Studies*, 19, 517–539.

Andresen, M. A. and M. Felson (2010). "The impact of co-offending", *British Journal of Criminology*, 50, 66–81.

Becker, R. and G. Mehlkop (2006). "Social class and delinquency: An empirical utilization of rational choice theory with cross-sectional data of the 1990 and 2000 German General Population Surveys (ALLBUS)", *Rationality and Society*, 18, 193–235.

Bellair, P. (1997). "Social interaction and community crime: Examining the importance of neighbor networks", *Criminology*, 35, 677–703.

Botchkovar, E. V., C. R. Tittle, and O. Antonaccio (2009). "General strain theory: Additional evidence using cross-cultural data", *Criminology*, 47, 131–176.

Bottoms, A. E., A. Claytor, and P. Wiles (1992). "Housing markets and residential community crime careers", pp. 118–144 in *Crime, Policing, and Place: Essays in Environmental Criminology*. Eds. D. J. Evans, D. T. Herbert, and N. R. Fyfe. London: Taylor & Francis Routledge.

Bottoms, A. E. and P. Wiles (1986). "Housing tenure and residential community crime careers in Britain", pp. 101–162 in *Communities and Crime (*series: *Crime and Justice)*. Eds. A. J. Reiss and M. Tonry. Chicago: University of Chicago Press.

Braithwaite, J. (1981). "The myth of social class and criminality reconsidered", *American Sociological Review*, 46, 36–57.

Browning, C. R., S. L. Feinberg, and R. D. Dietz (2004). "The paradox of social organization: Networks, collective efficacy, and violent crime in urban neighborhoods", *Social Forces*, 83, 503–534.

Bursik, R. J. (1988). "Social disorganization and theories of crime and delinquency: Problems and prospects", *Criminology*, 26, 519–551.

Bursik, R. J. and H. G. Grasmick (1993). *Neighborhoods and Crime. The Dimensions of Effective Community Control*. New York: Lexington.

Cantor, D. and K. C. Land (1985). "Unemployment and crime rates in the Post-World War II United States: A theoretical and empirical analysis", *American Sociological Review*, 50, 317–332.

Chamlin, M. B., J. K. Cochran, and C. T. Lowenkamp (2002). "A longitudinal analysis of the welfare-homicide relationship: Testing two (nonreductionist) macro-level theories", *Homicide Studies*, 6, 39–60.

Cloward, R. A. and L. E. Ohlin (1960). *Delinquency and Opportunity. A Theory of Delinquent Gangs*. Glencoe: Free Press.

Cohen, L. E. and M. Felson (1979). "Social change and crime rate trends: A routine activity approach", *American Sociological Review*, 44, 588–608.

Cohen, L. E., J. R. Kluegel, and K. C. Land (1981). "Social inequality and predatory criminal victimization: An exposition and test of a formal theory", *American Sociological Review*, 46, 505–524.

Dahlbäck, O. (1996a). "Urban place of residence and individual criminality", *British Journal of Criminology*, 36, 529–545.

Dahlbäck, O. (1996b). "Constructing and using a multiplicative model of the impact of societal changes on violent crime", *Quality & Quantity*, 30, 277–300.

Dahlbäck, O. (1998a). "Modelling the influence of societal factors on municipal theft rates in Sweden: Methodological concerns and substantive findings", *Acta Sociologica*, 41, 37–57.

Dahlbäck, O, (1998b). "The individualism-holism problem in sociological research", *Journal for the Theory of Social Behaviour*, 28, 237–272.

Dahlbäck, O. (2001). "Using single-equation models of function-of-functions type in sociological research", *Quality & Quantity*, 35, 173–189.

Dahlbäck, O. (2003). *Analyzing Rational Crime – Models and Methods*. Theory and Decision Library, Series A: Philosophy and Methodology of the Social Sciences. Dordrecht: Kluwer Academic Publishers.

DeFronzo, J. and L. Hannon (1998). "Welfare assistance levels and homicide rates", *Homicide Studies*, 2, 31–45.

Diesen, C. (2005). "Processrättsligt perspektiv" (Perspective of the law of legal procedure), pp. 181–390 in *Likhet inför lagen* (Equality before the law). Eds. C. Diesen, C. Lernestedt, T. Lindholm, and T. Pettersson. Stockholm: Natur och Kultur.

Dunaway, R. G., F. T. Cullen, V. S. Burton, Jr., and T. D. Evans (2000). "The myth of social class and crime revisited: An examination of class and adult criminality", *Criminology*, 38, 589–632.

Duncan, G. J. and K. A. Magnuson (2003). "The promise of random-assignment social experiments for understanding well-being and behavior", *Current Sociology*, 51, 529–541.

Elliott, D. S., W. J. Wilson, D. Huizinga, R. J. Sampson, A. Elliott, and B. Rankin (1996). "The effects of neighborhood disadvantage on adolescent development", *Journal of Research in Crime and Delinquency*, 33, 389–426.

Farrington, D. P. (1993). "Have any individual, family or neighbourhood influences on offending been demonstrated conclusively?", pp. 7–37 in *Integrating Individual and Ecological Aspects of Crime*. Eds. D. P. Farrington, R. J. Sampson, and P.-O. Wikström. The Swedish Council for Crime Prevention (Brottsförebyggande rådet), Report 1993:1.

Farrington, D. P. (2005). "Childhood origins of antisocial behavior", *Clinical Psychology and Psychotherapy*, 12, 177–190.

Feins, J. D. and M. D. Shroder (2005). "Moving to opportunity: The demonstration's design and its effects on mobility", *Urban Studies*, 42, 1275–1299.

Felson, M. and L. E. Cohen (1980). "Human ecology and crime: A routine activity approach", *Human Ecology*, 8, 389–406.

Fergusson, D., N. Swain-Campell, and J. Horwood (2004). "How does childhood economic disadvantage lead to crime?", *Journal of Child Psychology and Psychiatry*, 45, 956–966.

Fischer, C. (1995). "The subcultural theory of urbanism: A twentieth-year assessment", *American Journal of Sociology*, 101, 543–577.

Froggio, G. (2007). "Strain and juvenile delinquency: A critical review of Agnew's general strain theory", *Journal of Loss and Trauma*, 12, 383–418.

Froggio, G., N. Zamaro, and M. Lori (2009). "Exploring the relationship between strain and some neutralization techniques", *European Journal of Criminology*, 6, 73–88.

Gottfredson, D. C., R. J. McNeil III, and G. D. Gottfredson (1991). "Social area influences on delinquency: A multilevel analysis", *Journal of Research in Crime and Delinquency*, 28, 197–226.

Harcourt, B. E. and J. Ludwig (2006). "Broken windows: New evidence from New York City and a five-city social experiment", *The University of Chicago Law Review*, 73, 271–320.

Harper, C. C. and S. S. McLanahan (2004). "Father absence and youth incarceration", *Journal of Research on Adolescence*, 14, 369–397.

Hay, C., E. N. Fortson, D. R. Hollist, I. Altheimer, and L. M. Schaible (2006). "The impact of community disadvantage on the relationship between the family and juvenile crime", *Journal of Research in Crime and Delinquency*, 43, 326–356.

Haynie, D. L., E. Silver, and B. Teasdale (2006). "Neighborhood characteristics, peer networks, and adolescent violence", *Journal of Quantitative Criminology*, 22, 147–169.

Hipp, J. R. (2010). "A dynamic view of neighborhoods: The reciprocal relationship between crime and neighborhood structural characteristics", *Social Problems*, 57, 205–230.

Hipp, J. R., G. E. Tita, and L. N. Boggess (2009a). "Intergroup and intragroup violence: Is violent crime an expression of group conflict or social disorganization?", *Criminology*, 47, 521–564.

Hipp, J. R., G. E. Tita, and R. T. Greenbaum (2009b). "Drive-bys and trade-ups: Examining the directionality of the crime and residential instability relationship", *Social Forces*, 87, 1777–1812.

Hirschi, T. (1969). *Causes of Delinquency*. Berkeley, CA: University of California Press.

Jarjoura, G. R., R. A Triplett, and G. P. Brinker (2002). "Growing up poor: Examining the link between persistent childhood poverty and delinquency", *Journal of Quantitative Criminology*, 18, 159–187.

Juby, H. and D. P. Farrington (2001). "Disentangling the link between disrupted families and delinquency", *British Journal of Criminology*, 41, 22–40

Kling, J. R., J. Ludwig, and L. F. Katz (2005). "Neighborhood effects on crime for female and male youth: Evidence from a randomized housing voucher experiment", *The Quarterly Journal of Economics*, 87–130.

Krivo, L. J. and R. D. Peterson (1996). "Extremely disadvantaged neighborhoods and urban crime", *Social Forces*, 75, 619–650.

Land, K. C., P. L. McCall, and L. E. Cohen (1990). "Structural covariates of homicide rates: Are there any invariances across time and social space?", *American Journal of Sociology*, 95, 922–963.

Laub, J. H. and R. J. Sampson (1993). "Turning points in the life course: Why change matters to the study of crime", *Criminology*, 31, 301–325.

McNulty, T. (1999). "More on the costs of racial exclusion: Race and violent crime in New York City, 1980–1990", *Race & Society*, 2, 51–68.

Martens, P. and S. Holmberg (2005). *Brottslighet bland personer födda i Sverige och i utlandet* (Crime among Persons Born in Sweden and in Other Countries). Swedish Council for Crime Prevention (Brottsförebyggande rådet), Report 2005:17.

Mazerolle, P. and J. Maahs (2000). "General strain and delinquency: An alternative examination of conditioning influences", *Justice Quarterly*, 17, 753–778.

Merton. R. K. (1968). *Social Theory and Social Structure*. New York: The Free Press.

Morenoff, J. D., R. J. Sampson, and S. W. Raudenbush (2001). "Neighborhood inequality, collective efficacy, and the spatial dynamics of urban violence", *Criminology*, 39, 517–559.

Mosier, C. I. (1943). "On the reliability of a weighted composite", *Psychometrika*, 8, 161–168.

Oberwittler, D. (2004). "A multilevel analysis of neighbourhood contextual effects on serious juvenile offending: The role of subcultural values and social disorganization", *European Journal of Criminology*, 1, 201–235.

Peeples, F. and R. Loeber (1994). "Do individual factors and neighborhood context explain ethnic differences in juvenile delinquency?", *Journal of Quantitative Criminology*, 10, 141–157.

Piquero, N. L., A. R. Grover, J. M. MacDonald, and A. R. Piquero (2005). "The influence of delinquent peers on delinquency: Does gender matter?", *Youth Society*, 36, 251–275.

Portes, A. (1998). "Social capital: Its origins and applications in modern sociology", *Annual Review of Sociology*, 24, 1–24.

Rankin, J. H. and R. Kern (1994). "Parental attachments and delinquency", *Criminology*, 32, 495–515.

Rebellon, C. J., N. L. Piquero, A. R. Piquero, and S. Thaxton (2009). "Do frustrated economic expectations and objective economic inequality promote crime? A randomized experiment testing Agnew's general strain theory", *European Journal of Criminology*, 6, 47–71.

Reid, L. W., H. E. Weiss, R. M. Adelman, and C. Jaret (2005). "The immigration-crime relationship: Evidence across US metropolitan areas", *Social Science Research*, 34, 757–780.

Ring, J. and R. Svensson (2007). "Social class and criminality among young people: A study considering the effects of school achievement as a mediating factor on the basis of Swedish register and self-report data", *Journal of Scandinavian Studies in Criminology and Crime Prevention*, 8, 210–233.

Rosenbaum, E. and L. E. Harris (2001). "Low-income families in their new neighborhoods", *Journal of Family Issues*, 22, 183–210.

Rosenfeld, R. and R. Fornango (2007). "The impact of economic conditions on robbery and property crime: The role of consumer sentiment", *Criminology*, 45, 735–769.

Salmi, V. and J. Kivivuori (2006). "The association between social capital and juvenile crime: The role of individual and structural factors", *European Journal of Criminology*, 3, 123–148.

Sampson, R. J. (2008). "Moving to inequality: Neighborhood effects and experiments meet social structure", *American Journal of Sociology*, 114, 189–231.

Sampson, R. and B. Groves (1989). "Community structure and crime: Testing the social-disorganization theory", *American Journal of Sociology*, 94, 774–802.

Sampson, R. J. and J. H. Laub (1990). "Crime and deviance over the life course: The salience of adult social bonds", *American Sociological Review*, 55, 609–627.

Sampson, R. J. and J. H. Laub (1992). "Crime and deviance in the life course", *Annual Review of Sociology*, 18, 63–84.

Sampson, R. J., J. D. Morenoff, and T. Gannon-Rowley (2002). "Assessing 'neighborhood effects': Social processes and new directions in research", *Annual Review of Sociology*, 28, 443–478.

Sampson, R., S. Raudenbush, and F. Earls (1997). "Neighborhoods and violent crime: A multilevel study of collective efficacy", *Science*, 277, 918–924.

Savage, J., R. R. Bennett, and M. Danner (2008). "Economic assistance and crime: A cross-national investigation", *European Journal of Criminology*, 5, 217–238.

Savolainen, J. (2009). "Work, family and criminal desistance. Adult social bonds in a Nordic welfare state", *British Journal of Criminology*, 49, 285–304.

Schneiders, J., M. Drukker, J. van der Ende, F. C. Verhulst, J. van Os, and N. A. Nicolson (2003). "Neighbourhood, socioeconomic disadvantage and behavioural problems from late childhood into early adolescence", *Journal of Epidemiological & Community Health*, 57, 699–703.

Shaw, C. and H. McKay (rev. ed. 1969 [1942]). *Juvenile Delinquency and Urban Areas*. Chicago: University of Chicago Press.

Simcha-Fagan, O. and J. E. Schwartz (1986). "Neighborhood and delinquency: An assessment of contextual effects", *Criminology*, 24, 667–703.

Skarðhamar, T. (2009). "Family dissolution and children's criminal careers", *European Journal of Criminology*, 6, 203–223.

SOU 2006:30 (2006). The Government's Official Report 2006:30.

South, S. J. and S. F. Messner (2000). "Crime and demography: Multiple linkages, reciprocal relations", *Annual Review of Sociology*, 26, 83–106.

Steffensmeier, D. and D. Haynie (2000). "Gender, structure disadvantage, and urban crime: Do macrosocial variables also explain female offending rates?", *Criminology*, 38, 403–438.

Stowell, J. I., S. F. Messner, K. F. McGeever, and L. E. Raffalovich (2009). "Immigration and the recent violent crime drop in the United States: A pooled, cross-sectional time-series analysis of metropolitan areas", *Criminology*, 47, 889–928.

Tittle, C. R. and R. F. Meier (1990). "Specifying the SES/Delinquency relationship", *Criminology*, 28, 271–299.

Tittle, C. R., W. J. Villemez, and D. A. Smith (1978). "The myth of social class and criminality: An empirical assessment of the empirical evidence", *American Sociological Review*, 43, 643–656.

Veysey, B. M. and S. E. Messner (1999). "Further testing of social disorganization theory: An elaboration of Sampson and Groves's 'Community Structure and Crime'", *Journal of Research in Crime and Delinquency*, 36, 156–174.

Weijters, G., P. Scheepers, and J. Gerris (2007). "Distinguishing the city, neighbourhood and individual level in the explanation of youth delinquency: A multilevel approach", *European Journal of Criminology*, 4, 87–108.

Wellman, B. (1979). "The community question: The intimate networks of East Yorkers", *American Journal of Sociology*, 84, 1201–1231.

Wikström, P.-O. (1991). *Urban Crime, Criminals, and Victims*. New York: Springer.

Wikström, P.-O. (1998). "Communities and crime", pp. 269–301 in *The Handbook of Crime and Punishment*. Oxford: Oxford University Press.

Yearbook of Judicial Statistics 1990. Official Statistics of Sweden, Statistics Sweden, Stockholm 1990 (Rättsstatistisk årsbok 1990, Sveriges officiella statistik, Statistiska centralbyrån, Stockholm 1990).

# Appendices I-V

# Appendix I
# Definition of Areas

The list below describes the compass of the areas studied by referring to the 1990 official statistics of districts in the City of Stockholm. Studied areas are defined with respect to the parishes and to the subdistrict/s/ of parishes in which they are located. If a whole parish is included in an area, its subdistricts are not described. A map in Appendix III shows the geographical location of the areas.

**Table I.i    Definition of areas**

| No. | Parish | Subdiscrict/s/ |
|---|---|---|
| **Inner City** | | |
| *Old Town/central city* | | |
| 01 | Domkyrko-församl. | Storkyrkan/Klara/Jakob |
| *Vasastaden* | | |
| 02 | Adolf Fredrik | - |
| 03 | Gustav Vasa | - |
| 04 | Matteus | Östra Matteus |
| 05 | Matteus | Västra Matteus |
| 06 | Johnannes | - |
| *Östermalm Area* | | |
| 07 | Engelbrekt | Engelbrekts kyrka |
| 08 | Engelbrekt | Tekniska Högskolan/Universitetet/ Hjorthagen-Värtahamen |
| 09 | Hedvig Eleonora | - |
| 10 | Oscar | Oscars kyrka/Djurgården |
| 11 | Oscar | Gärdet |
| *Kungsholm Area* | | |
| 12 | Kungsholm | - |
| 13 | S:t Göran | Östra S:t Göran |
| 14 | S:t Göran | Marieberg/Fredhäll |
| 15 | S:t Göran | Stadshagen/Kristineberg |
| 16 | Essinge | - |

| No. | Parish | Subdiscrict/s/ |
| --- | --- | --- |
| *Södermalm Area* | | |
| 17 | Katarina<br>Maria | Västra Katarina<br>Södra Station Öst |
| 18 | Katarina | Östra Katarina |
| 19 | Sofia | Norra Sofia |
| 20 | Sofia | Södra Sofia/Södra Hammarbyhamnen |
| 21 | Maria | Mariatorget |
| 22 | Högalid | Norra Högalid/Reimersholme-Långholmen |
| 23 | Högalid<br>Maria | Mellersta Högalid/Södra Högalid<br>Södra Station Väst |

## Outer City

*Southern Areas*

| No. | Parish | Subdiscrict/s/ |
| --- | --- | --- |
| 24 | Hägersten | Aspudden |
| 25 | Hägersten | Gröndal/Liljeholmen |
| 26 | Hägersten | Hägersten |
| 27 | Hägersten | Hägerstensåsen |
| 28 | Hägersten | Midsommarkransen/Västberga |
| 29 | Hägersten | Mälarhöjden |
| 30 | Brännkyrka | Fruängen |
| 31 | Brännkyrka | Herrängen/Långsjö |
| 32 | Brännkyrka | Liseberg/Örby Slott/Östberga |
| 33 | Brännkyrka | Långbro/Älvsjö |
| 34 | Brännkyrka | Solberga |
| 35 | Brännkyrka | Västertorp |
| 36 | Vantör | Bandhagen |
| 37 | Vantör | Högdalen |
| 38 | Vantör | Rågsved |
| 39 | Vantör | Stureby |
| 40 | Vantör | Örby |
| 41 | Vantör | Hagsätra |
| 42 | Enskede | Enskedefältet/Enskede Gård |
| 43 | Enskede | Gamla Enskede |
| 44 | Enskede | Johanneshov |
| 45 | Enskede | Årsta |
| 46 | Skarpnäck | Björkhagen |
| 47 | Skarpnäck | Enskededalen/Kärrtorp |

| No. | Parish | Subdiscrict/s/ |
| --- | --- | --- |
| 48 | Skarpnäck | Flaten/Orhem/Skarpnäcks Gård/Skrubba |
| 49 | Skarpnäck | Hammarbyhöjden |
| 50 | Skarpnäck | Bagarmossen |
| 51 | Farsta | Fagersjö |
| 52 | Farsta | Farsta/Larsboda |
| 53 | Farsta | Farsta Strand/Farstanäset |
| 54 | Farsta | Gubbängen |
| 55 | Farsta | Hökarängen |
| 56 | Farsta | Sköndal |
| 57 | Farsta | Svedmyra/Tallkrogen |
| 58 | Skärholmen | Bredäng |
| 59 | Skärholmen | Sätra |
| 60 | Skärholmen | Skärholmen |
| 61 | Skärholmen | Vårberg |
| *Western Areas* | | |
| 62 | Bromma | Abrahamsberg/Riksby/Åkeshov/Åkeslund |
| 63 | Bromma Vällingby | Beckomberga Råcksta |
| 64 | Bromma | Blackeberg |
| 65 | Bromma | Bromma kyrka/Eneby/Norra Ängby/Södra Ängby |
| 66 | Bromma Spånga | Bällsta Bromsten/Flysta/Sundby |
| 67 | Bromma | Mariehäll/Ulvsunda industriområde |
| 68 | Västerled | Alvik/Traneberg/Ulvsunda |
| 69 | Västerled | Höglandet/Olovslund/Ålsten |
| 70 | Västerled | Nockeby/Nockebyhov |
| 71 | Västerled | Smedslätten/Stora Mossen/Äppelviken |
| 72 | Vällingby | Grimsta/Vällingby |
| 73 | Vällingby | Kälvesta/Vinsta |
| 74 | Vällingby | Nälsta |
| 75 | Spånga | Lunda/Solhem |
| 76 | Spånga | Rinkeby |
| 77 | Spånga | Tensta |
| 78 | Hässelby | Hässelby Gård |
| 79 | Hässelby | Hässelby Strand |

| No. | Parish | Subdiscrict/s/ |
| --- | --- | --- |
| 80 | Hässelby | Hässelby Villastad |
| 81 | Kista | Akalla |
| 82 | Kista | Husby |
| 83 | Kista | Kista |

# Appendix II
# Populations of Areas

The populations of the studied areas in 1970, 1980 and 1990 are shown below.  Data on where individuals lived come from the Censuses of Population and Housing.

**Table II.i    Populations of areas**

| No. | 1970 | 1980 | 1990 | No. | 1970 | 1980 | 1990 |
|---|---|---|---|---|---|---|---|
| 01 | 5,217 | 3,500 | 3,354 | 26 | 7,607 | 6,459 | 7,237 |
| 02 | 7,447 | 5,824 | 6,281 | 27 | 7,299 | 5,253 | 4,965 |
| 03 | 11,695 | 10,139 | 11,415 | 28 | 14,184 | 10,228 | 9,742 |
| 04 | 12,465 | 9,955 | 10,566 | 29 | 3,717 | 3,192 | 3,843 |
| 05 | 15,198 | 11,458 | 12,709 | 30 | 8,173 | 6,055 | 6,313 |
| 06 | 10,616 | 8,017 | 9,992 | 31 | 5,552 | 5,190 | 5,380 |
| 07 | 10,697 | 9,238 | 9,339 | 32 | 9,539 | 7,815 | 7,091 |
| 08 | 7,681 | 6,335 | 6,388 | 33 | 5,794 | 4,837 | 4,984 |
| 09 | 11,026 | 9,329 | 9,424 | 34 | 6,939 | 5,196 | 6,085 |
| 10 | 16,366 | 15,324 | 15,069 | 35 | 8,140 | 5,765 | 5,206 |
| 11 | 17,828 | 14,947 | 14,779 | 36 | 7,219 | 5,090 | 4,624 |
| 12 | 17,333 | 13,897 | 15,024 | 37 | 11,528 | 8,002 | 7,396 |
| 13 | 14,029 | 11,571 | 11,697 | 38 | 11,431 | 7,872 | 9,110 |
| 14 | 8,716 | 6,721 | 6,893 | 39 | 8,251 | 6,374 | 5,942 |
| 15 | 7,260 | 6,087 | 6,040 | 40 | 5,158 | 4,524 | 4,386 |
| 16 | 7,136 | 5,621 | 5,534 | 41 | 10,028 | 7,422 | 6,586 |
| 17 | 11,318 | 9,274 | 11,901 | 42 | 3,392 | 3,027 | 3,821 |
| 18 | 21,221 | 16,616 | 18,039 | 43 | 6,196 | 7,190 | 8,764 |
| 19 | 8,913 | 7,010 | 7,168 | 44 | 7,589 | 5,633 | 5,219 |
| 20 | 7,882 | 6,197 | 7,651 | 45 | 19,800 | 14,183 | 13,401 |
| 21 | 12,629 | 10,277 | 12,401 | 46 | 6,771 | 4,832 | 4,655 |
| 22 | 16,522 | 13,343 | 14,710 | 47 | 7,938 | 5,913 | 5,700 |
| 23 | 13,037 | 11,195 | 14,354 | 48 | 2,558 | 2,155 | 10,228 |
| 24 | 9,059 | 6,679 | 7,570 | 49 | 8,085 | 5,817 | 6,036 |
| 25 | 8,918 | 6,485 | 8,407 | 50 | 10,514 | 10,138 | 9,454 |

| No. | 1970 | 1980 | 1990 | | No. | 1970 | 1980 | 1990 |
|---|---|---|---|---|---|---|---|---|
| 51 | 3,366 | 2,489 | 2,328 | | 71 | 5,620 | 5,062 | 4,900 |
| 52 | 16,815 | 12,267 | 11,173 | | 72 | 13,360 | 9,672 | 8,580 |
| 53 | 5,820 | 4,633 | 4,154 | | 73 | 2,265 | 6,835 | 7,462 |
| 54 | 5,888 | 4,026 | 3,940 | | 74 | 3,919 | 4,462 | 4,261 |
| 55 | 12,231 | 8,079 | 7,460 | | 75 | 5,696 | 6,253 | 6,666 |
| 56 | 8,595 | 7,394 | 6,685 | | 76 | 6,846 | 13,645 | 13,400 |
| 57 | 8,031 | 6,198 | 6,040 | | 77 | 13,053 | 15,066 | 15,362 |
| 58 | 11,986 | 8,953 | 8,123 | | 78 | 11,823 | 8,608 | 8,080 |
| 59 | 7,798 | 6,551 | 5,940 | | 79 | 8,850 | 6,341 | 5,510 |
| 60 | 9,053 | 7,298 | 7,049 | | 80 | 4,953 | 13,590 | 17,055 |
| 61 | 8,259 | 8,334 | 7,858 | | 81 | - | 8,571 | 8,154 |
| 62 | 12,353 | 9,181 | 8,510 | | 82 | - | 9,243 | 9,767 |
| 63 | 6,379 | 5,437 | 5,197 | | 83 | - | 8,078 | 7,715 |
| 64 | 8,045 | 5,598 | 5,231 | | | | | |
| 65 | 8,778 | 8,087 | 8,738 | | | | | |
| 66 | 7,939 | 7,336 | 8,845 | | | | | |
| 67 | 4,508 | 3,067 | 3,470 | | | | | |
| 68 | 8,602 | 6,473 | 8,358 | | | | | |
| 69 | 4,895 | 4,620 | 4,736 | | | | | |
| 70 | 5,245 | 4,983 | 5,319 | | | | | |

# Appendix III

# Maps

Six maps are shown in this appendix. The first one (Figure III.i) shows the studied areas' boundaries and serial numbers as given in Appendix I. The other maps (Figures III.ii – III.vi) show the area distribution of categorized values in 1990 of the crime factor (C), the rate of multi-family houses (MULTHS), the mean income for men (INCMULT, here reflected), the rate of foreigners (FORGN) and the rate of unskilled workers (OCCDICH). All variables are constituted so that high values can be assumed to have caused high values of crime. The values of each property are divided into four categories. Areas' belongingness to these categories is indicated with grades from a gray scale, which go from white (indicating values that can be assumed to have caused low crime) to black (indicating values that can be assumed to have caused high crime).

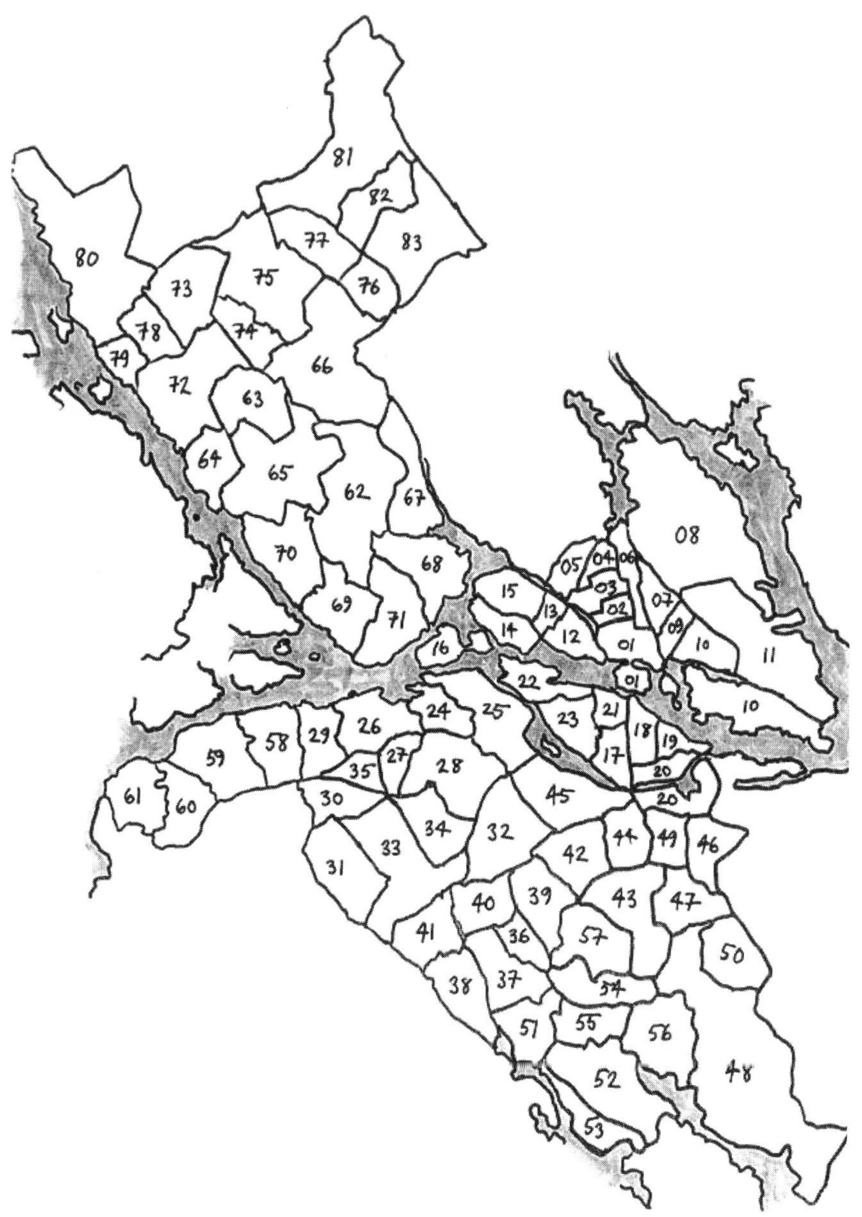



**Figure III.i　Boundaries and serial numbers of areas**

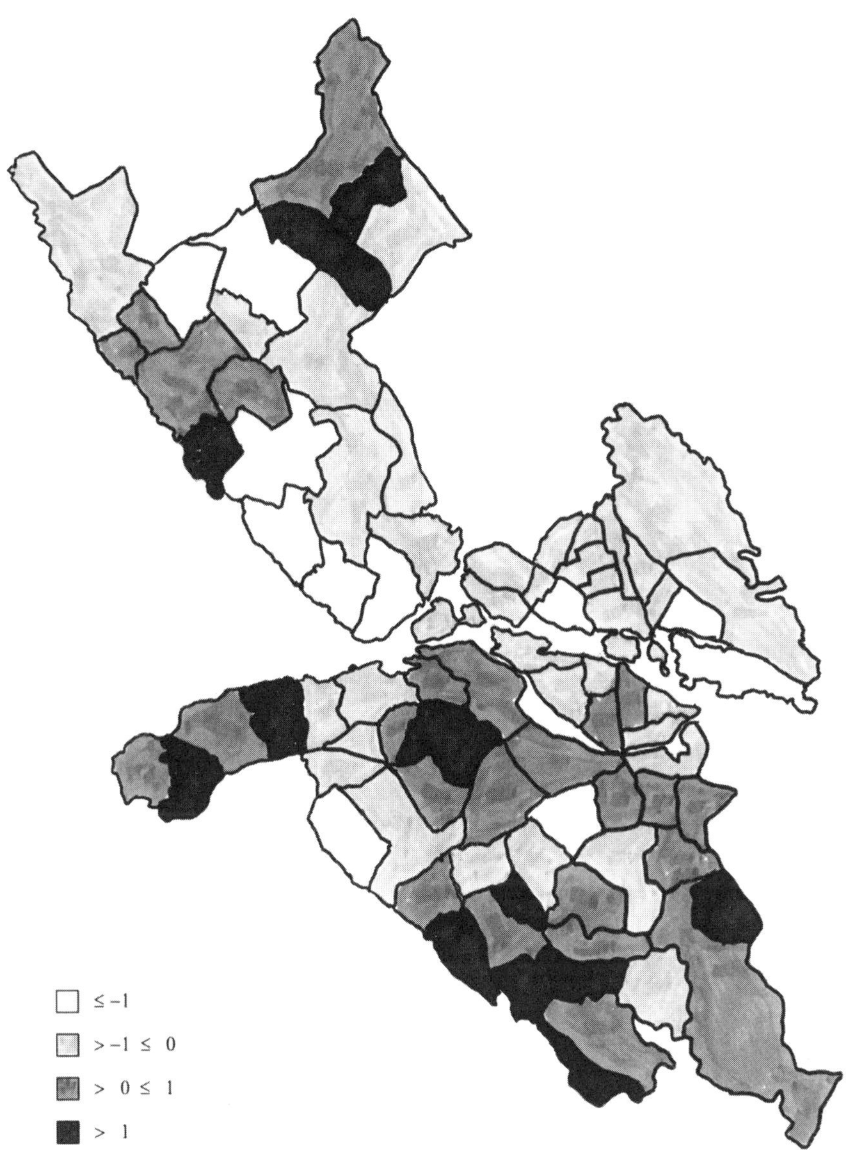



**Figure III.ii  Standardized values of the crime factor**

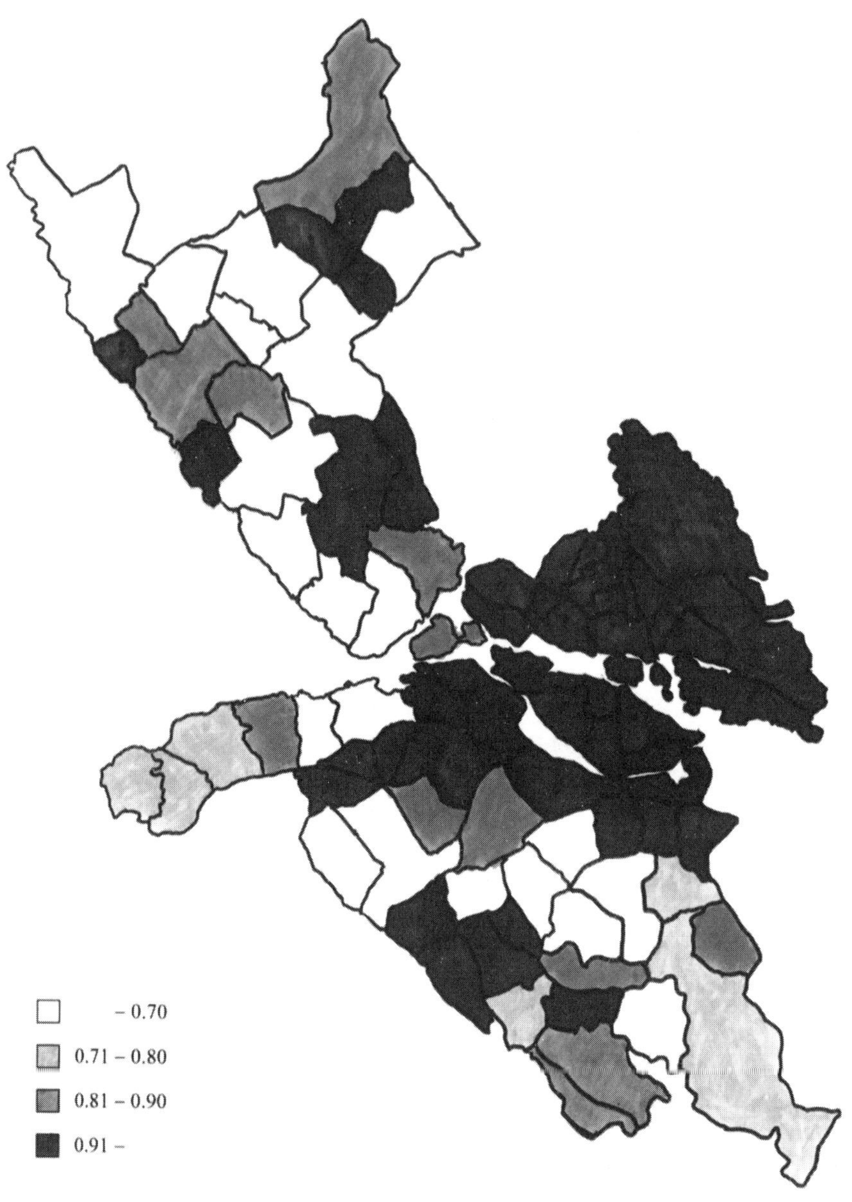



**Figure III.iii  Rates of multi-family houses**

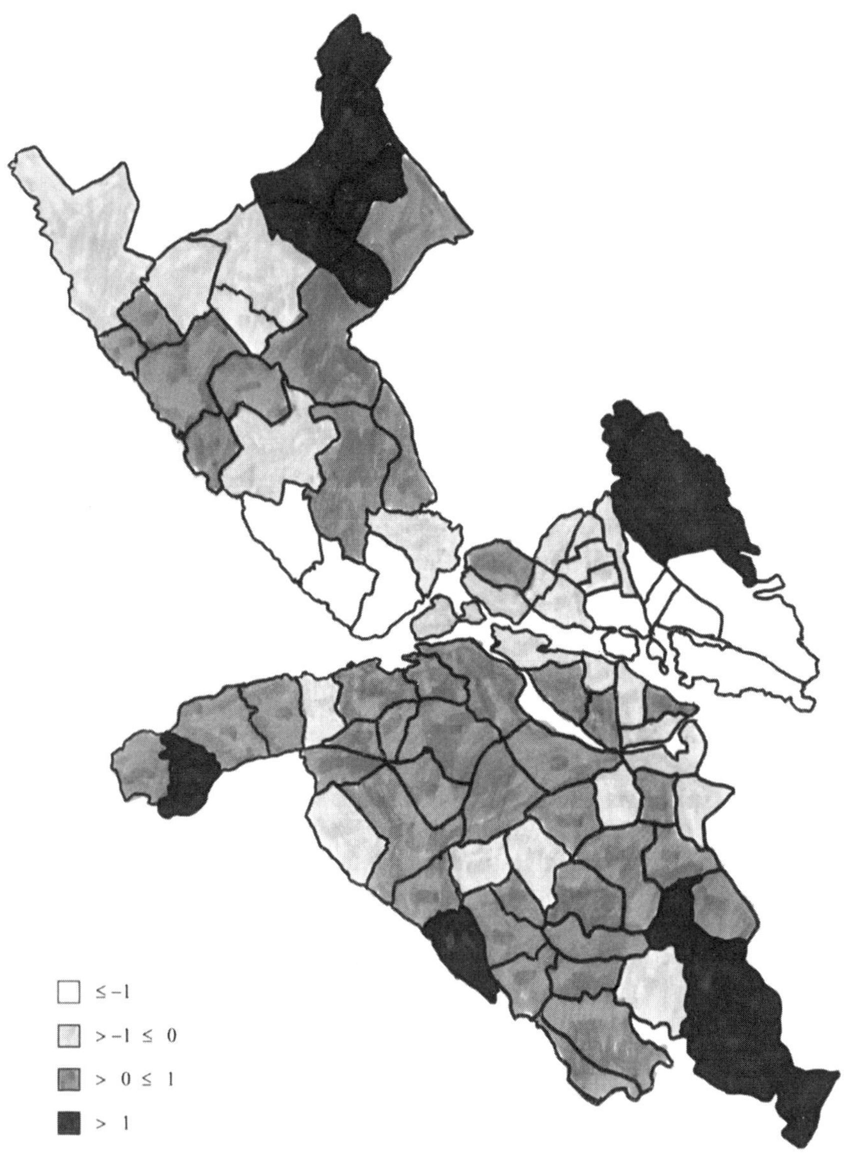



**Figure III.iv  Reflected standardized values of mean incomes**

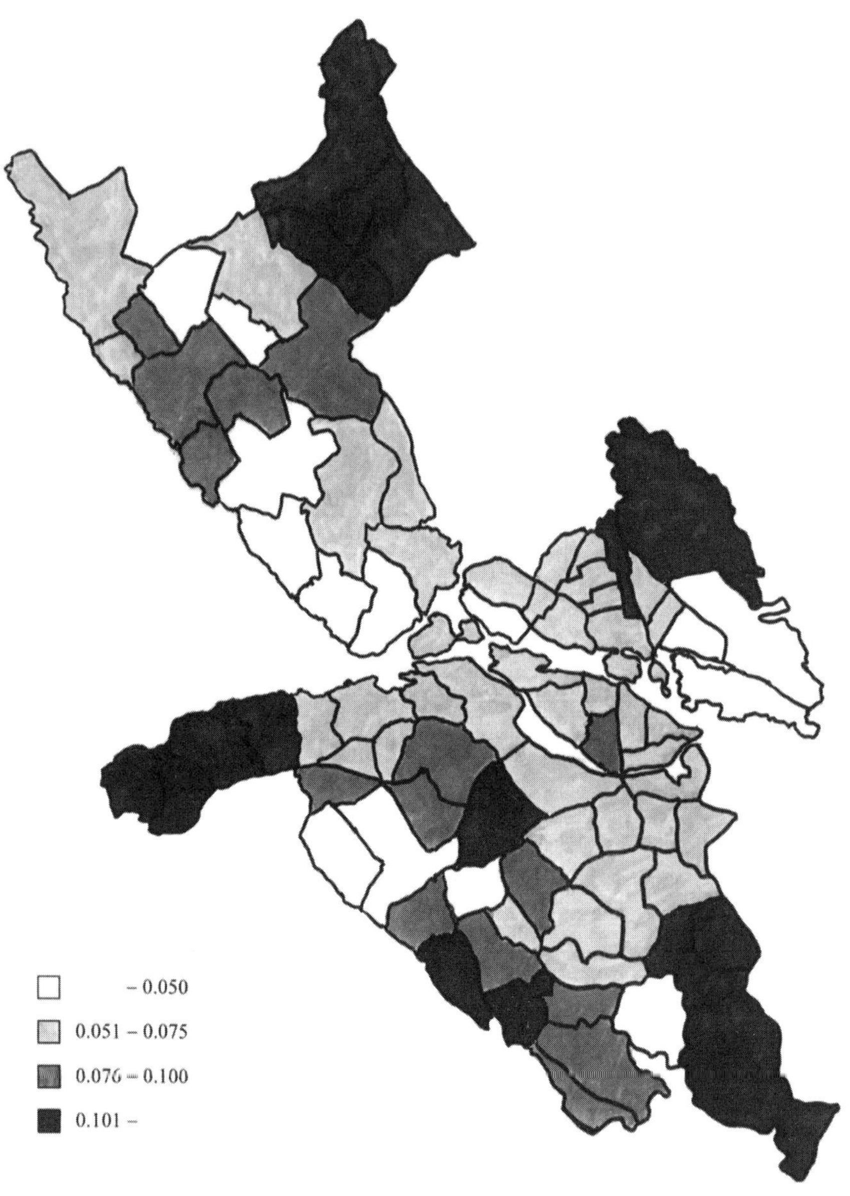


**Figure III.v   Rates of foreigners**

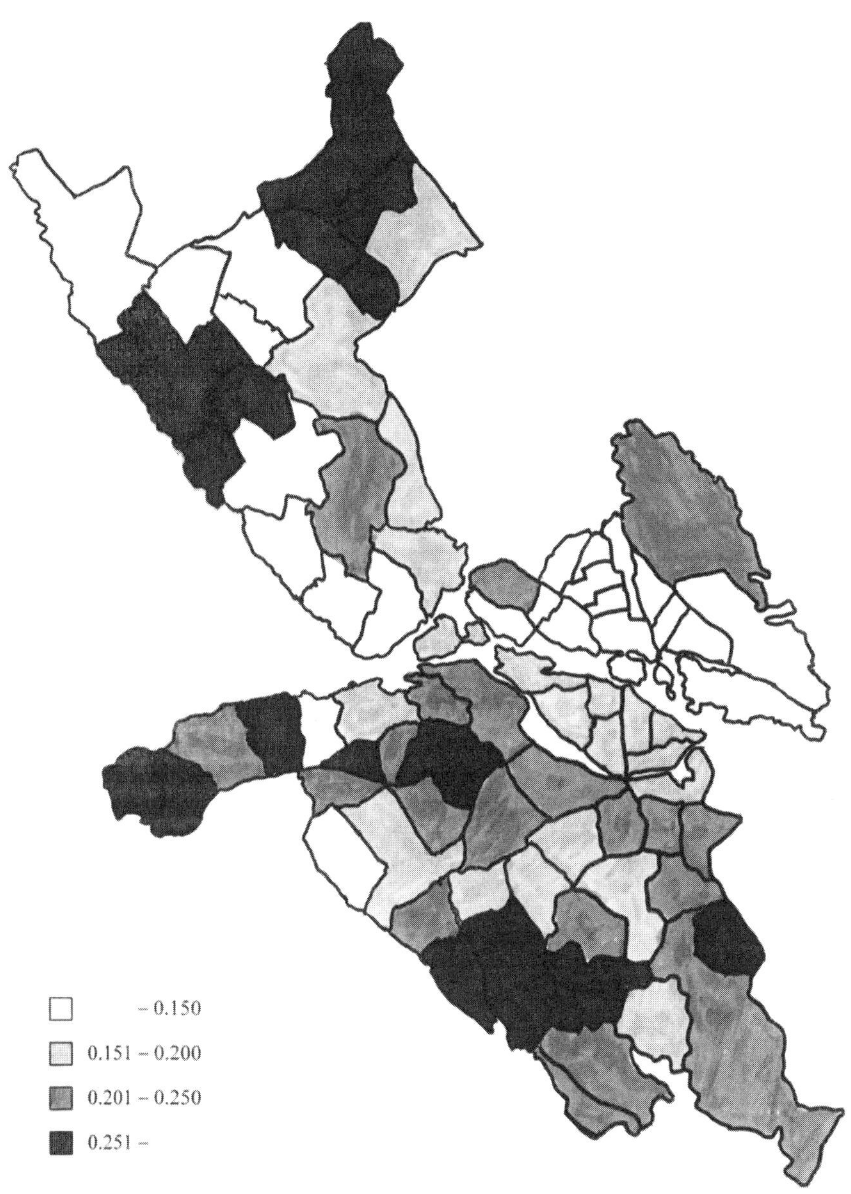



**Figure III.vi  Rates of unskilled workers**

# Construction of a Measure of Crime in Adjacent Areas

The measure of crime in adjacent areas is constructed by considering following areas.

**Table IV.i   Construction of a measure of adjacent areas' crime**

| No. | Considered areas | No. | Considered areas | No. | Considered areas |
|---|---|---|---|---|---|
| 01 | 02, 09, 18, 21 | 26 | 24, 27, 29, 35 | 51 | 37, 38, 52, 55 |
| 02 | 01, 03, 06 | 27 | 24, 26, 28, 35 | 52 | 53, 55, 56 |
| 03 | 02, 04, 05, 06 | 28 | 24, 25, 27, 32, 34 | 53 | 52 |
| 04 | 03, 05, 06 | 29 | 26, 30, 35, 58 | 54 | 55, 57 |
| 05 | 03, 04 | 30 | 29, 31, 33, 35 | 55 | 52, 54, 56 |
| 06 | 02, 03, 04, 07, 08 | 31 | 30, 33 | 56 | 48, 52, 54, 55 |
| 07 | 06, 09 | 32 | 28, 34, 39, 40, 42, 45 | 57 | 39, 43, 54 |
| 08 | 06, 07, 11 | 33 | 30, 31, 34, 40, 41 | 58 | 29, 59 |
| 09 | 01, 07, 10, 11 | 34 | 28, 32, 33 | 59 | 58, 60 |
| 10 | 09, 11 | 35 | 26, 27, 29, 30 | 60 | 59, 61 |
| 11 | 08, 09, 10 | 36 | 37, 39, 40 | 61 | 60 |
| 12 | 03, 13 | 37 | 36, 38, 40, 41 | 62 | 68, 69, 70, 71 |
| 13 | 05, 12, 14, 15 | 38 | 37, 41 | 63 | 64, 65, 66, 72, 74 |
| 14 | 13, 15, 16 | 39 | 32, 36, 40, 42, 57 | 64 | 63, 65 |
| 15 | 13, 14 | 40 | 32, 36, 37, 39, 41 | 65 | 62, 63, 64, 70 |
| 16 | 14 | 41 | 37, 38, 40 | 66 | 74, 75, 76 |
| 17 | 18, 20, 21, 23 | 42 | 32, 39, 43, 44, 45 | 67 | 62, 68 |
| 18 | 17, 19, 20, 21 | 43 | 39, 42, 44, 47, 49, 57 | 68 | 62, 67, 71 |
| 19 | 18, 20 | 44 | 42, 43, 45, 49 | 69 | 62, 70, 71 |
| 20 | 17, 18, 19 | 45 | 32, 42, 44 | 70 | 62, 65, 69 |
| 21 | 17, 18, 22, 23 | 46 | 47, 49 | 71 | 62, 68, 69 |
| 22 | 21, 23 | 47 | 43, 46, 48, 49, 50 | 72 | 63, 73, 74, 78 |
| 23 | 17, 21, 22 | 48 | 47, 50, 56 | 73 | 72, 74, 75, 78 |
| 24 | 25, 26, 27, 28 | 49 | 43, 44, 46, 47 | 74 | 63, 66, 72, 73, 75 |
| 25 | 24, 28 | 50 | 47, 48 | 75 | 66, 73, 74, 77 |

| No. | Considered areas |
|-----|------------------|
| 76  | 66, 77 |
| 77  | 75, 76 |
| 78  | 72, 73, 79, 80 |
| 79  | 78, 80 |
| 80  | 73, 78, 79 |
| 81  | 82 |
| 82  | 81, 83 |
| 83  | 82 |

# Appendix V
# Tables

**Table V.i**  **Results of regression analyses using basic independent properties of long-term residents (Group A) and of newcomers (Group B). For 1985/1990 data (n=166). Independent variables standardized**

| Independent property | Linear model A | B | Quasi-lin. model A | B | Product model I A | B | Product model II A | B |
|---|---|---|---|---|---|---|---|---|
| *Age and sex* | | | | | | | | |
| YNGMALE | .35 | −.14 | .38 | −.14 | .14 | −.02 | .14 | −.05 |
| YNGFEML | −.32 | −.19 | −.29 | −.17 | −.21 | −.03 | −.19 | −.01 |
| MDLMALE | −.01 | −.02 | −.02 | −.04 | −.01 | .13 | −.04 | .11 |
| MDLFEML | −.62 | −.14 | −.57 | −.14 | −.13 | −.03 | −.14 | −.01 |
| OLDMALE | .03 | .35 | .04 | .33 | −.03 | .34 | .04 | .37 |
| OLDFEML | −.57 | −.61 | −.48 | −.62 | −.03 | −.26 | −.08 | −.27 |
| *Social control* | | | | | | | | |
| FORGN | −.03 | .12 | −.07 | .09 | .10 | −.07 | −.02 | .19 |
| SINGLE | .08 | .06 | .10 | .02 | .07 | .21 | .05 | .14 |
| DIVOR | .66 | .08 | .51 | .18 | .15 | .02 | .17 | −.00 |
| *Social resources* | | | | | | | | |
| INCMULT | −.12 | .11 | −.10 | .09 | .01 | −.05 | −.01 | −.11 |
| SOCAID | .21 | −.15 | .21 | −.08 | .01 | .10 | .07 | −.14 |
| OCCDICH | .07 | .38 | .08 | .34 | .01 | .19 | −.01 | .16 |
| *Dwelling envir.* | | | | | | | | |
| MULTHS | −.28 | .22 | −.25 | .20 | −.18 | .08 | −.15 | .13 |
| PUBLIC | .21 | −.11 | .20 | −.12 | .05 | −.10 | .02 | −.04 |
| OVERCR | .02 | .25 | .10 | .19 | .06 | .09 | .08 | .06 |
| $const_{90}/g_{90}\,q/d_{90}$ | 2.72 | | 2.79 | | 2.71 | | 2.61 | |
| $const_{85}/g_{85}\,q/d_{85}$ | 2.52 | | 2.46 | | 2.45 | | 2.47 | |
| Expl. proportion of variance (uncorr.) | .89 | | .89 | | .91 | | .91 | |

**Table V.ii     Explaining crime with simultaneous and earlier values of independent properties. Linear regression analysis. Variables standardized**

| Independent property | 1990 (n=83) | | 1990 (n=80) | | | 1985/90 (n=166) | | 1980/ 85/90 (n=248) | |
|---|---|---|---|---|---|---|---|---|---|
| Period | 1990 | 1985 | 1990 | 1980 | 1970 | 1 | 2 | 1 | 2 |
| *Age and sex* | | | | | | | | | |
| YNGMALE | −.05 | - | −.01 | - | - | .06 | - | .09 | - |
| YNGFEML | −.20 | - | −.16 | - | - | −.17 | - | −.10 | - |
| MDLMALE | −.43 | - | −.30 | - | - | −.18 | - | −.12 | - |
| MDLFEML | −.18 | - | .01 | - | - | −.26 | - | −.41 | - |
| OLDMALE | .04 | - | .22 | - | - | .16 | - | .04 | - |
| OLDFEML | −.90 | - | −.73 | - | - | −.68 | - | −.59 | - |
| *Social control* | | | | | | | | | |
| FORGN | 1.03 | −1.22 | .58 | −.58 | −.10 | .57 | −.56 | .29 | −.13 |
| SINGLE | −.24 | −.09 | −.36 | .13 | .20 | −.07 | .06 | .11 | .00 |
| DIVOR | .04 | .48 | .19 | .45 | −.09 | −.21 | .85 | .12 | .59 |
| *Social resources* | | | | | | | | | |
| INCMULT | −.13 | .25 | −.01 | - | −.09 | .46 | −.42 | .38 | −.45 |
| SOCAID | −.13 | .51 | .17 | - | - | .11 | - | - | - |
| OCCDICH | .52 | .10 | .44 | - | - | .37 | - | - | - |
| *Dwelling envir.* | | | | | | | | | |
| MULTHS | .11 | - | .12 | - | −.09 | −.08 | - | −.09 | - |
| PUBLIC | −.03 | - | .06 | - | −.18 | .09 | - | .25 | - |
| OVERCR | .22 | −.04 | .21 | −.13 | −.06 | .16 | .01 | .11 | .06 |
| *Constants* | | | | | | | | | |
| 1990 | .00 | | −.01 | | | −.07 | | .15 | |
| 1985 | - | | - | | | .07 | | .02 | |
| 1980 | - | | - | | | - | | −.17 | |
| Expl. proportion of variance (corr.) | .91 | | .89 | | | .87 | | .84 | |

**Table V.iii**  **Explaining change in crime with changes in independent properties. Linear regression analysis. Variables standardized**

| Independent property | C90 – C85 (n=82) | | | C90 – C85/ C85 – C80 (n=162) | | | C90 – C80 (n=80) | | | |
|---|---|---|---|---|---|---|---|---|---|---|
| Period | 1 | 2 | 3 | 1 | 2 | 3 | 1 | 2 | 1 | 2 |
| *Age and sex* | | | | | | | | | | |
| YNGMALE | .07 | - | - | .04 | –.00 | - | –.19 | –.39 | –.00 | - |
| YNGFEML | –.39 | - | - | –.06 | –.12 | - | –.06 | .63 | –.23 | - |
| MDLMALE | –.18 | - | - | –.00 | –.64 | - | –.94 | –.71 | –.48 | - |
| MDLFEML | .20 | - | - | .40 | –.32 | - | 1.64 | .52 | 1.35 | - |
| OLDMALE | .09 | - | - | .06 | –.00 | - | –.53 | .33 | –.00 | - |
| OLDFEML | –.08 | - | - | .31 | –.85 | - | .69 | –.33 | .51 | - |
| *Social control* | | | | | | | | | | |
| FORGN | .34 | –.03 | –.08 | .35 | .08 | .04 | .52 | .16 | .55 | .04 |
| SINGLE | .23 | .02 | –.09 | –.08 | –.24 | –.21 | –.67 | –.79 | –.44 | –.36 |
| DIVOR | .12 | .41 | .01 | –.09 | .21 | .01 | .39 | .31 | .32 | .29 |
| *Social resources* | | | | | | | | | | |
| INCMULT | –.12 | –.09 | –.01 | –.02 | –.10 | .07 | –.07 | –.23 | –.04 | –.05 |
| SOCAID | –.12 | - | - | - | - | - | - | - | - | - |
| OCCDICH | .03 | - | - | - | - | - | - | - | - | - |
| *Dwelling envir.* | | | | | | | | | | |
| MULTHS | –.03 | –.09 | –.06 | .15 | .17 | –.01 | .04 | –.12 | .17 | –.09 |
| PUBLIC | –.22 | .11 | .26 | –.13 | .00 | .10 | .11 | .32 | .05 | .11 |
| OVERCR | .15 | .15 | .37 | .09 | .03 | –.22 | .21 | .33 | .15 | .35 |
| *Constants* | | | | | | | | | | |
| C90 – C85 | –.01 | | | –.21 | | | - | | - | |
| C85 – C80 | - | | | .23 | | | - | | - | |
| C90 – C80 | - | | | - | | | .05 | | .04 | |
| Expl. proportion of variance (corr.) | .20 | | | .18 | | | .47 | | .42 | |

**Table V.iv**  **Explaining change in crime with simultaneous changes in basic properties for Groups D and E. Linear regression analysis. Data adjusted for relative group size. Variables standardized**

| Independent property | C90 – C85 (n=83) | | C90 – C85/ C85 – C80 (n=166) | |
| --- | --- | --- | --- | --- |
| | D | E | D | E |
| *Age and sex* | | | | |
| YNGMALE | .29 | –.03 | .04 | .07 |
| YNGFEML | –.47 | .15 | –.02 | .26 |
| MDLMALE | .11 | –.10 | .28 | .21 |
| MDLFEML | –.26 | .28 | –.26 | .20 |
| OLDMALE | .28 | .20 | .31 | .06 |
| OLDFEML | –.15 | –.12 | –.22 | .42 |
| *Social control* | | | | |
| FORGN | .29 | .10 | .02 | .54 |
| SINGLE | .02 | –.20 | .01 | .01 |
| DIVOR | .25 | –.15 | –.07 | –.13 |
| *Social resources* | | | | |
| INCMULT | –.06 | –.09 | –.03 | –.00 |
| SOCAID | –.10 | .07 | - | - |
| OCCDICH | –.24 | .46 | - | - |
| *Dwelling environment* | | | | |
| MULTHS | .07 | –.05 | .03 | .02 |
| PUBLIC | –.28 | .17 | –.16 | .13 |
| OVERCR | .39 | .01 | –.02 | .12 |
| *Constant* | .00 | | .20 | |
| *Dummy90–85* | - | | –.39 | |
| Expl. proportion of variance (corr.) | .34 | | .14 | |

# Index